In praise of The Desktop Publisher's Idea Book

"*The Desktop Publisher's Idea Book* brims with powerful ideas, presented simply and engagingly. I'd say it is mandatory reading for anyone who takes their marketing seriously and wants to unleash the creativity that exists with them."

> Jay Conrad Levinson, Author,
> *Guerrilla Marketing*

"Chuck Green has made an extremely difficult subject as simple as it's going to get!"

> John McWade, Publisher and Creative Director,
> *Before & After Magazine*

"If you're getting bored producing the same, old promotions and publications, this book is a great idea generator. And it explains projects and techniques in a way that makes readers say, 'I can do that!'"

> Catharine Fishel, Editor,
> *Dynamic Graphics Magazine*

"Chuck is the type of artist I'd love to be and when I use his designs I get to be that."

> Jim Meade, Author,
> Lotus *SmartSuite Desktop Companion*
> and *Ami Pro for Dummies*

"I have genuine admiration for the clarity and teaching value of Chuck Green's writing and illustration style....and so do participants in my design seminars."

> Roger C. Parker, Author,
> *Looking Good In Print* and *Web Page and Desktop Publishing Design for Dummies*

"Chuck Green is the ultimate desktop publisher—nobody gets more impact from fonts, clip-art, black ink, and white paper. If you can use a word processor, you can create every design in this book."

> Mark Scapicchio, Contributing Editor,
> *The Word on Word Processing,* IDG Newsletters

"This book has it all—great designs and complete instructions on how to recreate them. You can't find a better designer/teacher than Chuck Green."

> Daniel Will-Harris, Publisher,
> *EsperFonto* at www.will-harris.com

"Chuck Green is the master! If you thought desktop publishing meant boring, think again. The tips, the techniques, the tricks and the examples in this book can make any business a better guerrilla marketer."

> Seth Godin, Co-author, *How to Get What You Deserve: Guerrilla Marketing Yourself*

"At last, a cure for 'blank screen syndrome.' Chuck Green's book provides stumped desktop publishers with the inspiration and the instructions for creating dozens of useful, unusual projects with a computer. Definitely not the same old stuff."

> Susan Rich Brooke,
> Senior Editor, *Home Office Computing*

"Even the experienced designer is likely to find some new ideas and approaches here that will provide a spark of inspiration, a sense of 'Gee, why didn't I think of that?'"

> Nicholas Allison, Editor, *Aldus Magazine*

THE
DESKTOP PUBLISHER'S IDEA BOOK

2nd Edition

One-of-a-kind projects, expert tips, and hard-to-find sources

Chuck Green

This is a revised and updated edition of The Desktop Publisher's Idea Book, published in 1993.

Library of Congress Cataloging-in-Publication Data
Green, Chuck (Charles K.)
      The desktop publisher's idea book : one-of-a-kind projects, expert
tips, and hard-to-find sources / Chuck Green. – 2nd ed.
          p.   cm.
      ISBN 0-679-78006-8
      1. Desktop publishing. I. Title.
Z253.53.G74 1997
686.2'2544416–dc21   97-21539
                                                           CIP

This book is available for special purchases in bulk by organizations and institutions, not for resale, at special discounts. Please direct your inquiries to the Random House Special Sales Department, toll-free 888-591-1200 or fax 212-572-4961.

Please address inquiries about electronic licensing of this division's products, for use on a network or in software or on CD-ROM, to the Subsidiary Rights Department, Random House Reference & Information Publishing, fax 212-940-7370.

Typeset and printed in the United States of America.

Visit the Random House Web site at www.randomhouse.com

Second Edition
0 9 8 7 6 5 4 3 2
September 1998
ISBN 0-679-78006-8

New York   Toronto   London   Sydney   Auckland

To my parents,
Shirley F. and Charles K. Green, Sr.

Contents

Acknowledgments

Many thanks to all of the individuals and companies that supplied the clip art and production materials used throughout *The Desktop Publisher's Idea Book*.

Thanks to Dennis McWaters for his superb photography, to Rob Whittet for his printing insights, to my dear friend, Jack Flynn, for his vote of confidence, to Roger Parker for his kind words and encouragement, and to Charles Levine, Jennifer Dowling, Megan Schade, and the other professionals at Random House with whom I have had the pleasure of working.

Finally, thanks to my wife Leslie, and sons Jeffrey and Robert for supplying the support and energy that has allowed me to weave my small thread into the ever-growing fabric of ideas.

Foreword

An article or book by Chuck Green is always good news for those interested in the good-looking, easy-to-read page. This is especially true in the case of a book which Chuck has had several years to fine-tune and refine—as is the case of second edition of his *Desktop Publisher's Idea Book* which first appeared in 1993.

Several things set *The Desktop Publisher's Idea Book* apart from similar books. Some are obvious, such as the quality of the design of the book itself. (Ever notice how many ugly desktop publishing design books there are?— it's not easy balancing text and illustrations.) Chuck's page layouts, like the hundreds of sample illustrations which they contain, are simple and to the point, always focused on the message and its purpose.

Another difference is the emphasis upon what Chuck calls "the design and function of everyday documents…and ways to maximize their effectiveness." In contrast to fancy "portfolio" books written by fancy New York City art directors serving clients with megabuck four-color advertising budgets, Chuck writes for real people in real situations. Hence the emphasis upon bookmarks, invoices, simple newsletters, tags, envelopes, flyers, and forms. Not everyone has the luxury of four-color annual reports!

The key word that best describes this book, as the above quote from Chuck's Introduction emphasizes, is "function." It's instructive that Chapter One focuses on "Turning Ideas into Results" and only following that is there a discussion of the tools of graphic design.

The Desktop Publisher's Idea Book is a book to be used not just read once and then put away in a bookshelf. Chuck encourages you to freely adopt ideas from the illustrations, and—if you want to exactly replicate his results—shows you where to purchase the typeface and clip art employed.

As a result, *The Desktop Publisher's Idea Book* is as much a reference book as it is a resource book, written with simplicity and occasional touches of humor. I particularly like the remote control imagery used for the Web site navigation tool in Chapter 19.

Roger C. Parker

Author, *Looking Good in Print* (Ventana), *the One-Minute Designer* (Que), and *Web Page and Print Design for Dummies* (IDG Books).

http://www.rcparker.com

Introduction

Your computer, software, and laser printer provide you with all the basic publishing tools—a sophisticated typesetting machine, a reduction and enlargement camera, a production drafting board, and a short-run printing press. That they fit on your desktop is an amazement surpassed only by the fact that just fifteen short years ago, the equivalent would have cost over a hundred thousand dollars.

But the wonderment has just begun. With a connection to the Internet, a few megabytes of storage space on a server, and some simple web publishing tools, you can now publish your ideas worldwide. Imagine—the tools to publish words, still and moving pictures, and sound within the grasp of anyone with a computer and a modem.

The computer, conceived to perform a few simple tasks, has evolved into a primary cog in the wheel. It has revolutionized number and name crunching by means of spreadsheets and databases. Word processing has transformed the art of writing and the task of typing. Desktop publishing programs and the visual word processors are recasting the course of publishing and design. And the World Wide Web promises to redefine the very nature of communication.

But we're still in the early stages of desktop publishing's evolution. Even now, the majority of computer generated documents, paper or electronic, follow standardized formats used for a surprisingly limited range of applications.

The Desktop Publisher's Idea Book is about breaking new ground. Beyond the obvious newsletters, envelopes, and letterheads, there are a wealth of useful, eye-catching, and unusual projects perfectly suited to your desktop system. It's time to rethink the design and function of everyday documents and explore ways to maximize their effectiveness.

On the pages that follow, you'll find the project ideas, tips, and hard-to-find sources that will unleash your creativity and help you tap the real power of your ever expanding toolbox.

This book is for you

A professionally presented message is a proven method for distinguishing yourself, your product, or service from the crowd.

Whether you're a new computer user with no design experience, or an experienced pro with hundreds of projects under your belt, *The Desktop Publisher's Idea Book* will plant the ideas that put the power of print to work for you.

What do you need?

This is not a book about how to use a certain computer system or software program. Most hardware/software configurations allow you to do the basics: create and edit text, choose and size fonts and graphics, and publish the finished product.

We'll assume you're using desktop publishing software or one of the more sophisticated visual word processing programs on a microcomputer, and that you have access to a laser or a very good graphics printer. For the web projects you'll need a connection to the Internet and the software tools for creating graphics and web pages.

What's inside?

It's not enough to see what can be done, you have to understand how to get from the idea to the published piece. In Chapter 1 you'll learn just that—a simple step-by-step method for establishing a goal, composing a message, and producing a winning design.

Chapter 2 fills in the necessary details. You'll find tips on working with type, clip art, and photography, finding and working with illustrators, photographers, and printers, and how to choose paper types, finishes, and weights.

Chapters 3 through 19 are the meat of the order—a diverse collection of desktop publishing project ideas. Each project includes a sample project, a layout of the actual page, suggestions for how you might use the same idea, and information about sources that will help you get the job done.

A different kind of desktop publishing book

Most books on desktop publishing show you examples created by designers for their clients with the idea that you'll apply the same principles to your own work. The unwritten rule is that you don't copy the designs or contents verbatim.

But the projects in *The Desktop Publisher's Idea Book* were created exclusively for you to integrate into your own work. You are free to copy any element of a project—the design, the production techniques, the font choices, even the headline and text ideas.

The only thing you can't do is scan or copy the graphics or clip art; they are copyrighted by the companies that supply them. But, if you want to use the same image, the graphics are clearly labeled and readily available from the sources listed.

Each project is described and diagramed in detail, and in many cases is accompanied by a photograph that shows you how the project looks in final form:

1 · Layouts show all the design elements in detail.

2 · Illustrations and photographs show the results in finished form.

3 · Layout captions specify the name, size, and alignment of each font and the sources of clip art and photographs.

4 · Rulers measure the exact size and positioning of each element in inches.

5 · Source captions direct you to out-of-the-ordinary products or services used to produce the finished project.

Expert help and hard-to-find sources

Even the most sophisticated professional rarely performs all the roles of designer, writer, production artist, web programmer, and printer on all projects. You take on the roles you can handle and delegate the rest. *The Desktop Publisher's Idea Book* is filled with sources for materials, products, and services that will help you fill in the gaps. In addition to those found throughout the book, you'll find a detailed listing and explanation of more of my favorites in the *Sources* section beginning on page 323.

How this book is designed

A microwave is a terrific gadget for cooking popcorn, but it makes a lousy toaster. My desktop publishing system is a terrific tool for certain projects, but I don't believe that everything can or should be created using the computer.

A fellow designer called me one afternoon and asked me how I was able to print a particularly complex image at a slant. He could barely contain himself because rotating images was something he had long wanted to do and something his software denied him. He knew I was using the same program and was certain I had discovered a way. "I'm afraid I've got disappointing news," I told him, "I cut it out and pasted it down."

I've done the same thing before myself. I got stuck thinking that I had to do everything with the computer and rather than expanding my sights, I ended up narrowing them. By integrating the computer with conventional production techniques and sources you will rapidly increase the productive uses of your system.

To that end, you'll find that this book is part sketchbook, part desktop publishing, and part imagination. And, if I've done my job, you'll come away from *The Desktop Publisher's Idea Book* with a new perspective on your desktop system and a collection of ideas that demonstrate the variety, excitement, and power of publishing and design.

Continue the discussion at www.ideabook.com

To reach the Idea Book web site, type the following line into the "Address" or "Location" box of your web browser:

http://www.ideabook.com/

I love ideas. Thinking of new ways of doing things. Looking at problems from different angles. Digging for treasure in cultivated earth.

Whether I'm writing a book, designing a brochure, or building a web site—the process is the same—I look at the obvious solutions and try to take them a step further. Am I always successful? Not hardly. What may be a new wrinkle to me may well be old hat to you.

Which leads me to the purpose of my web site—www.ideabook.com. It's a place to continue the discussion. A place to trade ideas. A place for you to learn a little more about me and, hopefully, for me to hear about you. Between the two of us, we may even get the next visitor to pause for a second or two and pay us the ultimate compliment— "Hey, why didn't I think of that?"

If you have ideas and tips you'd like to share, or comments and suggestions about the Idea Book, come by and have a look around.

Chuck Green
P.O. Box 3192
Glen Allen, Virginia 23058-3192
www.ideabook.com
E-mail: chuckgreen@ideabook.com

CHAPTER 1
Turning Ideas Into Results

Introduction

Robert Frost said "An idea is a feat of association."

An accomplished desktop publisher learns to gather ideas while looking at the work of others. You mentally file away the design, how the writer crafted the message, which fonts were used, how major points were illustrated, and details about how the final piece was produced and printed.

Later, you craft your own documents by blending, not copying, the best of these ideas with your own knowledge and experience. Use their influence to develop ideas of your own.

The goal of *The Desktop Publisher's Idea Book* is to advance that process. With this book you *can* copy a project exactly or use bits and pieces to inspire your own designs.

Along with over 100 different types of projects, the Idea Book contains literally thousands of designs, text concepts, and production details. Everything is included, from the dimensions of the page, to the font selections, and the illustrations and sources for unusual materials.

The basics of project production

If you're not already familiar with taking a project from beginning to end, you can simplify the process by looking at production as a series of steps. These are not hard and fast rules that apply to every type of project, but they are the basis of most.

1. SET YOUR GOAL

No matter what kind of product, service, or cause you're promoting, begin each project by establishing a clear goal. Ask yourself what you must achieve to consider your effort a success—an inquiry, a documented change in the reader's thinking, a purchase? Decide up front who your audience is and find out everything you can about them—research where you are likely to find them, what their tastes are, what other types of information they respond to.

2. COMPOSE YOUR MESSAGE

The message is king. Even the best design, the most dramatic illustration, and the most expensive printing can't save the wrong message.

Most effective marketing materials telegraph the same main message: "This is what we can do for you." "This is how you will look or feel once you've take the action described." They don't waste space trying to convince you how great their organization is or how many features their product has; they transform their image, and the facts, figures, and options surrounding it, into benefits.

This reader-centered message is just as important to a simple form as it is to the most sophisticated brochure—if you can't promise a little enjoyment or ease a little pain, few readers will take notice.

3. CHOOSE THE MEDIUM

Next, choose the vehicle for the message. Which type of layout works best: a brochure, a flyer, a self mailer, a web page? Sometimes, as with a business card, the medium is obvious. Other times, your message may work in a whole range of layouts.

Imagine your information in place on the Idea Book examples. Throughout the projects, the terms "sampler" and "example" are used where you will typically insert your or your organization's name.

4. SELECT A DESIGN

Once you have a winning message, organize your design around it. Decide which Idea Book layout best targets your audience and re-create the fonts, spacing, and positioning on your version.

Obviously, you don't have to use the same design as the Idea Book project you've chosen. Browse through the others and find a design or font combination that you like and apply it to any project.

Look carefully at the fonts and graphics and exactly how they're organized on the page. Believe it or not, a designer can spend hours adjusting the placement of elements, and the size and spacing of text. The difference between a design that works and one that doesn't is often hidden in these details.

5. ILLUSTRATE YOUR MESSAGE

The purpose of an illustration or photograph is to emphasize your words or to show what you can't say. That doesn't mean that you can't use graphics merely to set the tone or draw attention, but whenever possible, make the illustration work for you and with you.

You are not permitted to scan or copy the clip art in the Idea Book, but if you see an image you like, the graphics used are clearly labeled and readily available from the sources listed.

6. PREPARE YOUR ARTWORK

Next, prepare the artwork in the proper size and print it out. If you're taking it to a commercial printer, output the final copy on high-quality laser paper. Be sure there are lines or crop marks that show the borders of the page and the folds. (*See* "Working with a commercial printer," page 20.)

If you're creating a web page, take a look a your pages on other computers and other computer platforms using different browers and color palettes.

7. CHECK THE ARTWORK AND TEXT FOR ERRORS

Let the finished artwork sit for a day or two, then review it from the reader's point of view. Does the main message ring true? Have you supplied all of the information necessary for the reader to take action?

Check for typographical errors. Double-check spelling and grammar, and triple-check your phone number, address, and other contact information. Once you're certain you've uncovered every possible problem, have someone else proof it. They're sure to find at least one or two more mistakes. Make the corrections and repeat the process.

The same applies to your web pages with the addition of checking links and graphics.

8. PRINT OR PUBLISH YOUR PROJECT

Print multiple copies of your finished artwork from your computer or take it to a commercial or specialty printer to have it reproduced in quantity. (*See* "Working with a commercial printer" and "Working with a specialty printer," pages 20-23.) Or load your web pages to the host.

In Chapter 2, we'll look at some people and products that can make the difference between good and great.

CHAPTER 2
Adding the
Professional
Touches

You don't need to be a creative genius to produce top-quality work with your desktop publishing system. With a carefully chosen collection of fonts, clip art, photographs, and the services of outside experts, great things are possible.

The following are tips for finding and working with people and products that will make your documents a cut above the rest.

Selecting typefaces

Why adjust the alignment and spacing of your type?

How you break lines of text and adjust the space between individual characters and lines of type, has a subtle but significant effect on your overall design.

Why adjust the alignment and spacing of your type?

Typefaces have a profound effect on the design of your documents. Each has a personality of its own.

The Idea Book follows a few simple guidelines on the use of type. To explain, let's divide them into three separate groups: display, serif, and sans serif. (We use the term typeface to describe a family of individual fonts, i.e., Helvetica is a typeface, Helvetica Light and Bold are fonts.)

The easiest way to describe *display fonts* is to define how they are *not* used. Typically, they are not used for body text. Display fonts are designed primarily for headlines, subheads, titles, and other short text blocks sized 20 points or larger.

Throughout the Idea Book you'll see that most body text is made up of *serif fonts* (fonts with "feet" at the tops and bottoms of the characters). Although these fonts also work well as headlines and subheads, they are designed primarily for running text.

Serif fonts, in general, are more readable than sans serif or display fonts. Theories why range from speculation that the "feet" lead your eye from one character to the next, to the belief that you are simply accustomed to reading them in books, magazines, and newspapers.

Sans serif fonts (without serifs) are also used for body text and display purposes but they are generally more difficult to read than serif fonts. Sans serif fonts are particularly good for captions, very small text (6 point and under), and for titles and subheads to contrast body text.

Take particular note of the alignment (center, justified, flush left or right), the space between lines of type (leading), and the space between individual characters (kerning). All software programs allow you to control these spaces to some degree. Equalizing the visual space between lines and characters can have a dramatic effect on the results.

As you see in the list below, you don't need hundreds of different typefaces to recreate the Idea Book projects, nor do you need the exact *same* fonts. You can use fonts that are roughly the same or substitute the fonts you have available.

Below, the column to the left shows the names of the actual typefaces used in the Idea Book; on the right are examples of fonts you could use in their place. The fact is, most Idea Book projects could easily be recreated with one serif, one sans serif, and two or three display typefaces. All of the typefaces used in the Idea Book are available from Adobe Systems. See the *Fonts* section of the *Sources* directory (page 332) for a detailed listing of producers.

DISPLAY TYPEFACES

Arcadia	Willow
Boulevard	Shelley Allegro
Brush Script	Minstral
Carta	ITC Zapf Dingbats
Charlemagne	Trajan
Copperplate Gothic	Universe Extended
Fette Fraktur	ITC Zapf Chancery
Impact	Helvetica Compressed
Shelley Allegro	Snell Roundhand

SERIF TYPEFACES

Adobe Caslon	Palatino
Century Old Style	New Century Schoolbook
Cochin	Garamond
Courier	ITC American Typewriter
Minion	Garamond
Times New Roman	Times Roman

SANS SERIF TYPEFACES

Formata	Helvetica
Franklin Gothic	Futura
Frutiger	Gill Sans
Gill Sans	Frutiger
Helvetica	Univers
Trebuchet MS	Helvetica

Choosing clip art

All of the illustrations used with the Idea Book projects are from collections of conventional or electronic clip art. Because the subject matter of clip art is generic, the challenge is to find artwork that is more than mere decoration.

One constructive and obvious application of clip art is to visually telegraph your message. A bouquet, for example, identifies a florist (page 108), a microscope symbolizes a lab (page 252) and a phone represents a "call with questions" request (page 284).

Better yet is to use an illustration to show something words can't describe. For instance, an illustration of enterprising business people transmits a positive message about a training company (page 81); and a shower of fireworks creates a sense of excitement for a party invitation (page 135).

Use other images to establish a tone. A cartoon shows your sense of humor (page 218), and an elegant flower adds a touch of class (page 282).

With the price of a single custom illustration or photograph generally starting at $100 or more; it's easy to understand how finding a few useful images may justify the cost of an entire clip art collection.

A less costly alternative to electronic clip art is conventional clip art books and services. These sources supply artwork printed in book or catalog form that you cut out and paste on your finished artwork. For example, the *Bookmark Gift Card* (page 46) includes a silhouette illustration from a clip art book.

Each time an image is used in one of the Idea Book projects, the name of the company that supplied it is listed. See the *Clip Art* section of the *Sources* directory (page 328) for a detailed listing of these and other clip art producers.

Using royalty-free and stock photography

The photographic equivalent of clip art is royalty-free photography. Collections of photographs on CD-ROM that you pay for one time and are free to use, in most cases, anyway you like. Like clip art, the subject matter is necessarily generic but the categories are growing by leaps and bounds. You'll find city skylines, food, business people, families, money, backgrounds, antiquities—you name it. See the *Royalty Free & Stock Photography* section of the *Sources* directory (page 331) for a list of some of the better collections.

The term "stock" illustrations and photographs ordinarily means that the material is governed by a more restrictive agreement. The royalty you pay to use a stock image is most often based on criteria such as the type of project, the size of the potential audience, and/or the number of copies you plan to print.

Though they typically cost more, the top stock houses have libraries of hundreds of thousands, even millions of photographs from which to choose. Subject matter includes photographs staged for advertising and a mind-boggling array of historic subjects, movie stills, and news photos.

The process for finding what you want is simple. You describe the subject matter you're looking for and the company searches its files and sends you copies of photographs that meet your criteria. (They generally charge a research fee that is applied toward the royalty.)

Some royalty-free and stock providers are now allowing you to search for and purchase images online.

Commissioning custom illustrations and photographs

Electronic clip art and stock photography are just the tip of the illustration iceberg. There are far more illustrations and photographs commissioned each year for individual projects. After all, an image that speaks directly to your audience can pay off in a big way. It makes the publication uniquely yours.

If you have never commissioned an illustration or a photograph, the process can seem a bit intimidating, but it's really quite simple.

A WORD ABOUT COPYRIGHT
Remember, when you purchase clip art and stock photography you buy the right to use it; you do not own it. Before you use images on projects that will be resold (i.e., T-shirts, rubber stamps, etc.), be sure to check the legalese. Some manufacturers don't allow you to use their artwork on products for resale when the value of the product is in the art itself.

The first step is to find an artist whose style you like. Illustration styles range from near photographic realism to abstract symbolism. The techniques include electronic drawing and painting, pen and ink, scratch board, 3D sculptures, airbrush, pencils, and many different types of painting. Photography styles also run the gamut. A skilled photographer uses props, effects, and lighting to create a unique look.

Creative source books are an excellent way to make contacts. The artists or their agents buy space in these directories to present full color reprints of their best work. You'll find international, national, and regional books through graphic arts book clubs and design magazines. Here are two good examples:

The American Showcase Series, 212-673-6600, 915 Broadway #14, New York, NY 10010. Each year, American Showcase publishes a series of source books on photography, illustration, and graphic design, including one volume that focuses on corporate design and another dedicated to digital technology.

The Creative Black Book, 212-539-9800, 10 Astor Place, 6th floor, New York, NY 10003. This group annually publishes a well-respected set of source books for photography, illustration, print, film, and video.

Another way to find photographers and illustrators is to look on the Net and in newsletters, newspapers, and magazines. A call to the art director of the publication will usually yield the artist's name and address. Local artists are also often listed in your Yellow Pages.

Working with an illustrator

As you can imagine, custom illustration is not inexpensive, but it may be less than you think. Charges vary widely; a local illustrator may charge $200 for an illustration for which a nationally known illustrator can charge upwards of $2000.

If you haven't used an illustrator before, there are a few tips that will help make your first experience a positive one.

Begin with a phone call to explain your project and expectations. Describe how the illustration will be used and in what type of publication.

You'll get the most from artists by giving them some breathing room. Describing an assignment to "symbolize the global economy" will give the artist much more opportunity to be creative than saying "I want a drawing of a globe on a one dollar bill."

Discuss the medium they use (i.e., pen and ink, electronic, water-colors, etc.) and how it reproduces in the process you'll use to print it. Don't forget to point out whether you will be printing the finished art in black and white or in color.

Before you talk price, reach an understanding about the rights you

These are samples of the work by accomplished illustrators, all of whom we contacted after seeing their work in magazines or newspapers. The illustration on the far right was produced by a service that specializes in black and white line art.

Jennifer Hewitson Illustration, Cardiff, CA. © Jennifer Hewitson. All rights reserved

Peter Hoey, Washington, DC © Peter Hoey. All rights reserved

are buying. It's important to understand that illustrations and photographs remain the property of the artists. By law, they can reuse the image and charge you a fee if you ever want to reprint a publication using the same illustration. If you need exclusive rights, or rights to reprint the work, ask up front.

Next, negotiate the price. If it's too high, don't hesitate to offer what you can afford. Most artists are willing to work with you in the hope you'll use them again in the future. *The Graphic Artist's Guild Handbook, Pricing and Ethical Guidelines* is a valuable resource for gauging fair prices (available from the Graphic Artist's Guild, 212-463-7730, 11 West 20th Street, New York, NY 10011, www.gag.org).

Once they understand the assignment and you have agreed to a price, set a deadline allowing yourself a few days for the possibility of changes or delays.

Now it's time to stand back and let them work their magic. Generally, the illustrator will rough out several different ideas for you to choose from. Select the one that works best and point out anything that is out of place or technically inaccurate. If you make changes after this stage, it will be expensive.

Working with a photographer

Some photographers charge by the day, some by the assignment. Many will accept a variety of assignments, others specialize in either studio or location work.

Studio photography requires that you bring your people or subjects to the studio and set up within reach of the photographer's equipment. A good studio photographer can re-create just about any imaginable scene or mood with a combination of lighting, props, and sets. You'd be surprised how many of the photographs you see are actually staged in a studio.

A location photographer shoots everything on site. Sometimes it's as simple as traveling to your location to photograph the subject with available light. Other projects might require elaborate preparation, props, and special lighting.

The practice of working with a photographer is much the same as working with an illustrator. You explain the project, set a deadline, and describe how and where the finished photograph will be used to establish the rights and price.

While many photographers prefer the same creative freedom you might afford an illustrator, others prefer a more specific assignment. Photography is typically a bit more literal than illustration, so there are often more details to cover.

Once you're under way, usually, photographers will explain their ideas, sketch them out, or maybe show you photographs of similar subject matter they have taken. Most will want you to be present so that you can answer questions that arise as they compose the picture. If you can't, be sure to cover every conceivable question beforehand.

When you see the final photograph or illustration printed on your document, you'll have a new appreciation of just how valuable a custom image can be.

Scanning and copyright

Scanning is a terrific way to incorporate custom illustrations and photographs in your artwork. But you must own the artwork before you can use it. Illustrators and photographers hold legal rights to their creations from the moment they produce them, and you can't use them without written permission.

And just because you change an image doesn't nullify the copyright and confer it to you. In one recent case, the artist reproduced his version of a copyrighted photograph as a computer drawing. He added elements, changed colors, and used no physical portion of the original, but was still charged with infringement. As Tad Crawford writes in the *Legal Guide for the Visual Artist* (Allworth Press, New York, 1995), "What is the test for copyright infringement? It is whether an ordinary observer, looking at the original work and the work allegedly copied from it, recognizes that a copying has taken place." In other words, you would have to literally transform an image to call it your own.

With the proliferation of computers and scanners, it's a fair bet that the art world will continue to actively search for opportunities to test and reinforce copyright. You don't want to be the next landmark case.

Reproducing the print projects

There are three basic ways to reproduce the Idea Book projects. You can output the final project in small quantities directly from your computer's laser or graphics printer, use the computer printer output as master artwork to be reproduced on a high-quality copier, or use the output to be reproduced on a printing press by a commercial or specialty printer. Each project description includes recommendations for which method to use.

Generally speaking, your laser or graphics printer is ideal for small quantity projects that can be printed on standard 8 1/2" by 11" or 8 1/2" by 14" papers and labels designed especially for a computer printer.

Once you get above a quantity of 50 to 100 copies of a single page, the laser printer becomes less practical and you're ready to switch to a high-quality copier.

Projects that require paper heavier than your computer printer or copier can handle, colored ink, or 500 or more copies are best reproduced by a commercial printer on a printing press.

Working with a service bureau

The master artwork for all of the Idea Book projects shown in the photographs throughout the book was output from a standard laser printer at a resolution of 300 dots per inch (DPI). But if you have detailed artwork or a particularly important job and you plan to reproduce the artwork on a copier or printing press, you may choose to output it at a higher resolution. In fact, we opted to print the final pages of the Idea Book at 1270 DPI. To do this, we engaged the services of a *desktop publishing service bureau*, a company that specializes in outputting computer desktop publishing files on an expensive, high-resolution printer.

Most service bureaus offer printouts on a per-page basis at resolutions of 1200 DPI and higher. The pages are usually output on a glossy photographic paper to guarantee a sharp, clean image. When you contact them they'll tell you all about the capabilities of the hardware they're using, and provide you with specific instructions on how to save your files for their printer. They can print your pages on paper or film, and typically, offer a whole range of other production services.

Another advantage of using a service bureau is that they have hundreds, if not thousands, of different fonts from which to choose. Some will sell you screen versions of these fonts for a fraction of the cost of a printer font. You are able to see the font on your screen, but it prints only on the service bureau's printer. This isn't very practical for day-to-day work, but it is a good way to take advantage of fonts you will use only occasionally.

Desktop publishing service bureaus are available in virtually all metropolitan areas and plenty of smaller cities and towns. To find one, look under typesetting or desktop publishing in your Yellow Pages, or contact a regional or national service bureau through desktop publishing publications.

The pages for *The Desktop Publisher's Idea Book* were output by Riddick Corporate Marketing, Inc., 804-780-0006, 700 East Main Street, Suite 1801, Richmond, VA 23219.

Working with a commercial printer

If you are doing any serious desktop publishing, a commercial printer is an important resource. Although many of the Idea Book projects can be reproduced in small quantities directly from your computer, a commercial printer with a small printing press can generally save you time and money when you're printing more than 500 pages.

An outside printer is also essential for printing projects that require the use of papers heavier than your printer can handle or for large projects that require folding and binding.

FINDING A QUALITY PRINTER

Printing quality varies widely. The best and most obvious way to find out if printers meet your standards is to review their work and have them print a small project for you.

Below is a list of four fundamentals to look for. These are not legal definitions of good printing, but simple indicators of the minimum acceptable quality.

Reproduction quality—The printed piece should not be noticeably less sharp and clear than the original.

Positioning—The artwork should be positioned on the page within 1/16" of where you laid it out, top and bottom, left and right. It should not slant on the page unless your original did.

Ink coverage—The ink color (black is considered a color) should be the same shade and density on all parts of the page and throughout the document. Text that is noticeably heavier or lighter than the original may have been printed using too much or too little ink.

Dust and debris—There should not be noticeable dust or debris that didn't appear on the original artwork. An occasional spot on a limited number of copies is unpreventable, but an attentive printer will catch and discard the majority of these pages.

If the printer is using a high-speed copier, they have less control of these fundamentals, so when in doubt, opt for printing on a press versus a copier.

GETTING A FAIR PRICE

Printing prices vary widely. Some printers estimate jobs based on changing criteria such as how busy they are or how well-suited your job is to the equipment they use. Other printers follow a strict computer formula. In any case, to ensure you're getting a reasonable price, it's best to get price estimates from two or three different printers.

PREPARING YOUR ARTWORK

Today, many printers prefer a computer file to a camera-ready pasteup of the art on a board (a mechanical). But there are still plenty of places that work the conventional way—you supply a mechanical and they shoot a negative of it to create the printing plate. In that case, the better prepared your artwork is, the more likely your job will return from the printer as you envisioned it. If you are not clear about how to prepare the artwork, ask the printer what they require.

Obviously, if you are simply copying a standard 8 1/2" by 11" page, you normally don't need additional preparation. But if your pages are an odd size or they will be folded and bound, you are responsible for giving the printer complete instructions.

There are many good books on preparing pasteup and mechanical artwork, but for the Idea Book projects, the following preparation should be enough for most printers.

Protect your artwork—To keep pages from being damaged, mount your final artwork on pasteup or poster board with an additional 1" border around the edges. Use spray adhesive to mount the pages and cover them by taping a sheet of tracing paper over the artwork. This protects the art and doubles as a convenient place to write printing instructions.

Show where to trim and fold—Use crop marks to show how you want the final pages trimmed. Crop marks are a "Print" option of all desktop publishing programs and some of the more advanced word processors.

If there isn't room for crop marks, add a thin line around the outside edge and instruct the printer not to print the line but to use it as the trim guide. Use broken (dotted) crop marks outside the print area to show if and where you want pages folded.

Clean it up—Opaque-out any dust and dirt with white paint or typewriter correction fluid.

Supply complete instructions—When it comes to printing, you can't supply too much information. Give the printer complete written instructions, including the ink color(s), what brand, weight, and finish of paper to use, and any special instructions on folding and binding. Be sure to read the printer's contract terms so you clearly understand who is responsible for what.

Before settling on the quantity, ask about the printer's policy on under- and overruns. It is accepted practice for printers to be 10 percent over or under the quantity you request and to charge an equal amount more or less. So, if you need a minimum of 5,000 postcards, you may need to order 5,500.

Create a mock-up—Even for something as simple as an 8 1/2" by 11" sheet printed on both sides, you should create a miniature mockup of how you want the final pages arranged. It doesn't have to be elaborate, just blank paper folded and marked to show what pages print where.

In the case of a brochure, you might want to show the direction of the folds. If you're creating a multipage document, trim out miniature pages, fold and number them to show how the finished pages should be assembled.

Sign off on a proof—Most printers can provide you with a photographic print of the negative they use to make the printing plates for your job (called a blueline). If your project represents a significant cost or is at all complicated, a blueline is your insurance that everything is positioned correctly.

The blueline shows all of the artwork in place, trimmed, folded, and bound. The only thing you can't check on the blueline is color. If the color arrangement is complex, the printer can provide a separate color proof for an additional charge.

Check the blueline to confirm that everything is in place and that pages are in the right order. Point out any missing elements, dust spots, debris, or anything that doesn't look exactly as you expected.

Double-check the finished job—When you accept delivery of the final job, check to see that you're getting roughly the right quantity of pieces. If you have a number of packages or boxes, take a random sample from each to ensure that printing quality is consistent throughout.

Working with a specialty printer

A specialty printer has the equipment and expertise to print a particular type of project like decals, pocket folders, or envelopes. Sometimes, a source halfway across the country will beat a local price or provide a higher-quality job simply because they specialize in that service.

Just about all of the basics covered in the previous section on commercial printers also apply here. Printing on coasters or T-shirts is not nearly as easy as printing on paper, so you'll probably have to be a bit more tolerant about production quality and variances in positioning.

Before you use a specialty printer, even those listed among the Idea Book sources, be sure to contact them for a description of services, pricing, and for samples to ensure they meet your expectations.

If you ask, most printers are more than happy to provide verbal or written details about how you should prepare your artwork for their process.

The more complex the job and equipment, the more printing becomes an art rather than a technical skill. A printer who cares about quality and knows how to achieve it is a key element in successful desktop publishing.

Choosing paper

Whether you print directly from your computer or have your project reproduced by a commercial printer, paper obviously plays an important role in desktop publishing.

DESKTOP PUBLISHING PAPERS

There are many papers specially designed for use with computer printers: super-smooth papers for printing final artwork, fine stationery papers and envelopes, and general use papers in an amazing variety of colors and textures.

Many computer software and office supply stores stock these papers and at least three direct mail companies specialize in them. They are:

Baudeville, 800-728-0888, 5380 52nd St., SE, Grand Rapids, MI 49512-9765, www.baudville.com

The Baudeville catalog includes a big collection of papers and seals for certificates and an excellent selection of papers, picture frames, postcards, tentcards, badges, etc.

PaperDirect, 800-272-7377, P.O. Box 64429, St. Paul, MN 55164-0429. The PaperDirect catalog includes papers, general desktop publishing supplies, and all the Avery Laser Labels used with the Idea Book projects.

Queblo, 800-523-9080, P.O. Box 8465, Mankato, MN 5600. The Queblo catalog features an equally interesting selection of blank and preprinted papers, and desktop publishing products.

STOCK FOR COMMERCIAL PRINTING

Paper is called "stock" in the printing trade. There are literally thousands of different weights, colors, and finishes.

Costs vary widely and can represent a significant portion of your printing bill, especially when you print in large quantities. So be sure to ask your printer to show you the same type of paper in different price ranges and to explain the advantages of each.

Many of the Idea Book projects include suggestions for stock selections, including the category, weight, color, and finish.

Categories and weights—The Idea Book text refers to three different categories of stock: bond, text, and cover. Each category is available in a variety of weights.

Bond is the stock you probably buy for everyday use with your printer or copier. It ranges from high-quality sheets for stationery to inexpensive sheets for copiers. It is available in a good variety of colors, but does not offer nearly the variety available in text stock. The most common bond weights are 20 lb, 24 lb, 28 lb, and 32 lb.

The *text* category (sometimes called book) includes literally thousands of different sheets used for books, brochures, and other projects that require a light to medium weight stock. The text category includes stock in every imaginable color and finish. The Idea Book refers to text weights ranging from 60 lb to 100 lb.

Cover stock is used to cover booklets, paperbacks, pocket folders, business cards, and other projects that require a rigid sheet. The Idea Book refers to cover weights between 60 lb and 100 lb.

FINISHES—Besides various weights, you can choose from a seemingly endless selection of surface finishes.

Uncoated stock may have a smooth or textured surface. For example, a "laid" finish has a series of tiny ridges that run parallel down the page; a "pebbled" finish looks just like it sounds. Your printer can show you everything from a conventional smooth finish to a finish that simulates leather.

Coated stock is finished with a very thin layer of clay that provides an excellent surface for printing. It's easy to spot a coated stock by the obvious gloss.

To ensure that you get what you expect, ask your printer for samples. They have hundreds of different types and weights of paper available from paper manufacturers and they'll be happy to help you choose a stock appropriate for your project.

If you are creating a multipage brochure or booklet, many printers will make a "dummy" for you using the actual paper to show you how the final piece will look and feel.

CHAPTER 3
Binder & Folder Projects

Instant Binder

Create a custom presentation in a matter of minutes

A custom presentation binder adds an air of substance to a presentation that few other mediums can. When you imprint the client's name on the cover, they know at a glance this is no canned proposal. A ring binder gives you the freedom to reorganize information and add last minute facts and figures.

The Idea Book example shows how a teacher's association might use the binder to make a presentation to the school board (*see* Source:).

For your version you'll need the artwork and a ring binder with a clear plastic cover. (*See* the layouts on pages 30-31.) Position your organization's name and logo on the top layout, and the name of the group to which you're presenting on the bottom.

Print both sheets directly from your computer and trim them to size. Use white stock for the top section and color stock for the bottom. Butt the sheets edge to edge and use spray adhesive to mount them on a third, heavier sheet. A rigid sheet will be easier to position once you insert it in the pocket on the ring binder.

Trim the final insert 1/4" smaller than the overall size of the pocket and insert it so there's an equal amount of space on all sides.

More binder ideas:

Audio cassette packages
Catalogs
Handbooks
Manuals
Personal organizers
Proposals
Reports
Software packages
Videotape packages
Workbooks

The Idea Book example shows how a teachers' association might use the binder to make a presentation to the school board.

Source: Clear Cover Binders

The "Cardinal ClearVue RoundRing Binder" (5/8") is available through your local office supply dealer.

Sampler Teacher's Association

Presentation to the
Sampler County
Board of Supervisors

**Instant Binder
Layout: Top**

*1 · Apple Clip
Art: From Logic
Arts, 804-266-
7996, 11475
Chickahominy
Branch, Glen
Allen, VA 23060
© Logic Arts
Corp. All rights
reserved*

*2 · Organization
Name: Helvetica
Black, 18/17pt,
flush left,
reverse (white)
on a black
background box*

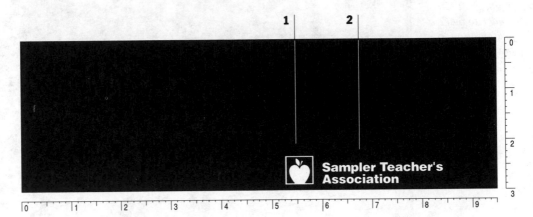

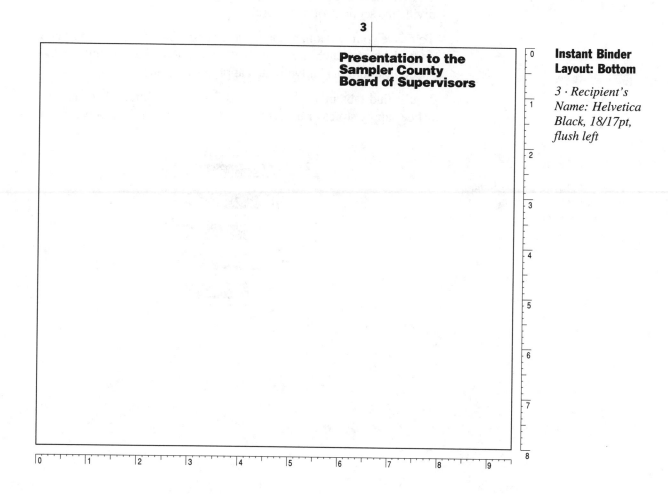

3

**Presentation to the
Sampler County
Board of Supervisors**

**Instant Binder
Layout: Bottom**

*3 · Recipient's
Name: Helvetica
Black, 18/17pt,
flush left*

Binder Index Tabs

Organize in record time

When you're presenting a significant amount of information in a presentation binder, a set of index tabs makes finding details easy.

The example shows how a recording studio might use the tabs to divide the sections of a proposal.

To create your version, produce the artwork for one set of labels and copy them to match the number of transparent laser labels on the sheet. Print the final artwork and apply them to the tabs.

You'll find tabs in sets of 3, 5, and 8, and matching labels at your office supply stores or in sets from Avery Dennison (*see* Source:).

Index Labels Layout

1 · Tab Text: Adobe Caslon Bold, 14pt, flush left, reverse (white) on a black background box

2 · Large Initial: Shelley Allegro, 36pt, flush left

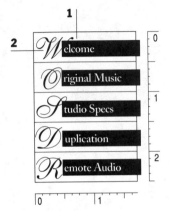

The example shows how a recording studio might use the tabs to divide the sections of a proposal.

Source: Index Labels & Tabs

"Index Maker" includes sets of tabs and sheets of clear labels to fit. From Avery Dennison, 800-252-8379, 818 Oak Park Road, Covina, CA 91724

Gift Folder

Make an eloquent statement with a simple gift

Here is an attractive way to personalize your gift of currency, tickets to an event, or a gift certificate from a favorite store.

Start your version by centering the greeting on the cover. In place of "Congratulations," your cover could read "Happy Birthday," "For Your 40th Anniversary," or feature a favorite quotation. On the inside, print your name or add a verse and sign it like a greeting card.

Print the artwork directly from your computer on white stock and use spray adhesive to mount it to a second, color sheet. To maximize the contrast between the cover and inside pocket, choose a high-quality textured stock in a rich, dark color. Trim the assembled sheet, score and fold it using the marks on the layout.

Gift Folder Layout

1 · Sender's Signature: Shelley Allegro, 24pt, centered

2 · Greeting: "Congratulations": Shelley Allegro, 40pt, centered. "Martin & Diane" is Shelley Allegro, 50pt, centered

The dotted lines represent folds.

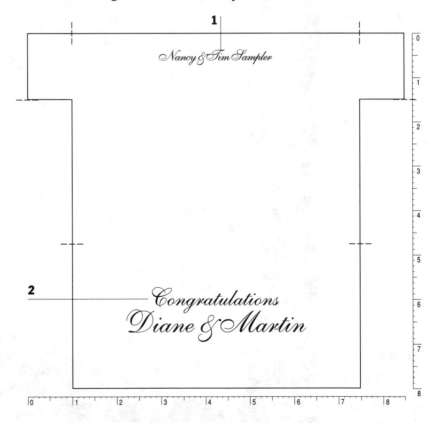

The Idea Book example shows how a wedding guest might add his or her personal touch to a gift.

Pocket Folder

Define the big picture

If you make lots of proposals or send out an ever-changing combination of marketing materials, this *Pocket Folder* is essential. Instead of including just a name or logo on the cover, take advantage of the opportunity to state your organization's mission and set the tone for the materials inside.

The Idea Book example shows how an engineering firm might use the folder in the form of a dictionary definition to state its mission.

To create your version, choose the word that best describes your profession and compose a cover definition. (*See* the layouts on pages 38-39.) On the inside flap, define your organization's name (read the layout for the full effect). Include the organization's name, address, and phone number on the back cover.

Print one master copy of the front and back covers, and the inside flaps and assemble them as shown.

Send the artwork to a printer that specializes in pocket folders (*see* Source:). Because they already have the expensive dies used to trim this and other layouts, a specialty printer will probably be able to print the folder for less. If you want to insert your business card on the inside flap, ask the printer to use a die that cuts the necessary slots.

The Idea Book example was printed on 10 point coated cover stock and covered with a high-gloss protective coating called U.V. ClearCote.

Pocket Folder Layout

1 · To prepare the artwork for a commercial printer, arrange the four sheets (pages 40-41) and mount them to a heavy white board. The dotted lines represent folds.

The Idea Book example shows how an engineering firm might use the folder to state its mission in the form of a dictionary definition .

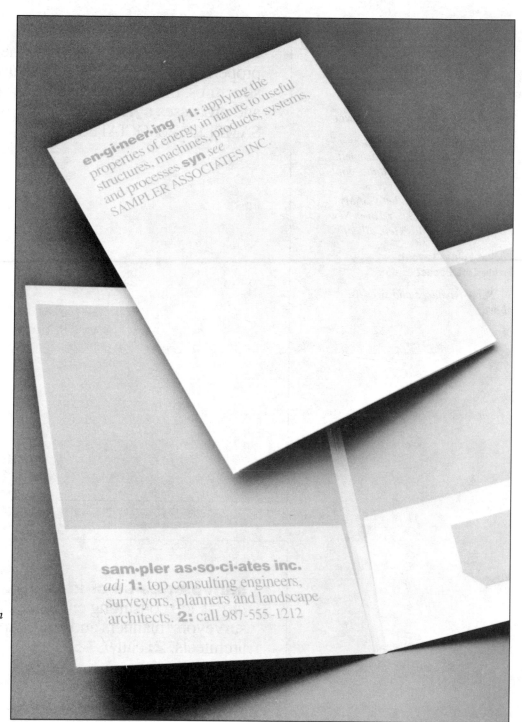

Source: Custom Printed Pocket Folder

The folder pictured (style RG) and many other variations are available from Gentile Brothers Folder Factory, 800-368-5270, 116-A High St., PO Box 429, Edinburg, VA 22824

Pocket Folder Layout: Front Cover

2 · "engineering," "1:," and "syn": Helvetica Black, 32/35pt, flush left. "n": Times New Roman Italic, 36pt. "applying the...": Times New Roman, 36/35pt, flush left. "SAMPLER ASSOCIATES...": Times New Roman, 32/35pt, flush left, all caps

Pocket Folder Layout: Inside-Left Pocket

3 · Same typefaces and sizes as above

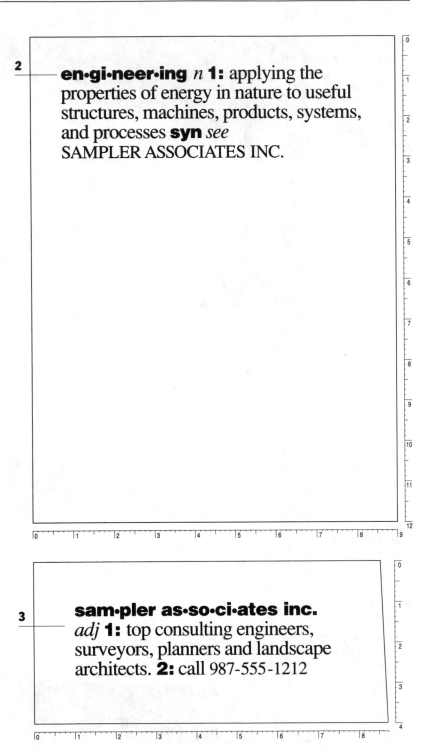

en·gi·neer·ing *n* **1:** applying the properties of energy in nature to useful structures, machines, products, systems, and processes **syn** *see* SAMPLER ASSOCIATES INC.

sam·pler as·so·ci·ates inc. *adj* **1:** top consulting engineers, surveyors, planners and landscape architects. **2:** call 987-555-1212

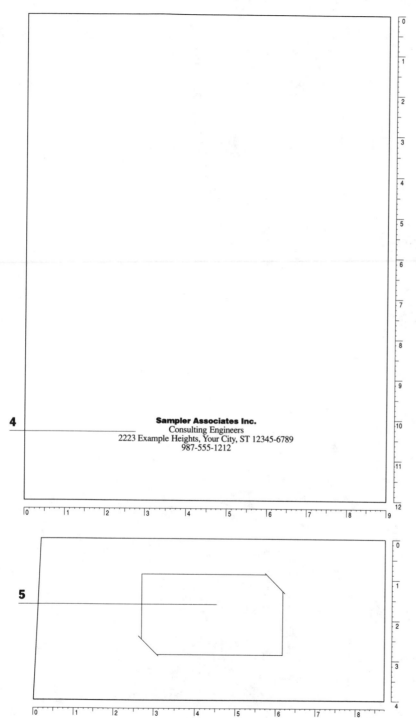

4

Sampler Associates Inc.
Consulting Engineers
2223 Example Heights, Your City, ST 12345-6789
987-555-1212

5

Pocket Folder Layout: Back Cover

4 · Organization's Name: Helvetica Black, 14pt, centered. Tag Line and Address: Times New Roman, 16/16pt, centered

Pocket Folder Layout: Inside-Right Pocket

5 · Tell the printer if you want slots cut in this position to hold your business card.

CHAPTER 4
Book & Booklet Projects

Appointment Calendar

Keep your name prominent all year long

A well-organized personal calendar is a helpful tool for anyone with even a moderately busy schedule. This custom version is a useful incentive that keeps your organization's name in front of customers all year long.

The Idea Book example shows how a commercial printer might imprint its name on a one-page-per-week layout.

For your version, start at the top of column one with your organization's name, address, and phone number. Use the remainder of the column for a to-do or task list. Divide the next two columns into six equal boxes; Monday through Friday each get a block with 8am to 6pm listings; Saturday and Sunday share the last block. Leave a wide margin on the left-hand side for a hole punch. Add scheduling terms, events, and other details specific to your field to make your version truly unique.

To use the calendar, fill in the month and week in the left-hand column and date each day in the small gray boxes. Because the pages are not preprinted with dates, you can make mistakes or reschedule a week simply by inserting a clean sheet.

Print one master copy of the calendar and take it to a commercial printer to have it reproduced on 24 lb uncoated bond stock.

A year's worth of pages inside a high-quality ring binder makes a unique and useful business gift.

More calendar headings

Activity summary
Appointments
Assignments
Book/article list
Call list
Diary
Events
Expenses
Holidays
Ideas
Mileage
Military hours
Next week or month
Notes
Priority numbering scheme
Time record

Appointment Calendar Layout

1 · Day: Century Old Style Italic, 14pt, flush left, 1pt line above

2 · Schedule Fill-In: Century Old Style Italic, 6/18pt, flush left, .5pt lines

3 · Date Fill-In: The user writes the date (usually by hand) in this box. The background box is filled with a 10% shade of black.

4 · Organization Name: Helvetica Black Italic, 14pt, flush left. Address and Phone: Century Old Style Italic, 10/11pt, flush left. Both are reverse (white) on a black background.

5 · Task List Fill-In: Century Old Style Italic, 10/18pt, flush left. The background box is filled with a 10% shade of black.

6 · Hole Punch

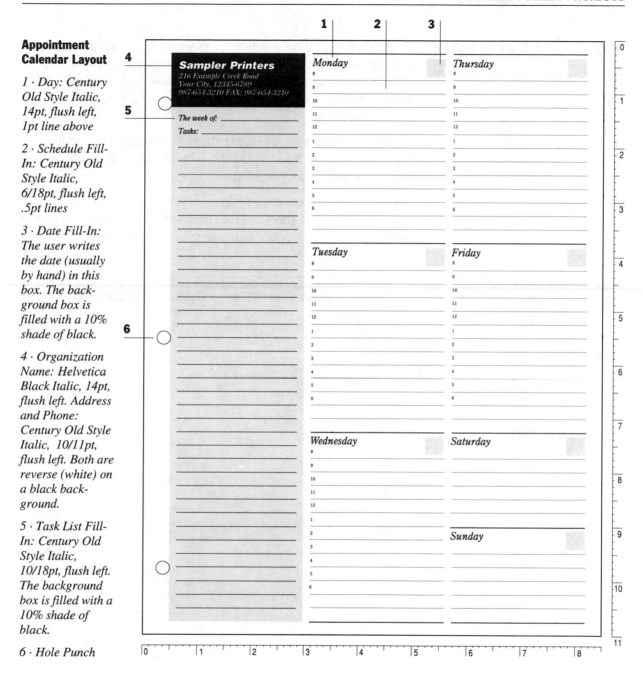

Book Jacket Index

Create a quick reference of important passages

If you have ever used a yellow highlighter to mark the significant passages in a book, the resulting clutter probably left you wishing for a better way. A clever alternative is this *Book Jacket Index*, a single sheet that lists the subject and location of each excerpt without marring the book.

To create your version, substitute your name and address on the left-hand side. Use the fill-in to list the subject and page number of the passages you ordinarily highlight.

Print the index sheets directly from your computer on white 24 lb bond stock. Fold the sheet and trim the bottom to match the height of the book. Secure the jacket with tape at the top and bottom.

Book Jacket Index Layout

1 · Heading: Helvetica Black Italic, 10pt, flush left, all caps, reverse (white) on a black background box

2 · Fill-In Lines: .5pt

3 · Name, Address, and Phone: Helvetica Black Italic, 11/13pt, flush left

The dotted lines on the top and bottom edge represent folds.

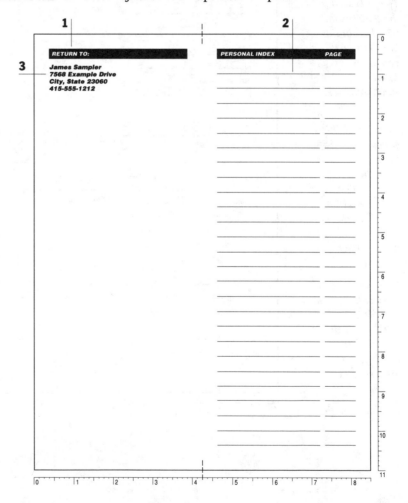

RETURN TO:

James Sampler
7568 Example Drive
City, State 23060
415-555-1212

PERSONAL INDEX   PAGE

The Book Jacket Index is printed on a standard 8.5" by 11" sheet and trimmed to match the height of the book.

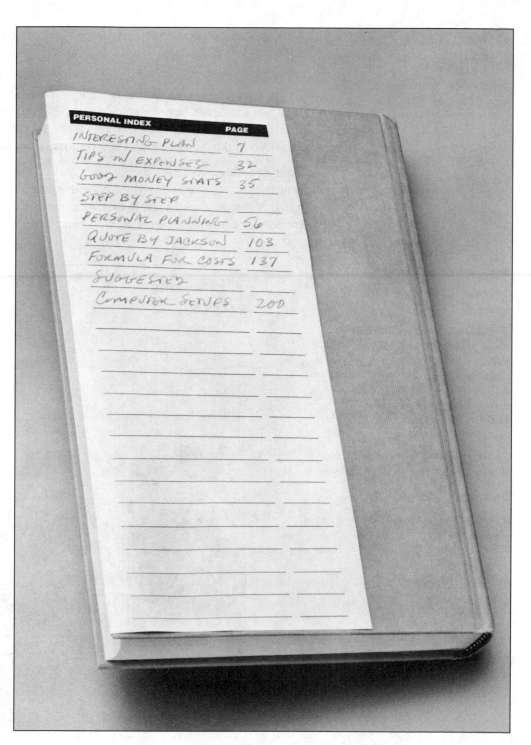

Bookmark Gift Card

Send a bookmark that doubles as a gift card

This combination bookmark/gift card is a natural giveaway for businesses that deal in books, or a fun project for anyone giving one as a gift.

Begin your version by finding a fitting verse or message for the occasion and illustrations to match. Position the text and image on the front and add your "To:" and "From:" message at the bottom. On the back, repeat the illustration and add your name and address.

Print one master copy of the artwork and take it to a commercial printer to have it reproduced on 65 lb (or heavier) uncoated cover stock. If you only need a few bookmarks, construct a heavier stock by mounting two or three sheets of 24 lb bond stock, back to back.

Bookmark Layout: Front

1 · Headline: Cochin, 28/28pt, flush left

2 · Illustrations: From "Silhouettes, A Pictorial Archive of Varied Illustrations," edited by Carol Belanger Grafton, from Dover Publications, Inc., 516-294-7000, 31 East 2nd Street, Mineola, NY 11501 © Dover Publications, Inc. All rights reserved

3 · To and From: Formata Bold, 10pt, flush left, on a white background box

Bookmark Layout: Back

4 · Organization Name: Cochin, 18pt, flush left. Address and Phone: Formata Bold, 9/11pt, flush left. Both are reverse (white) on a black background box.

The Idea Book example shows how a bookstore might customize the bookmark with its name and address.

Bookplate

Personalize your library

For hundreds of years, lovers of the written word have used *Bookplates* to identify their libraries. *Ex libris*, the Latin for "from the library of," is the most common inscription, but just one of many possibilities.

The first Idea Book example (top-left) shows how one reader might label his or her personal collection. The second example (top-right) shows how a library might identify the donor of a collection. The last example (bottom) shows how a parent might label children's books.

The simpler you make your version, the more likely it will blend with the design of the book. Print the designs directly from your computer on 3 1/3" by 4" labels (*see* Source:). Center the finished labels inside the front cover of your book.

Bookplate Layout: Top-Left

1 · "Ex Libris": Fette Fraktur, 32pt, centered. "Margaret Sampler": Fette Fraktur, 42/36pt, centered. Both are reverse (white) on a black background box

2 · Book Clip Art: From Logic Arts, 804-266-7996, 11475 Chickahominy Branch, Glen Allen, VA 23060 © Logic Arts Corp. All rights reserved

Bookplate Layout: Top-Right

3 · Line: .5pt

4 · "Malcolm" and "Collection": Adobe Caslon Italic, 30pt, centered. "S" in SAMPLER: Adobe Caslon Swash Italic, 50pt. "Sampler": Adobe Caslon Regular, 40pt, centered, all caps

5 · Date: Copperplate Gothic 33BC, 18pt, centered

Bookplate Layout: Bottom

6 ·"This book...": Formata Light, 18/18pt, centered. "Alice Sampler": Formata Bold, 18pt, centered

7 · Bear Clip Art: From Designer's Club by Dynamic Graphics, 800-255-8800, 6000 N. Forest Park Dr., Peoria, IL 61614-3592 © Dynamic Graphics, Inc. All rights reserved

8 · Line: .5pt

Print the designs directly from your computer on 3 1/3" by 4" labels and center the finished labels inside the front cover of your book.

Source: Bookplate Labels

The bookplates were printed on "Avery Laser Printer Labels" (3 1/3" by 4") from Avery Dennison, 800-252-8379, 818 Oak Park Road, Covina, CA 91724

Catalog

Catalog publishing is easier than you think

If you consider a catalog too complex a project to tackle, this simplified design may change your mind. The layout is particularly easy to execute because each product gets equal billing.

For your version, begin by dividing each page into a grid of four equal columns. (*See* the layouts on pages 52-53.) The cover features a collage of product photographs excerpted from the inside pages. Add the catalog title and replace the upper right photo with your organization's name and ordering details. If you plan to update the catalog often, add a publication date.

On the inside, use the first column of the left-hand page for a photograph or illustration. Use the second and third columns for the item number, the product name, and the product description. If your products don't require much text, divide the page into three equal columns and use the extra space for a larger photograph. Use the fourth column to list prices, color choices, sizes, availability, etc. Leave a wide left-hand margin for the hole punch.

Copy the same basic layout to produce the right-hand page but switch the photographs to the outside column to balance the left and right pages visually. Shift the page number so that it is flush right to the outside and leave extra margin space on the left for the hole punch.

Start each new product category on a new page. If you change categories in mid-page, leave the rest of the page blank.

Include solid black boxes where you want the photographs and have the commercial printer strip them in.

Print one master copy of the catalog and take it to a commercial printer to have it reproduced. Choose 80 lb coated text stock to maximize the reproduction quality of the photographs.

Have the pages printed side by side on 17" by 11" sheets, folded to 8 1/2" by 11" and saddle-stitched (bound with staples) in booklet form. Or have the pages printed on 8 1/2" by 11" sheets, hole punched; then distribute them in a ring binder.

**Catalog Layout:
Cover**

1 · Line: 8pt

2 · Line: 1pt

*3 · Catalog Title:
Helvetica Black,
24/22pt, flush left*

*4 · Organization
Name and Phone:
Times New
Roman, 20/20pt,
flush left*

*5 · Tag Line:
Times New
Roman, 12/14pt,
flush left*

6 · Photo area

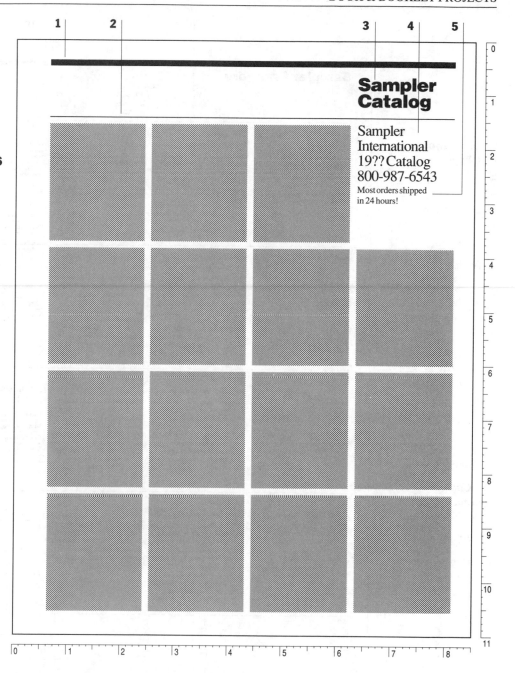

**Sampler
Catalog**

Sampler
International
19?? Catalog
800-987-6543

Most orders shipped
in 24 hours!

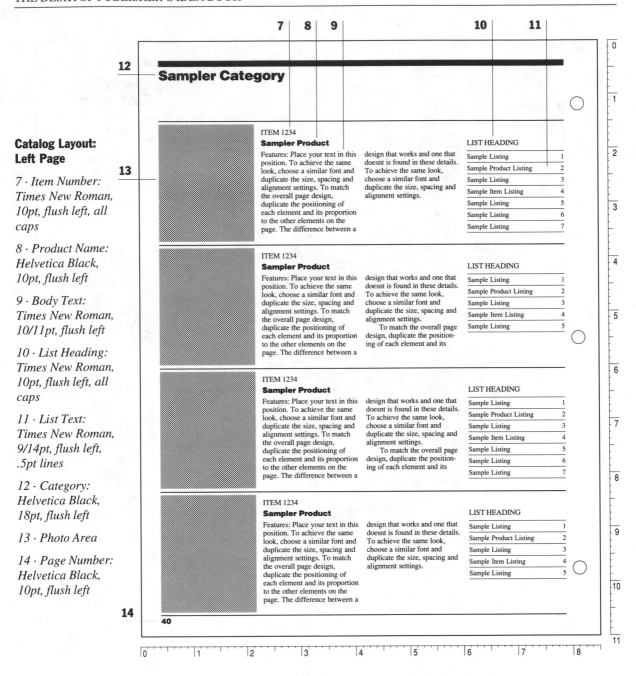

**Catalog Layout:
Left Page**

*7 · Item Number:
Times New Roman,
10pt, flush left, all
caps*

*8 · Product Name:
Helvetica Black,
10pt, flush left*

*9 · Body Text:
Times New Roman,
10/11pt, flush left*

*10 · List Heading:
Times New Roman,
10pt, flush left, all
caps*

*11 · List Text:
Times New Roman,
9/14pt, flush left,
.5pt lines*

*12 · Category:
Helvetica Black,
18pt, flush left*

13 · Photo Area

*14 · Page Number:
Helvetica Black,
10pt, flush left*

52

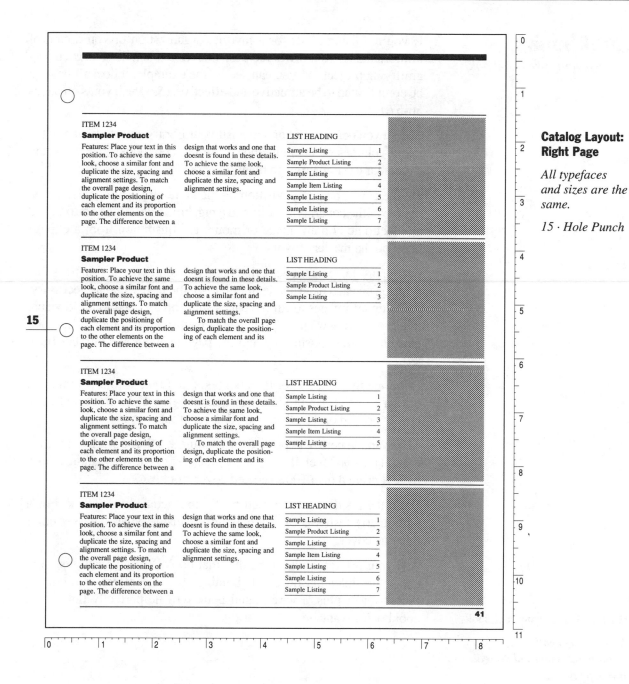

Catalog Layout: Right Page

All typefaces and sizes are the same.

15 · Hole Punch

53

Cookbook

Publish your own cookbook

If you're raising funds for a favorite organization or you dream of immortalizing your own recipes, this *Cookbook* is a particularly gratifying project. As you can see by the example, it doesn't have to be complicated to be attractive and effective. (*See* the layouts on pages 56-57.)

Before you begin your version, visit your library and study one of the many volumes on creating and marketing cookbooks. They contain details far too numerous to mention here.

On the cover, begin by positioning the name of your organization at the top of the cover. Follow it with a big, bold title. At the bottom, add an electronic clip art image or mount an illustration from a clip art book on the master artwork.

On the inside, feature one recipe per page. Start your text in the same position on each page and let it fall down the page as far as necessary. Add clip art images to fill the pages short on text and to build visual interest. If you want to print pages back to back, move the wide margin to the opposite side and the page heading and number flush left.

Print one master copy of the cookbook and take it to a commercial printer to have it reproduced in quantity. Have the front and back covers printed on 100 lb uncoated cover stock.

The example here was printed on a textured, colored stock to give it a natural look and feel. If you want your cover to withstand more abuse, have it printed on a 100 lb coated cover stock.

Have the inside pages printed on 60 lb uncoated text stock. For a particularly festive look, try making the inside pages a darker color than the cover.

Ask your printer to wire bind the final book. Wire typically is more expensive than plastic comb binding, but the effect is far more professional; plus, a wire-bound book will lie perfectly flat, a real cookbook advantage.

More topics for your cookbook

Acknowledgments
Definitions of unusual ingredients
Ingredients shopping list
Sample menus
A profile of your organization

The Idea Book example shows how a club might use a cookbook as a fundraiser.

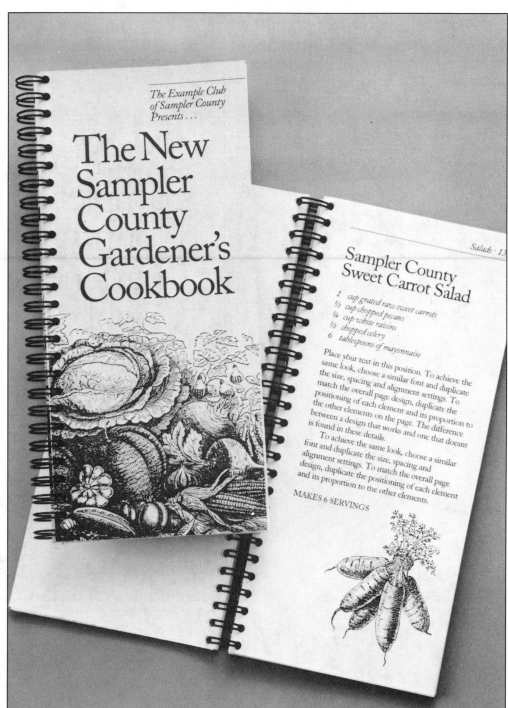

Source:
Wire Binding

The cookbook is bound using a "Wire-O" binding machine from Southern Binding & Supply, 800-331-5295, P.O. Box 21489, Hot Springs, AR 71903

Cookbook Layout: Cover

1 · Subtitle: Adobe Caslon Italic, 16/16pt, flush left, .5pt line above

2 · Title: Adobe Caslon Regular, 55/48pt, flush left

3 · Garden Illustrations: From "Food and Drink, A Pictorial Archive from Nineteenth-Century Sources," selected by Jim Harter, from Dover Publications, Inc., 516-294-7000, 31 East 2nd Street, Mineola, NY 11501
© Dover Publications, Inc. All rights reserved

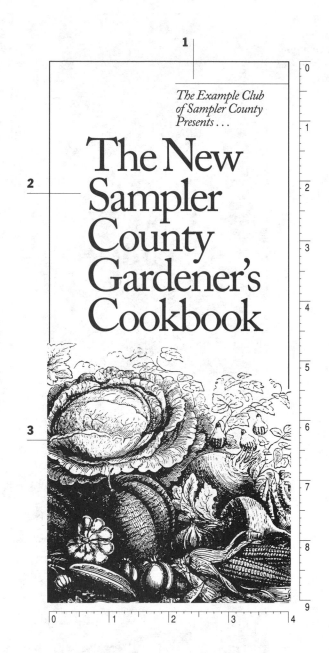

The Example Club
of Sampler County
Presents . . .

The New Sampler County Gardener's Cookbook

4

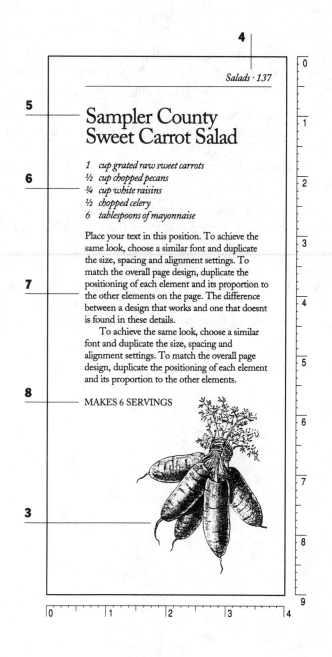

Salads · 137

5

Sampler County Sweet Carrot Salad

6

1 cup grated raw sweet carrots
½ cup chopped pecans
¾ cup white raisins
½ chopped celery
6 tablespoons of mayonnaise

7

Place your text in this position. To achieve the same look, choose a similar font and duplicate the size, spacing and alignment settings. To match the overall page design, duplicate the positioning of each element and its proportion to the other elements on the page. The difference between a design that works and one that doesnt is found in these details.

To achieve the same look, choose a similar font and duplicate the size, spacing and alignment settings. To match the overall page design, duplicate the positioning of each element and its proportion to the other elements.

8

MAKES 6 SERVINGS

3

Cookbook Layout: Inside Page

4 · Page Heading and Number: Adobe Caslon Italic, 13pt, flush right

5 · Recipe Title: Adobe Caslon Regular, 26/24pt, flush left

6 · Ingredients: Adobe Caslon Italic, 13/15pt, flush left

7 · Recipe Text: Adobe Caslon Regular, 12/14pt, flush left

8 · Servings: Adobe Caslon Regular, 11pt, flush left, all caps

Family Album

A memorable project for your family

The *Family Album* is not only a fun and fairly easy desktop publishing project, it may be one of the most meaningful gifts you'll ever give.

To create your version, you'll need the artwork, a ring binder with a clear plastic cover, a supply of 8 1/2" by 11" sheet protectors, and a package of old-fashioned photo mounting corners (*see* Source:).

First, produce the album cover artwork and trim it to 1/8" outside the border. (*See* the layouts on pages 60-61.) Use spray adhesive to mount it to a second, heavier white sheet. Trim the final insert 1/4" smaller than the overall size of the pocket and insert it so that there is an equal amount of space on all sides.

Next, compose the text column artwork and trim it to the outside edge. Use spray adhesive to mount the columns on the black construction paper insert that comes with the sheet protector.

Finally, arrange your photographs and attach them with old-fashioned photo mounting corners. You can also add other memorabilia like pressed flowers, announcements, invitations, and ticket stubs. Insert the finished page in the sheet protector and assemble all the pages in the binder.

Organize your family album by

Years or decades
Major events
Individual family members
Your family tree

Use the same basic layout for

A history of your organization
A school scrapbook
A travel diary
An anniversary or birthday gift

The Idea Book example shows how a family might divide the album into years or events.

**Source:
Clear Cover Binders**

The "Cardinal ClearVue RoundRing Binder" (5/8") available from your local office supply dealer.

**Source:
Album Pages**

The "Standard Sheet Protectors" (8 1/2" by 11") are available from 20th Century Plastics, 800-767-0777, 205 South Puente St., Brea, CA 90928

Family Album Cover Layout

1 · "THE": Adobe Caslon Regular, 24pt, centered, all caps

2 · Title: "S" in Sampler and the "F" in Family: Adobe Caslon Swash Italic, 72/58pt. "Sampler Family": Adobe Caslon Italic, 72/58pt, centered

3 · Date: Adobe Caslon Regular, 24pt, centered

4 · Line: .5pt

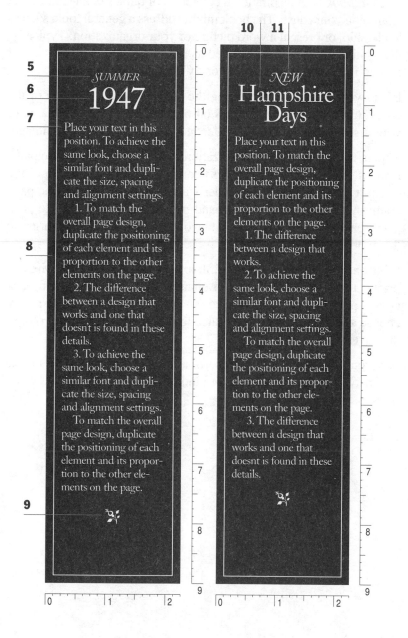

Text Column Layout: Left

5 · "S" in "SUMMER: Adobe Caslon Swash Italic, 13pt. "SUMMER": Adobe Caslon Italic, 13pt, centered, all caps. Both are reverse (white) on a black background box.

6 · "1947": Adobe Caslon Regular, 38pt, centered, reverse (white) on a black background

7 · Body Text: Adobe Caslon Regular, 14/16pt, flush left, reverse (white) on a black background

8 · Line: 1pt reverse (white) on a black background

9 · Ornament: Adobe Caslon Ornaments, 18pt, centered, reverse (white) on a black background

Text Column Layout: Right

10 · "Hampshire..." is Adobe Caslon Regular, 28/24pt, centered, reverse (white) on a black background box

11 · The "N" in NEW is Adobe Caslon Swash Italic, 16pt. "NEW" is Adobe Caslon Italic, 16pt, centered, all caps, reverse (white) on a black background

Giftbook

A special presentation with your signature

The *Giftbook* is an inspirational collection of quotes or anecdotes that champion your cause. The book might address a general topic such as leadership, or present a word picture of your organization. Typically, these miniature volumes are used as morale boosters, incentives for raising funds, or for setting the tone with potential customers.

Begin your version by centering the subtitle at the very top of the cover. (*See* the layouts on pages 64-65.) Follow it with the name of your organization, the book's title, and your logo or a clip art image.

Repeat the name of your organization at the top of each inside page. Limit the quotations or anecdotes to one per page no matter how long or short the text. Focus the reader's attention and increase the page count by printing on the right-hand page only. If you want to print pages back to back, use the same layout and shift the wide margin to the opposite side.

Print one master copy of the giftbook and take it to a commercial printer to have it reproduced in quantity. Have the front and back covers printed on 80 lb uncoated cover stock. For the inside pages, choose a bright white 70 lb uncoated text stock to contrast the color of the cover.

Ask your printer to wire bind the final book. Wire typically is more expensive than the plastic comb binding, but the effect is far more professional.

More pages for your giftbook

Biography of contributors
History of the organization
Index of contributors
Index of topics
Introduction
Space for a handwritten note

The Idea Book example shows how a school might use the layout to commemorate its 25th anniversary.

**Source:
Wire Binding**

The Giftbook is bound using a "Wire-O" binding machine from Southern Binding & Supply, 800-331-5295, P.O. Box 21489, Hot Springs, AR 71903

Giftbook Layout: Front Cover

1 · Subtitle: Copperplate Gothic 33BC, 11pt, centered, all caps, .5pt line below

2 · Title: "THE" is Minion Regular, 32pt, centered. "SAMPLER SCHOOL" is Minion Regular, 45/40pt, centered

3 · Line: .5pt

4 · Book Clip Art: From Logic Arts, 804-266-7996, 11475 Chickahominy Branch, Glen Allen, VA 23060 © Logic Arts Corp. All rights reserved

Gifbook Layout: Back Cover

5 · Organization Name: Copperplate Gothic 33BC, 11pt, centered, all caps. Address: Minion Regular, 11/12pt, centered

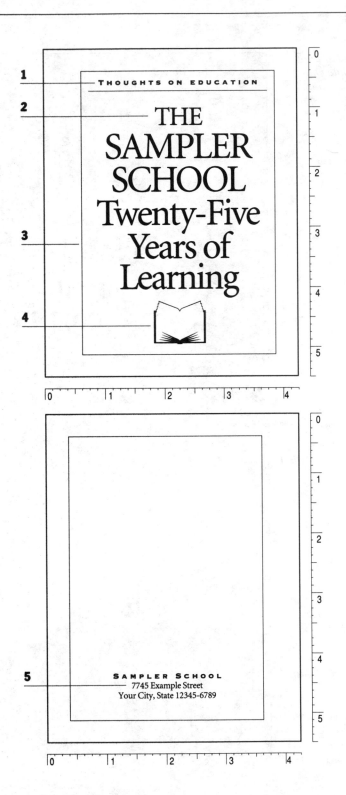

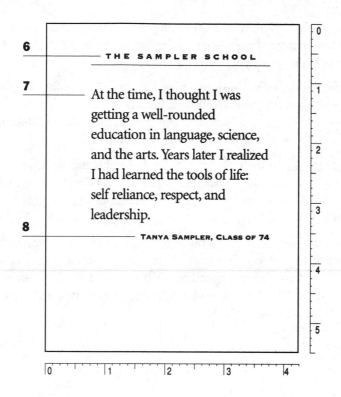

6

THE SAMPLER SCHOOL

7

At the time, I thought I was getting a well-rounded education in language, science, and the arts. Years later I realized I had learned the tools of life: self reliance, respect, and leadership.

8

TANYA SAMPLER, CLASS OF 74

Giftbook Layout: Inside Pages

6 · Organization Name: Copperplate Gothic 33BC, 11pt, centered, all caps, .5pt line below

7 · Body Text: Minion Regular, 18/24pt, flush left

8 · Credit: Copperplate Gothic 33BC, 11pt, flush right, all caps

Infobook

*Publish tips to promote
your business*

Before people commit to work with you, normally they want some indication that you know what you're talking about. This *Infobook* is one way to establish your credibility fast.

The Idea Book example shows how a painting contractor might use the Infobook to demonstrate his or her knowledge of painting older homes. But it's easy to see how this general format could apply to anyone in the business of selling his or her expertise.

Start your version with a headline that highlights the information you have to offer. (*See* the layouts on pages 68-69.) On the inside pages, stick to one topic per page. Reserve the last page to profile your organization.

Print one master copy of the book and take it to a commercial printer to have it reproduced in quantity and saddle-stitched (bound with staples). Have the cover printed on 80 lb uncoated cover stock. For the inside pages, choose a bright white 80 lb uncoated text stock to contrast the color of the cover.

The Idea Book example shows how a painting contractor might use the Infobook to demonstrate his or her knowledge of painting older homes.

10 big time myths about prepping and painting your older home...

BIG TIME MYTH FIVE:
Oil based paints are better than latex.

Place your text in this position. To achieve the same look, choose a similar font and duplicate the size, spacing and alignment settings. To match the overall page design, duplicate the positioning of each element and its proportion to the other elements on the page.

5

**Infobook Layout:
Back & Front
Covers**

*1 · Headline:
Minion Regular,
54/45pt, flush left*

*2 · Town House
Clip Art: From
Electronic Clipper
by Dynamic
Graphics, 800-255-
8800, 6000 N.
Forest Park Dr.,
Peoria, IL 61614-
3592 © Dynamic
Graphics, Inc. All
rights reserved*

*3 · Organization
Name, Phone, and
Address: Minion
Regular, 18/20pt,
centered*

*The dotted lines on
the top and bottom
edge represent
folds.*

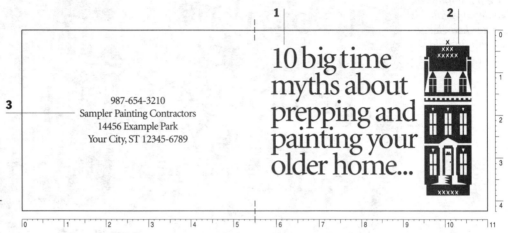

987-654-3210
Sampler Painting Contractors
14456 Example Park
Your City, ST 12345-6789

10 big time
myths about
prepping and
painting your
older home...

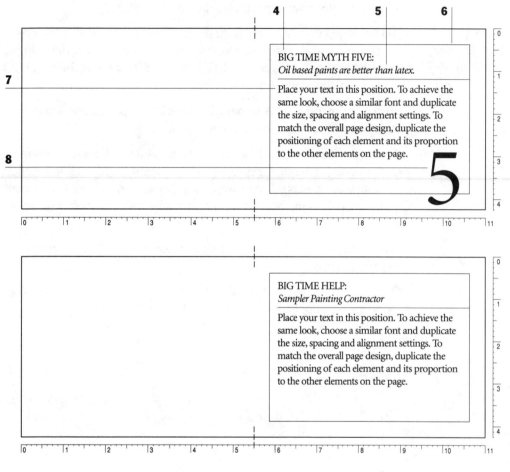

Infobook Layout: Inside Pages

4 · Lead-In: Minion Regular, 18pt, flush left, all caps

5 · Heading: Minion Italic, 18pt, flush left, .5pt line below

6 · Line: .5pt

7 · Body Text: Minion Regular, 18/20pt, flush left

8 · Large Number: Minion Regular, 140pt, flush left

Infobook Layout: Last Inside Page

All typefaces and sizes are the same as above.

The dotted lines on the top and bottom edge represent folds.

Within the layout image:

BIG TIME MYTH FIVE:
Oil based paints are better than latex.

Place your text in this position. To achieve the same look, choose a similar font and duplicate the size, spacing and alignment settings. To match the overall page design, duplicate the positioning of each element and its proportion to the other elements on the page.

BIG TIME HELP:
Sampler Painting Contractor

Place your text in this position. To achieve the same look, choose a similar font and duplicate the size, spacing and alignment settings. To match the overall page design, duplicate the positioning of each element and its proportion to the other elements on the page.

Phone Book

Spread the word at conferences, meetings, and tradeshows

Hand out a phone or address book at just the right time and people may start using it on the spot. Conferences, tradeshows, meetings, or anywhere else people collect names and numbers, are perfect opportunities to distribute your book. Once they start using it, it's guaranteed they'll see your message time and time again.

To create your version, position the book title at the top of the cover and the organization name, address, and phone number at the bottom. (*See* the layouts on pages 72-73.) Reserve the back cover for a detailed listing of your products and services.

Instead of preprinting A through Z on the inside pages, the user gets to choose how many pages to devote to each letter.

Print one master copy of the telephone book and take it to a commercial printer to have it reproduced in quantity and saddle-stitched (bound with staples). The example was printed on a bright fluorescent paper that gives the booklet a contemporary look and makes it easy to spot.

This type of booklet will incur lots of abuse, so have the cover printed on 80 lb uncoated cover stock.

To contrast the cover, print the inside pages on a bright white 24 lb bond stock. Supply at least one page for each letter of the alphabet.

Other ways to use the Phone Book layout

Address book
Expense book
Pocket-sized daily planner

The Idea Book example shows a miniature telephone book that a retailer might hand out to cellular phone buyers.

Phone Book Layout:
Back and Front Covers

1 · Marketing Information: "Sampler Cellular" : Minion Regular, 14pt, flush left. "The finest..." : Minion Regular, 9/12pt, flush left

2 · Title: Minion Regular, 22pt, flush left, .5pt line around. "Book" : Reverse white on a black background box

3 · Organization Name, Address, and Phone: Minion Regular, 9/12pt, flush left

The dotted lines on the top and bottom edge represent folds.

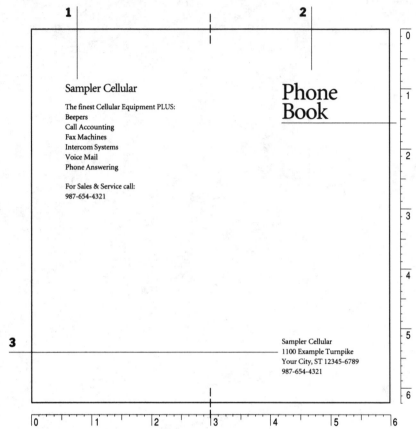

Sampler Cellular

The finest Cellular Equipment PLUS:
Beepers
Call Accounting
Fax Machines
Intercom Systems
Voice Mail
Phone Answering

For Sales & Service call:
987-654-4321

Phone
Book

Sampler Cellular
1100 Example Turnpike
Your City, ST 12345-6789
987-654-4321

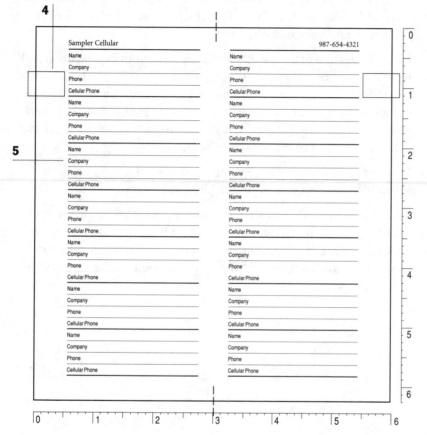

Phone Book Layout: Inside Pages

4 · Fill-In Box: This is where the user enters a letter of the alphabet. .5pt line around

5 · Name, Address, and Phone Fill-In: Helvetica Narrow, 7/14pt, flush left, .5pt lines

The dotted lines on the top and bottom edge represent folds.

Record Book

Help your customers track important information

Could you use a book that tells customers how valuable you are? This little *Record Book* is one way to help customers track facts and figures, and prompt them to use your products and services regularly.

The Idea Book example illustrates an auto service center. The book provides important facts about the vehicle, a record of services provided, and a maintenance checklist.

Start your version of the cover with the name of your organization and the title of the book. (*See* the layouts on pages 76-77.) Next, add a fill-in for details like the customer's name, ID numbers, dates, etc. At the bottom, include instructions about how to use the book. On the back cover list your organization's name, address, and phone. On the inside, create fill-in areas for the records.

Print one master copy of the Record Book and take it to a commercial printer to have it reproduced and saddle-stitched (bound with staples).

Have the cover printed on 80 lb uncoated cover stock to ensure that it survives frequent handling; or, choose a 65 lb stock and distribute the book in a clear vinyl pocket (*see* Source:). For the inside pages, choose a bright white 24 lb bond stock to contrast the color of the cover.

More uses for the Record Book

To document a financial plan
To keep home maintenance records
To record payments
To report expenses
To track a weight loss program

The Idea Book example illustrates an auto service center. The book provides important facts about the vehicle, a record of services provided, and a maintenance checklist.

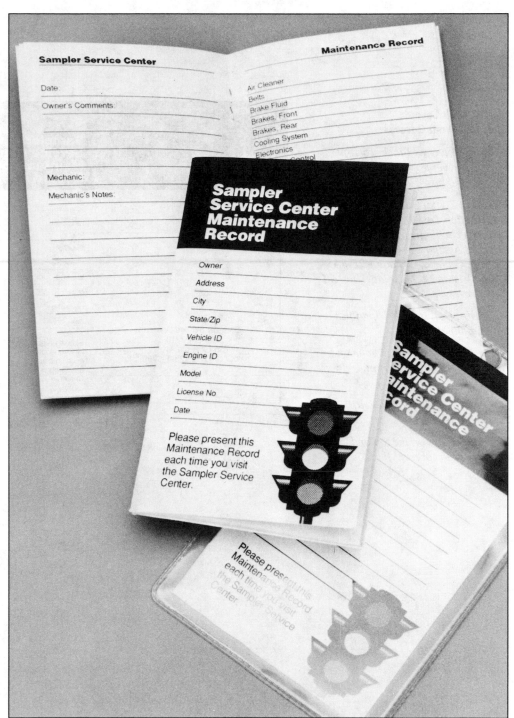

**Source:
Clear Vinyl
Pockets**

The Record Book is sized to fit in a 3 1/2" by 5 1/2" vinyl envelope from Bardes Products, 800-223-1357, 5245 West Clinton Ave., Milwaukee, WI 53223

Record Book Layout:
Back and Front Covers

1 · Title: Helvetica Black, 16/15pt, flush left, reverse (white) on a black background box

2 · Traffic Signal Clip Art: From Presentation Task Force by New Vision Technologies, Inc., 613-727-8184, 38 Auriga Drive, Unit 13, Nepean, Ontario, Canada K2E 8A5 © New Vision Technologies, Inc. All rights reserved

3 · Fill-In: Helvetica, 8/18pt, flush left, .5pt. lines

4 · Organization Name, Phone and Address: Helvetica, 11/12pt, centered

5 · Cover Message: Helvetica, 10/11pt, flush left

The dotted lines on the top and bottom edge represent folds.

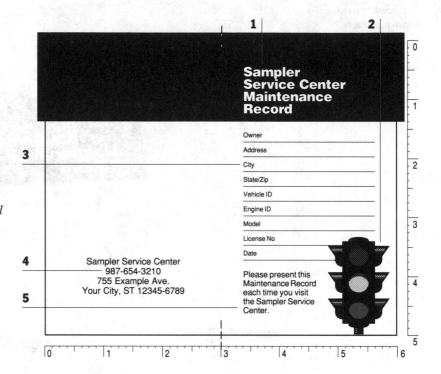

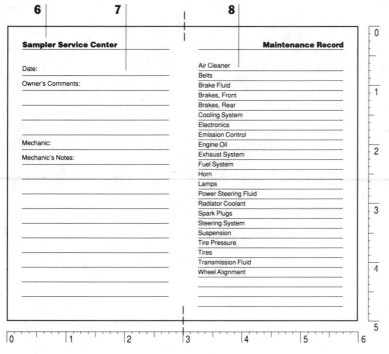

6　　**7**　　**8**

Sampler Service Center　　　　　　　　**Maintenance Record**

Date:

Owner's Comments:

Mechanic:

Mechanic's Notes:

Air Cleaner
Belts
Brake Fluid
Brakes, Front
Brakes, Rear
Cooling System
Electronics
Emission Control
Engine Oil
Exhaust System
Fuel System
Horn
Lamps
Power Steering Fluid
Radiator Coolant
Spark Plugs
Steering System
Suspension
Tire Pressure
Tires
Transmission Fluid
Wheel Alignment

**Record Book Layout:
Inside Pages**

*6 · Subhead: Helvetica Black, 9pt,
flush left on left page, flush right on
right page, .5pt line below*

*7 · Left Page Fill-In: Helvetica ,
8/18pt, flush left, .5pt lines*

*8 · Right Page Fill-In: Helvetica ,
8/12pt, flush left, .5pt lines*

*The dotted lines on the top and
bottom edge represent folds.*

CHAPTER 5
Brochure Projects

Brochure #10

Tailor your next brochure to a standard business envelope

Here is a sales representative you can send across town or around the country for the price of a stamp. It is a simple, clear brochure that tells the story of your business, trumpets the kind words of customers, and prompts the reader to take action.

The brochure is a standard 14" by 11" page folded in half, and in half again to fit a #10 business envelope.

Begin your version with a compelling cover headline. (*See* the layouts on pages 82-83.) Tell the big picture story on the next two pages and follow up on the inside spread with the details. Include two or three quotations from customers to endorse your claims. At the end of the text, conclude with a clear call to action.

Choose a clip art image for the cover that supports the headline and sets a professional tone. Use another appropriate image inside or repeat the cover illustration.

Print one master copy of the brochure, take it to a commercial printer, and have it reproduced on a high-quality 65 lb cover stock and machine folded.

If you're printing all the text and illustrations in black ink, choose an uncoated colored stock. If you're printing in color, a white, coated stock will net handsome results.

Customer questions your brochure should answer

What can you do for me?
What does it cost?
Why should I deal with you?
Are your other customers happy?
Will you help me with problems?
Why should I believe you?

The Idea Book example shows how a training center might use the brochure as a big picture marketing tool.

Brochure #10
Layout: Side One

1 · Cover Headline: Formata Bold, 40/38pt, flush left

2 · Organization Name: Times New Roman, 8pt, flush left, all caps

3 · Inside Headlines: Formata Bold, 30/30pt, flush left

4 · Body Text: Times New Roman, 12/14pt, flush left

5 · Line: .5pt

6 · Quotation: Times New Roman Italic, 18/20pt, flush left. Credit Line: Times New Roman, 12pt, flush right

7 · Work Group Clip Art: From Electronic Clipper by Dynamic Graphics, 800-255-8800, 6000 N. Forest Park Dr., Peoria, IL 61614-3592 © Dynamic Graphics, Inc. All rights reserved

8 · Organization Name: Formata Bold, 14pt, flush left. Address and Phones: Times New Roman, 12/14pt, flush left

The dotted lines on the top and bottom edges represent folds.

Within the layout image, the following text appears:

Sampler Training Center
2520 Example Grove Road
City, State 23060
800-555-1212 Fax 800-555-1313

SAMPLER TRAINING CENTER

SAMPLER TRAINING

Leave everyone wondering how you got so good so fast.

Real-world computer training with a bulletproof guarantee.

Place your text in this position. To achieve the same look, choose a similar font and duplicate the size, spacing and alignment settings. To match the overall page design, duplicate the positioning of each element and its proportion to the other elements on the page. The difference between a design that works and one that doesn't is found in these details.

To achieve the same look, choose a similar font and duplicate the size, spacing and alignment settings. To match the overall page design, duplicate the positioning of each element and its proportion to the other elements on the page. The difference between a design that works and one that doesn't is found in these details. To achieve the same look, choose a similar font and duplicate the size, spacing and alignment settings.

To match the overall page design, duplicate the positioning of each element and its proportion to the other elements on the page. The difference between a design that works and one that doesn't is found in these details. Place your text in this position. To achieve the same look, choose a similar font and duplicate the size, spacing and alignment settings. To match the overall page design, duplicate the positioning of each element and its proportion to the other elements on the page.

The difference between a design that works and one that doesn't is found in these details. Place your text in this position. To achieve the same look, choose a similar font and duplicate the size, spacing and alignment settings.

"The Sampler Training Center got our staff producing in a matter of hours."

Wendy Best, Example Corporation

82

SAMPLER TRAINING

Dollars and sense reasons for using our one-of-a-kind training center...

"The Sampler Training Center is a top-knotch facility with professionals that know their business."

To match the overall page design, duplicate the positioning of each element and its proportion to the other elements on the page. The difference between a design that works and one that doesn't is found in these details. Place your text in this position. To achieve the same look, choose a similar font and duplicate the size, spacing and alignment settings. To match the overall page design, duplicate the positioning of each element and its proportion to the other elements on the page.

The difference between a design that works and one that doesn't is found in these details. Place your text in this position. To

achieve the same look, choose a similar font and duplicate the size, spacing and alignment settings. To match the overall page design, duplicate the positioning of each element and its proportion to the other elements.

Place your text in this position. To achieve the same look, choose a similar font and duplicate the size, spacing and alignment settings. To match the overall page design, duplicate the positioning of each element and its proportion to the other elements on the page. The difference between a design that works and one that doesn't is found in these details.

To achieve the same look, choose a similar font and duplicate the size, spacing and alignment settings. To match the overall page design, duplicate the positioning of each element and its proportion to the other elements on the page. The difference between a design that works and one that doesn't is found in these position. To match the overall page design, duplicate the positioning of each element and its

proportion to the other elements on the page. The difference between a design that works and one that doesn't is found in these details. Place your text in this position. To achieve the same look, choose a similar font and duplicate the size, spacing and alignment settings. To match the overall page design, duplicate the positioning of each element and its proportion to the other elements.

The difference between a design that works and one that doesn't is found in these details. Place your text in this position. To achieve the same look, choose a similar font and duplicate the size, spacing and alignment settings. The difference between a design that works and

one that doesn't is found in these details.

To achieve the same look, choose a similar font and duplicate the size, spacing and alignment settings. To match the overall page design, duplicate the positioning of each element and its proportion to the other elements on the page. The difference between a design that works and one that doesn't is found in these details. Place your text in this position. To achieve the same look, choose a similar font and duplicate the size, spacing and alignment settings.

To match the overall page design, duplicate the positioning of each element and its proportion to the other elements on the page. The difference between a design that

Call today for a free one hour consultation...805-555-1212

Sampler Training Center
2520 Example Grove Road
City, State 23060
805-555-1212 Fax 805-555-1313

**Brochure #10
Layout: Side Two**

All of the typefaces and sizes are the same with one addition:

9 · Call To Action: Formata Bold, 14/16pt, flush left

The illustration from the cover is blown up, cropped, and re-used inside. The dotted lines on the top and bottom edges represent folds.

Brochure Book

*Tell your story with an
eye-catching miniature book*

If you're telling the story of how a product was made, the history of your organization or any other message that lends itself to a narrative format, this miniature book is worth a look. The inside pages of the brochure are printed and bound, then folded into a miniature dust jacket.

For your version, center the title and subtitle on the cover of the book jacket and the name of your organization on the back. (*See* the layouts on pages 86-87.) On the inside pages, present the text of the story and pepper it with quotations from the people involved.

Recreate the wallpaper background by typing, spacing, and repeating a single type of ornament. This design works best with a hefty number of inside pages, a minimum 16. If you're short on text, increase the page count by printing on the right-hand page only. If you want to print pages back to back, use the same layout and shift the wide margin to the opposite side.

Print master copies of the book jacket and the inside pages and take them to a commercial printer. Have the book jacket printed on a white 60 lb uncoated cover stock. Have the inside pages printed on 60 lb uncoated text stock, folded and saddle-stitched (bound with staples).

Assemble the final book by wrapping the jacket flaps around the first and last pages of the inside booklet.

The Idea Book example shows how a charitable organization might use the book to tell how one volunteer made a difference.

Brochure Book Layout:
Book Jacket

1 · Ornament: Adobe Caslon Ornaments, 30/28pt, flush left

2 · Organization Name: Charlemagne, 18pt, centered, all caps. Tag Line: Adobe Caslon Regular, 9pt, centered, .5pt line around

3 · Title: Charlemagne, 35/33pt, centered, all caps, reverse (white) on a black background box. Tag Line: Adobe Caslon Regular, 12pt, centered, .5pt line around

The dotted lines on the top and bottom edges represent folds.

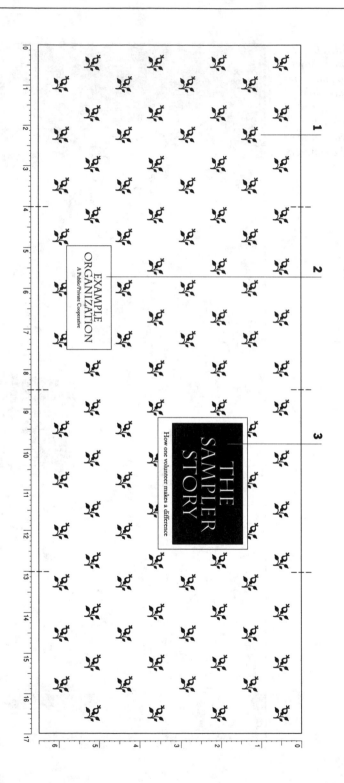

EXAMPLE ORGANIZATION
A Public/Private Cooperative

THE SAMPLER STORY
How one volunteer makes a difference

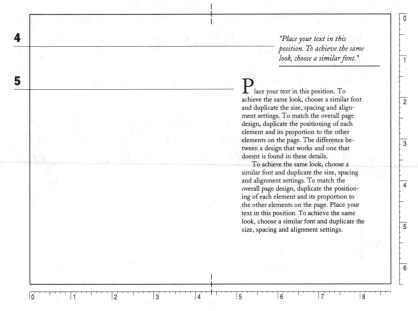

"Place your text in this position. To achieve the same look, choose a similar font."

Place your text in this position. To achieve the same look, choose a similar font and duplicate the size, spacing and alignment settings. To match the overall page design, duplicate the positioning of each element and its proportion to the other elements on the page. The difference between a design that works and one that doesnt is found in these details.

To achieve the same look, choose a similar font and duplicate the size, spacing and alignment settings. To match the overall page design, duplicate the positioning of each element and its proportion to the other elements on the page. Place your text in this position. To achieve the same look, choose a similar font and duplicate the size, spacing and alignment settings.

Brochure Book Layout: Inside Pages

4 · Quotation: Adobe Caslon Italic, 14/16pt, flush left, 1pt line below

5 · Large Initial: Adobe Caslon Regular, 36/14pt, flush left. Body Text: Adobe Caslon Regular, 36/14pt, flush left

The dotted lines on the top and bottom edges represent folds.

Brochure Wrap

Add updates and special offers to existing brochures

If you need to personalize a generic manufacturer's brochure or update your own, this design could save a big printing bill. It's the same idea used by countless magazines and mail order firms to add a personal touch to general publications.

To create your version, start with a headline that speaks to the reader one-on-one. Add your name and affiliation at the bottom and sign it like a letter. Center the organization, address, and phone number on the back.

Stick with black type on a white background so the wrap is less likely to clash with the design of the brochure.

Print the wrap directly from your computer on white 24 lb uncoated bond stock. Fold it and trim the bottom to match the height of the brochure. Attach the wrap to the spine of the brochure with a strip of double-sided tape.

Brochure Wrap Layout

1 · Headline: Cochin, 42/40pt, flush left

2 · Line: .5pt

3 · Symbol: Adobe Carta Font, 30pt, centered

4 · Organization Name, Address, and Phone: Cochin, 14/16pt, centered

5 · Headline Signature: Cochin Italic, 14/16pt, flush left

The dotted lines on the top and bottom edges represent the fold.

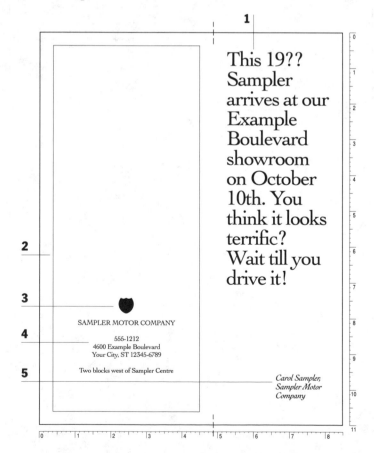

This 19?? Sampler arrives at our Example Boulevard showroom on October 10th. You think it looks terrific? Wait till you drive it!

SAMPLER MOTOR COMPANY

555-1212
4600 Example Boulevard
Your City, ST 12345-6789

Two blocks west of Sampler Centre

*Carol Sampler,
Sampler Motor
Company*

The Idea Book example shows how a car sales rep might use the wrap to alert special clients to the arrival of a new model.

PERSONAL LUXURY SEDAN

This 19?? Sampler arrives at our Example Boulevard showroom on October 10th. You think it looks terrific? Wait till you drive it!

Carol Sampler, Sampler Motor Company

SAMPLER MOTOR COMPANY

555-1212
4600 Example Boulevard
Your City, ST 12345-6789

Two blocks west of Sampler Centre

Quick-Change Menu

Respond quickly to changing information

With your desktop publishing system and these plastic display frames you can update menu items and prices before breakfast. But you don't have to be a restauranteur to use the idea. A banker could use the layout to display interest rates; a retailer might use it to announce daily specials.

To create your version, center the name of your organization over the box that frames the text. Choose a clip art image that reflects the subject matter and position it at the bottom.

Print the menus directly from your computer on a 24 lb uncoated bond stock and insert them in display frames (*see* Source:).

Quick-Change Menu Layout: Menu

1 · Restaurant Name: Charlemagne, 48pt, centered, all caps

2 · Headings: Times New Roman, 16pt, centered

3 · Listings: Times New Roman, 12/14pt, flush left. The prices are flush right.

4 · Food Basket Clip Art: From Designer's Club by Dynamic Graphics, 800-255-8800, 6000 N. Forest Park Dr., Peoria, IL 61614-3592 © Dynamic Graphics, Inc. All rights reserved

5 · Line: .5pt

Quick-Change Menu Layout: Wine List

On the small menu, all of the typefaces and sizes are the same.

The illustration is cropped differently and bleeds off the page (extends off the edge).

Instead of an eatery, a banker could use the layout to display interest rates; a retailer might use it to announce daily specials.

Source: Display Frames

The large menu is displayed in an "Acrylic Fabricated Display" (8.5" by 11", bottom load, double-sided) from Beemak Plastics, Inc., 800-421-4393, 16639 South Gramercy Place, Gardena, CA 90247

The small menu is displayed in a "Clear Plastic Frame" (5" by 7", top load, double-sided) from Siegel Display Products, 800-626-0322, PO Box 95, Minneapolis, MN 55440

RSVP Brochure

An instant response brochure

The customer's impression of your organization often spells the difference between success or failure. Yet many of us spend very little time finding out how we're doing.

The Idea Book example shows how a company might use the brochure to solicit valuable feedback.

Before you begin your version, visit the library and look through some of the books on research gathering. You'll find information on different ways to phrase the questions and gather answers.

Compose a cover headline that asks for the reader's help. (*See* the layouts on page 94-95.) Inside, explain why you're seeking the information and list your questions. Add check-off boxes rating performance from poor to excellent. Post your return address on the back cover so the customer can drop the completed brochure in the mail. The customer typically remains anonymous, but you could give them the option and space to fill in his or her name.

Print one master copy and take it to a commercial printer to have it reproduced on 65 lb uncoated cover stock and machine folded. Choose stock with a smooth, uncoated finish so it's easy to write on with pen or pencil. If you use a color, select a very light shade in case you later need to photocopy the responses.

Before you print, stop by the post office with the final artwork and a paper sample to confirm that your brochure meets postal regulations. Add return postage to each brochure before it goes out. For a large mailing, apply for a Business Reply Mail permit from the post office and print the panel using those guidelines.

Some fill-in question topics

Would you deal with us again?
How can we improve?
How else can we serve you?
Where did you hear about us?

The Idea Book example shows how a company might use the brochure to solicit valuable feedback.

RSVP Brochure Layout: Back and Front Covers

1 · Mailing Instructions: Helvetica Light, 11/12pt, centered, .5pt box around

2 · Return Address: Helvetica Light, 12/16pt, flush left

3 · Magnifying Glass Clip Art: From ClickArt EPS Business Art by T/Maker Company, 415-962-0195, 1390 Villa Street, Mountain View, CA 94041 © T/Maker Company. All rights reserved

4 · Title: Helvetica Light, 14pt, centered. Text In Magnifying Glass: Helvetica Light, 24pt, flush left

5 · Headline: Charlemagne, 60/55pt, centered, all caps

The dotted lines on the right and left edges represent folds.

Place Postage Here

Sampler Company
4577 Example Bluff
Your City, ST 12345-6789

A Sampler Company Survey

HOW ARE WE DOING?

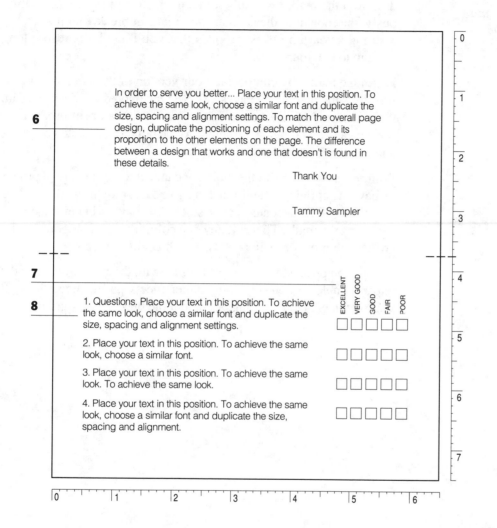

6

In order to serve you better... Place your text in this position. To achieve the same look, choose a similar font and duplicate the size, spacing and alignment settings. To match the overall page design, duplicate the positioning of each element and its proportion to the other elements on the page. The difference between a design that works and one that doesn't is found in these details.

Thank You

Tammy Sampler

7

8

1. Questions. Place your text in this position. To achieve the same look, choose a similar font and duplicate the size, spacing and alignment settings.

2. Place your text in this position. To achieve the same look, choose a similar font.

3. Place your text in this position. To achieve the same look. To achieve the same look.

4. Place your text in this position. To achieve the same look, choose a similar font and duplicate the size, spacing and alignment.

EXCELLENT
VERY GOOD
GOOD
FAIR
POOR

RSVP Brochure Layout: Inside

6 · Letter Text: Helvetica Light, 12/14pt, flush left

7 · Check Off Headings: Helvetica Light, 8/18pt, flush left, all caps, rotated

8 · Question Text: Helvetica Light, 12/14pt, flush left

The dotted lines on the right and left edges represent folds.

Self Mailer

Mail your next brochure without an envelope

Take a standard 8 1/2" by 11" sheet, fold it in thirds, add postage and drop it in the mail. It doesn't come much simpler or cheaper. Obviously, the content of the message will make or break your mailer, but a strong layout improves the odds that you'll hook the reader long enough to tell your story.

Begin the mailer by composing your version of the three-part headline. (*See* the layouts on pages 98-99.) Once you draw the reader in, the photograph or illustration sets the mood and a list of products or services and text provide the detail. At the bottom left, state your offer and call the reader to action.

Print one master copy of the mailer and take it to a commercial printer to have it reproduced and machine folded. You can mail a lighter stock, but 65 lb uncoated cover stock will have a better chance of surviving the mails. To test if any one color improves response, print an equal number of mailers on two or three different colors.

Before you print, stop by the post office with the final artwork and a paper sample to confirm your mailer meets postal regulations. If you're doing a large mailing, ask about the bulk mail program.

The Idea Book example shows how a landscaping company might use the mailer to generate phone calls for free estimates.

**Self Mailer
Layout: Outside**

*1 · Headline Two:
Adobe Caslon
Regular, 65/55pt,
centered. The
commas and the
ellipsis are
reduced to 45pt.*

*2 · Return
Address: Adobe
Caslon Regular,
12/14pt, flush left*

*3 · Recipient's
Address: Courier
Bold, 11/15pt,
flush left*

*4 · Headline One:
Adobe Caslon
Regular, 65/55pt,
centered. The
ellipsis at the end
is reduced to
45pt.*

*The dotted lines
on the right and
left edges
represent folds.*

5

To create your picture-perfect landscape

6

Call Sampler Landscaping for:
Planting
Mulching
Transplanting
Seeding
Pruning
Flower Beds
Grading
Top Soil
Lawn
Renovation
Insect Control
Fertilizer
Application
Soil Analysis
& Irrigation
Systems

7

8
9

For a FREE on-site estimate, call:

987-654-3210

10

Sampler Landscaping
1555 Example Springs
Your City, ST 12345

Our nursery is open 9-5 Monday-Saturday Take Route 1 North to Example Springs and turn left, Sampler Landscaping is 1.4 miles west.

Place your text in this position. To achieve the same look, choose a similar font and duplicate the size, spacing and alignment settings.

To match the overall page design, duplicate the positioning of each element and its proportion to the other elements on the page. The difference between a design that works and one that doesn't is found in these details.

To achieve the same look, choose a similar font and duplicate the size,

spacing and alignment settings. To match the overall page design, duplicate the positioning of each element and its proportion to the other elements on the page. The difference between a design that works and one that doesn't is found in these details.

Place your text in this position. To achieve the same look, choose a similar font and duplicate the size, spacing and alignment settings.

To match the overall page design, duplicate the positioning of each

Self Mailer Layout: Inside

5 · Headline Three: Adobe Caslon Regular, 65/55pt, centered

6 · List: Adobe Caslon Regular, 14/16pt, flush left, reverse (white) on a black background box

7 · Garden Stock Photo: From Electronic Clipper by Dynamic Graphics, 800-255-8800, 6000 N. Forest Park Dr., Peoria, IL 61614-3592 © Dynamic Graphics, Inc. All rights reserved

8 · Call To Action: Adobe Caslon Regular, 14/16pt, flush left

9 · Phone Number: Adobe Caslon Regular, 18pt, flush left

10 · Body Text: Adobe Caslon Regular, 14/16pt, flush left

The dotted lines on the right and left edges represent folds.

Take-A-Test Brochure

Demonstrate your marketing message

We all love a challenge and this layout offers one. If there are popular misconceptions about your field of expertise this *Take-A-Test Brochure* can help dispel them.

The cover of the brochure lists a series of questions the reader answers by checking true or false boxes. They then lift the cover to reveal the correct answers and gauge their knowledge of the subject.

The Idea Book example shows how a career consultant might shoot down myths about who and why organizations hire.

Start your version by composing your questions and answers, and positioning them as shown. (*See* the layouts on pages 102-103.) Add the phone number on the inside page as the call to action. If you need space for a longer message, include a paragraph or two on the back cover above the organization name and address.

Print one master copy of the artwork and take it to a commercial printer to have it reproduced on 65 lb uncoated cover stock and machine folded. Choose stock with a smooth, uncoated finish so it's easy to write on with pen or pencil. This example was printed on a bright colored stock to capture attention and add more interest to the all-type design.

The Idea Book example shows how a career consultant might shoot down myths about who and why organizations hire.

The Job Hunter's Test

Experience is the no longer the top small business hiring criteria.

Fortune 500 companies hire the majority of their workforce through Personnel Departments.

You should never apply for a position that requires a degree you don't have.

Poorly executed resumes eliminate twenty percent of all job applicants.

You must have inside contacts to get the top management positions.

Some surprising answers

True

False

False

True

False

To match the overall page design, duplicate the position. Place your text in this position. To achieve the same look, and duplicate the size, spacing and alignment settings.

Place your text in this position. To achieve the same look, choose a similar font and duplicate the size, spacing and alignment settings. To match the overall page design, duplicate the positioning of each element.

For expert career counseling call Sampler Career Consultants 987-654-3210

Take-A-Test Brochure: Back and Front Covers

1 · Title: Formata Bold, 24pt, flush left

2 · Question Text: Minion Display, 24/24pt, flush left

3 · Organization Name: Formata Bold, 14pt, centered. Address and Phone: Minion Display, 14/18pt, centered

The dotted lines on the top and bottom edges represent folds.

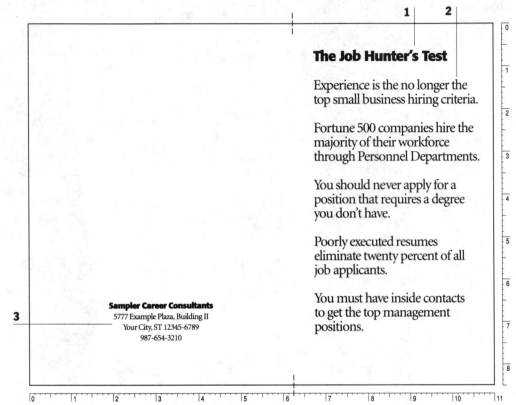

The Job Hunter's Test

Experience is the no longer the top small business hiring criteria.

Fortune 500 companies hire the majority of their workforce through Personnel Departments.

You should never apply for a position that requires a degree you don't have.

Poorly executed resumes eliminate twenty percent of all job applicants.

You must have inside contacts to get the top management positions.

Sampler Career Consultants
5777 Example Plaza, Building II
Your City, ST 12345-6789
987-654-3210

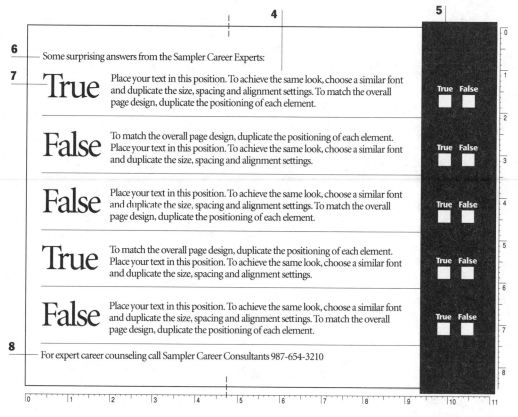

Some surprising answers from the Sampler Career Experts:

True

Place your text in this position. To achieve the same look, choose a similar font and duplicate the size, spacing and alignment settings. To match the overall page design, duplicate the positioning of each element.

False

To match the overall page design, duplicate the positioning of each element. Place your text in this position. To achieve the same look, choose a similar font and duplicate the size, spacing and alignment settings.

False

Place your text in this position. To achieve the same look, choose a similar font and duplicate the size, spacing and alignment settings. To match the overall page design, duplicate the positioning of each element.

True

To match the overall page design, duplicate the positioning of each element. Place your text in this position. To achieve the same look, choose a similar font and duplicate the size, spacing and alignment settings.

False

Place your text in this position. To achieve the same look, choose a similar font and duplicate the size, spacing and alignment settings. To match the overall page design, duplicate the positioning of each element.

For expert career counseling call Sampler Career Consultants 987-654-3210

**Take-A-Test
Brochure: Inside**

*4 · Answer Text:
Minion Display,
18/20pt, flush left*

*5 · Check-Off Box
Text: Formata
Bold, 14pt,
centered, reverse
(white) on a black
background box*

*6 · Lead In:
Minion Display,
18pt, flush left*

*7 · Answer
Headline: Minion
Display, 60pt,
flush left*

*8 · Call To Action:
Minion Display,
18pt, flush left*

*The dotted lines
on the top and
bottom edges
represent folds.*

CHAPTER 6
Card & Ticket Projects

Business Card

Your #1 marketing tool

A business card is probably your single best marketing opportunity. It is accepted practice to offer it in situations in which it would be awkward or inappropriate to offer a brochure.

To create your version, begin with the basics. Include your name, title, voice, fax, and page phone numbers; even consider adding telex or computer network ID numbers. List the organization name and address, and don't forget a one-sentence description of your business or mission, a key component left off many business cards.

Add your logo or a clip art symbol to represent your business. You may even want to compose one or two brief paragraphs about the organization for the back of the card.

Print one master copy of the card and take it to a commercial printer to have it reproduced on high-quality 80 lb uncoated cover stock.

Business Card Layout: Top

1 · Tree Clip Art: From Designer's Club by Dynamic Graphics, 800-255-8800, 6000 N. Forest Park Dr., Peoria, IL 61614-3592 © Dynamic Graphics, Inc. All rights reserved

2 · Description of Services and Phones: Adobe Caslon Regular, 8/8pt, centered. Name: Adobe Caslon Regular, 9pt, centered. Title: Adobe Caslon Italic, 8pt, centered

3 · Line: .5pt

4 · Organization Name: Adobe Caslon Bold Italic, 11/9pt, flush left

5 · Address: Adobe Caslon Regular, 8/9pt, flush left

Business Card Layout: Bottom

6 · Organization Name: Cochin Bold Italic, 18/14pt, flush left. Address: Cochin Bold, 8/9pt, flush left. Both are reverse (white) on a black background box

7 · Description of Services: Cochin, 8/8pt, flush left

8 · Name: Cochin, 9pt, flush left. Title: Cochin Italic, 8pt, flush left. Phone Numbers: Cochin, 8pt, flush right

The Idea Book example shows two different ways a landscaping company might use the layout.

**Source:
Lamination**

Also pictured is an adhesive backed "ad-a-tab" that converts your business card into a rotary file card. From DO-IT Corp., 800-426-4822, P.O. Box 592, South Haven, MI 49090

Business Card Brochure

Create the world's least expensive brochure

If a business card is your number one marketing tool, this card is a close second. Rather than focus on your name and title, the *Business Card Brochure* presents, in miniature, all of the key ingredients of a full-sized brochure. And because of its size, this brochure will make it to places a full-sized brochure won't.

Like its full-sized counterpart, begin your brochure cover with a compelling headline. Compose a paragraph about the organization on the inside-left page and follow it on the right with the organization name, phone, and a list of products or services. On the right, add an image that illustrates the headline. If you want your name on the card, position it above the organization name on the inside-right.

Print one master copy of the artwork and take it to a commercial printer to have it reproduced and machine folded. Have it printed on a high-quality 80 lb uncoated cover stock in white or a pastel color.

Business Card Brochure Layout: Back and Front Covers

1 · Address and Hours: Century Old Style, 10/12pt, flush left

2 · Organization Name: Charlemagne, 12pt, centered, all caps. Address: Century Old Style, 10pt, centered

3 · Headline: Charlemagne, 24/24pt, flush left, all caps

Business Card Brochure Layout: Inside

4 · Large Initial: Formata Bold, 18/18pt, centered, reverse (white) on a black background box

5 · Body Text: Century Old Style, 12/14pt, flush left

6 · Organization Name, Phone, and Services: Century Old Style, 12/14pt, flush left, reverse (white) on a black background box

7 · Bouquet Clip Art: From Electronic Clipper by Dynamic Graphics, 800-255-8800, 6000 N. Forest Park Dr., Peoria, IL 61614-3592 © Dynamic Graphics, Inc. All rights reserved

The dotted lines on the top and bottom edges represent folds.

The Idea Book example shows how a florist might use the card to remind customers of their phone number <u>and</u> their products.

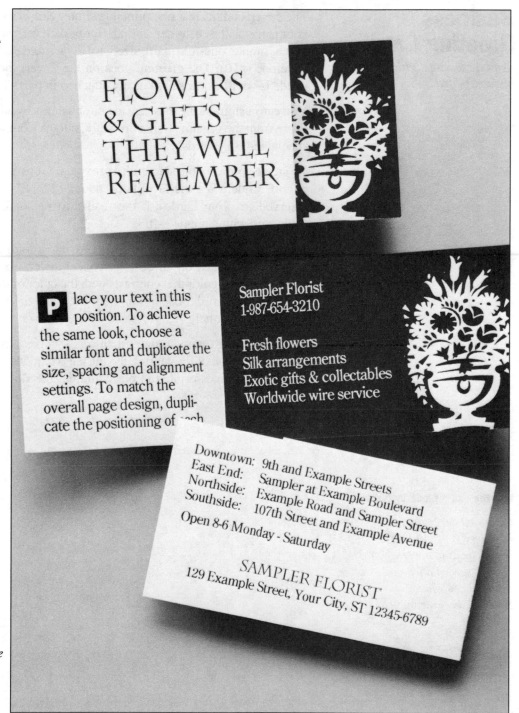

FLOWERS
& GIFTS
THEY WILL
REMEMBER

Place your text in this position. To achieve the same look, choose a similar font and duplicate the size, spacing and alignment settings. To match the overall page design, dupli-cate the positioning of each

Sampler Florist
1-987-654-3210

Fresh flowers
Silk arrangements
Exotic gifts & collectables
Worldwide wire service

Downtown: 9th and Example Streets
East End: Sampler at Example Boulevard
Northside: Example Road and Sampler Street
Southside: 107th Street and Example Avenue

Open 8-6 Monday - Saturday

SAMPLER FLORIST
129 Example Street, Your City, ST 12345-6789

**A brochure card
will fit into**

*A business card file
A wallet
A rotary card file
A shirt pocket*

Business Greeting Card

Send a message with your business card

The experts tell us that one principle strategy of marketing is to keep your name on the customer's mind. Here's a clever way to do just that. It's a simple one-fold card sized to fit a standard business sized envelope (#10). The greeting goes on the cover; the payoff on the inside is your business card neatly attached in two slots.

You can customize the message to your business by adding marketing prose from the organization's brochure, quotes from management, or special industry terms.

To create your version, start with a provocative cover headline and the payoff inside. (*See* the layouts on pages 112-113.) Below the area reserved for your card, ask the reader to respond, or promise to follow-up with a phone call.

Print one master copy of the card and take it to a commercial printer to have it reproduced on an 80 lb uncoated cover stock and machine folded. Select a color that contrasts with the color of the business card to set it off from the background and to make the presentation that much more dramatic.

If you're going to create more than a few copies, ask the printer to estimate the cost of die-cutting the business card slots for you. If not, have the slot lines printed in place and cut the slots yourself with a sharp art knife.

Use the same basic layout to

Follow up a meeting
Introduce your business
Invite clients to a workshop
Make a special offer
Send a thank you
Send holiday greetings

The Idea Book example shows how an office equipment company might use the card to solicit appointments.

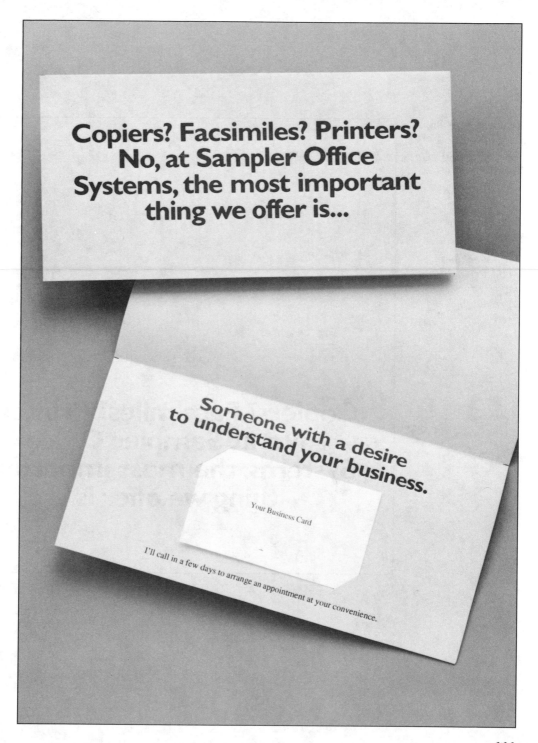

Copiers? Facsimiles? Printers? No, at Sampler Office Systems, the most important thing we offer is...

Someone with a desire to understand your business.

Your Business Card

I'll call in a few days to arrange an appointment at your convenience.

**Business Greeting
Card Layout:
Back and Front
Covers**

*1 · Cover Head-
line: Gill Sans
Bold, 38/36pt,
centered*

*The dotted lines
on the top and
bottom edges
represent folds.*

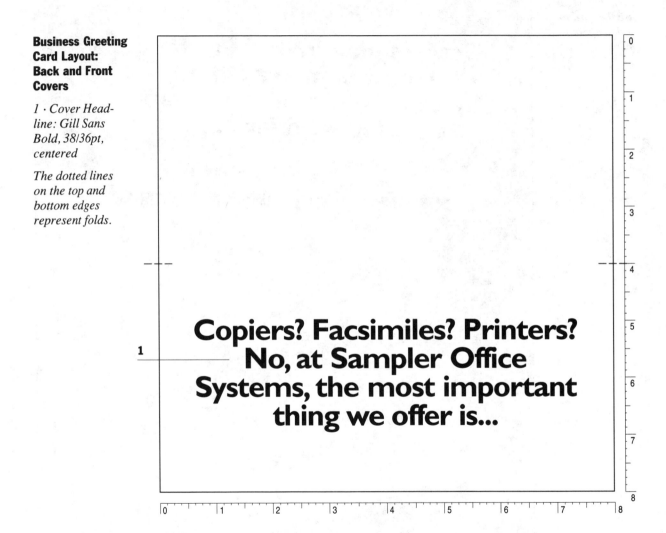

Copiers? Facsimiles? Printers? No, at Sampler Office Systems, the most important thing we offer is...

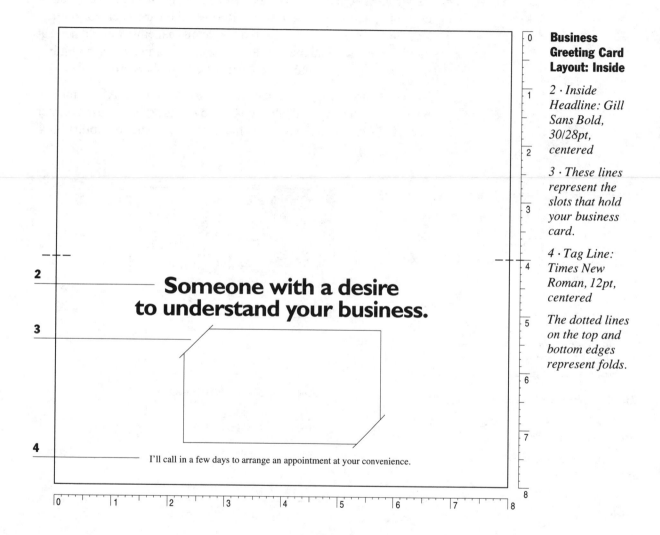

**Someone with a desire
to understand your business.**

I'll call in a few days to arrange an appointment at your convenience.

**Business
Greeting Card
Layout: Inside**

*2 · Inside
Headline: Gill
Sans Bold,
30/28pt,
centered*

*3 · These lines
represent the
slots that hold
your business
card.*

*4 · Tag Line:
Times New
Roman, 12pt,
centered*

*The dotted lines
on the top and
bottom edges
represent folds.*

Membership Card

Join the membership movement

Now, you can join the ever-growing number of organizations recasting customers as members. Participants earn discounts, prestige, and privileges unavailable to others.

The front of your card shows the name your organization, the group or club title, and states the reward. Reserve the card back for names, signatures, phone numbers, and other details a member might need at hand. Punch or initial the tally as the member completes each requirement, and award the incentive when all the numbers are marked.

Print one master copy of the card and take it to a commercial printer to have it reproduced on 100 lb uncoated cover stock; or, have the printer use 70 lb cover and laminate the cards for extra durability (*see* Source:).

Membership Card Layout: Front

1 · Child Swinging Clip Art: From Designer's Club by Dynamic Graphics, 800-255-8800, 6000 N. Forest Park Dr., Peoria, IL 61614-3592 © Dynamic Graphics, Inc. All rights reserved

2 · Organization Name: Adobe Caslon Italic, 14/12pt, flush left. Group Name: Adobe Caslon Regular, 32/28pt, flush left. Tag Line: Helvetica, 9/10pt, flush left

Membership Card Layout: Back

3 · Punch Tally: Helvetica Black, 8/13pt, centered, .5pt lines

4 · Group Details: Adobe Caslon Regular, 13/14pt, flush left

5 · Restrictions: Helvetica, 9pt, flush left

More card ideas

Admission card
Discount card
Preferred customer
Restaurant discount

The Idea Book example shows how a child care center might use the membership card to reward parents who use their service throughout the year.

**Source:
Do-It-Yourself
Laminating**

One of the cards pictured is laminated with "PRESAPLY," self-sealing laminating sheets. No special equipment required. From Avery Dennison, 800-252-8379, 818 Oak Park Road, Covina, CA 91724

115

Pop-Up Card

Add a surprise to your message

This is an idea bound to grab attention. Although most pop-ups require complex production, this *Pop-Up Card* is a simple way to get the same effect on a shoestring budget.

The Idea Book example shows how a company uses the card to announce a sales contest. In this case, two electronic clip art images are used to create the effect. The United States Capitol pops up and the airplane in the background enhances the effect.

Your version begins with a two-part headline on the cover and a pay-off on the inside left-hand panel. The last inside panel includes instructions and a description of the action you want the reader to take. Add lines to guide in cutting the slots on the printed card.

Print one master copy of the card and take it to a commercial printer to have it reproduced on 65 lb uncoated cover stock. Ask the printer to score the card on the folds but not to fold it. Cut the slots and fold the finished card as shown.

If you're going to create more than a few copies, ask printer to estimate the cost of die-cutting and hand-folding the cards for you.

Pop-Up Card Layout

1 · Cover Headline: Minion Regular, 42/40pt, centered

2 · Inside Headline: Minion Regular, 36/32pt, flush left

3 · These lines represent the cuts that make the Capitol pop-up when the card is opened.

4 · Clip Art: Both the Capitol and the aircraft are from Presentation Task Force by New Vision Technologies, Inc., 613-727-8184, 38 Auriga Drive, Unit 13, Nepean, Ontario, Canada K2E 8A5 © New Vision Technologies, Inc. All rights reserved

5 · Body Text: Minion Regular, 12/13pt, flush left

The dotted lines on the top and bottom edges represent folds.

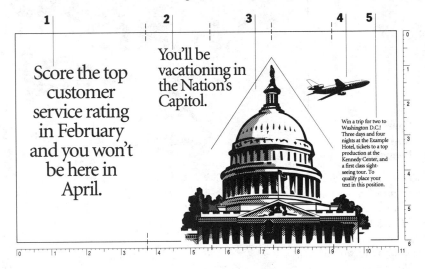

Score the top customer service rating in February and you won't be here in April.

You'll be vacationing in the Nation's Capitol.

Win a trip for two to Washington D.C.! Three days and four nights at the Example Hotel, tickets to a top production at the Kennedy Center, and a first class sightseeing tour. To qualify place your text in this position.

The Idea Book example shows how a company uses the card to announce a sales contest.

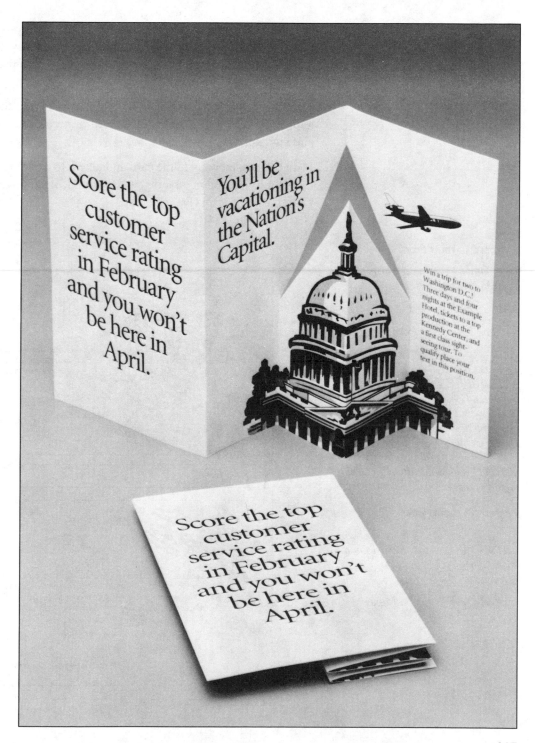

Score the top customer service rating in February and you won't be here in April.

You'll be vacationing in the Nation's Capital.

Win a trip for two to Washington D.C.! Three days and four nights at the Example Hotel, tickets to a top production at the Kennedy Center, and a first class sightseeing tour. To qualify place your text in this position.

Score the top customer service rating in February and you won't be here in April.

Postcard

Get the word out on time and under budget

If you have a brief message and a briefer budget consider this *Postcard* layout. Or use the same layout to create a purely decorative card using clip art you really like, but could never find a use for.

To create your version, begin by positioning the clip art image and return address on the front. Leave a minimum of half the cover for the address label and stamp. On the back, arrange your headline, message, and signature.

Print one master copy of the card and take it to a commercial printer to have it reproduced in quantity. A 100 lb uncoated cover stock should guarantee that it survives the mail.

Postcard Layout: Front

1 · *Recipient's Name: Courier Bold, 11/15pt, flush left*

2 · *Line: .5pt*

3 · *Return Address: Formata Light, 10/12pt, flush left*

4 · *Kids Group Clip Art: From ARTSOURCE Vol. 2: Borders, Symbols, Holidays, and Attention Getters, by The Church Art Works, available from Youth Specialties Order Center, 800-776-8008, PO Box 4406, Spartanburg, SC 29305-9976 © Youth Specialties Inc. All rights reserved*

Postcard Layout: Back

5 · *"GOOD JOB!" Clip Art: From ARTSOURCE Vol. 4: Phrases and Verses, from the same source as above*

6 · *Body Text: Formata Light, 12/14pt, flush left*

118

The Idea Book example shows how a school principal uses the card to communicate with parents.

Source: Laser Postcards

Or print yours directly from your computer on postcard sheets (four 5 1/2" by 4 1/4" cards per sheet). From Paper Direct, 800-272-7377, PO Box 64429, St. Paul, MN 55164-0429

Rotary File Card

Keep your name up front

Imagine two competing organizations that provide similar products or services. The first supplies customers with a rotary card that lists important contact information; the second assumes they'll look it up. Guess who has the best odds of getting the call?

For your version, start at the top of the card with your name and phone number. Below it, list all the details the customer might need, and a simple description of your organization's mission. Include the names of people to contact, FAX and telex numbers, computer network ID number, office hours, your address, and directions to your location.

Print the card directly from your computer on a sheet of 4" by 2 1/6" laser rotary cards (*see* Source:). Larger computer printer versions are also available, along with plastic and heavy paper versions from a variety of specialty printers.

Rotary File Card Layout

1 · Organization Name and Phone: Adobe Caslon Regular, 16pt, flush left, reverse (white) on a black background box

2 · Marketing Message: Adobe Caslon Italic, 11/11pt, flush left

3 · Medicines Clip Art: From Presentation Task Force by New Vision Technologies, Inc., 613-727-8184, 38 Auriga Drive, Unit 13, Nepean, Ontario, Canada K2E 8A5 © New Vision Technologies, Inc. All rights reserved

4 · Names, Hours, Address, etc: Adobe Caslon Regular, 11/12pt, flush left

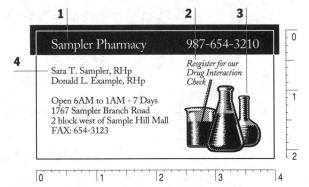

120

The Idea Book example shows how a pharmacy keeps its name up front.

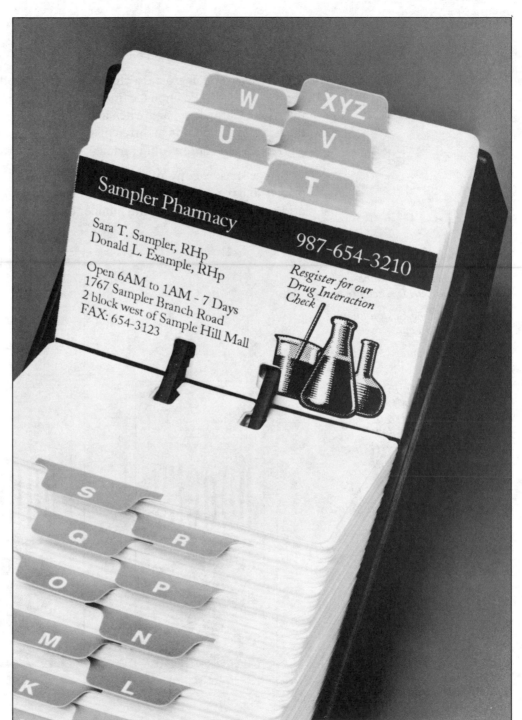

Source: Laser Rotary Cards

The "Laser Rotary Cards" (2 1/6" by 4") are from Avery Dennison, 800-252-8379, 818 Oak Park Road, Covina, CA 91724

Tickets

Design tickets with marketing clout

Next time your child promises his or her teacher that you'll head up the raffle, or a best friend volunteers you to chair the events committee, this ticket layout could be a lifesaver.

Center your version around a clip art image that reflects the excitement of the event. Position the title of the event above the image and the who, what, where, and when above that. Add other sections to the ticket for admission to different events, to register the holder for a prize, or to record his or her name, address, and phone.

Print one master copy of the ticket and take it to a commercial printer to have it reproduced on 65 lb uncoated cover stock. Most printers can also perforate and number the tickets sequentially.

Ticket Layout: Single

1 · Ticket Information: Adobe Caslon Regular, 9/11pt, centered

2 · Subhead: Adobe Caslon Regular, 12pt, centered, all caps

3 · Headline: Arcadia, 120pt, centered, all caps

4 · Dancing Clip Art: From Images With Impact!, People 1, by 3G Graphics, Inc., 800-456-0234, 23632 Highway 99 #F407, Edmonds, WA 98026 © 3G Graphics, Inc. All rights reserved

5 · Line: .5pt

6 · Consecutive Numbering: Courier Bold, 18pt, centered

Ticket Layout: Multi-Part

7 · Fill In Stub: Adobe Caslon Regular, 8pt, flush left, .5 lines

8 · Second Stub: Adobe Caslon Regular, 8pt, centered

The dotted lines represent perforations.

The Idea Book example shows how a club might publicize a New Year's Eve dance.

Trading Cards

A unique way to promote your organization

Beyond sports, the trading card industry now offers cards for a wide range of entertainment and educational topics. With these simple layouts, you can join the excitement. Kids who collect the cards earn them by demonstrating their knowledge, performing volunteer work, or participating in other ways.

Trading cards are terrific for promoting your hobby, a charitable cause, or a school or business. The Idea Book example shows two different possibilities: the first shows how a set of science cards might promote learning; the second, how a zoological park might promote their adopt-a-friend program.

Design your version of the cards around questions and answers, interesting facts, or pictures of people, places, and things. (*See* the layouts on pages 126-127.) Number the cards and publicize the number of cards available so collectors know how many cards make a complete set.

Print one master copy of each card and take it to a commercial printer to have it reproduced on a 12 point cover stock, coated on one side (front). If you plan to produce more than one set of cards, consider selecting a different colored stock for each.

The Idea Book example shows two different possibilities: the first shows how a set of science cards might promote learning; the second, how a zoological park might promote their adopt-a-friend program.

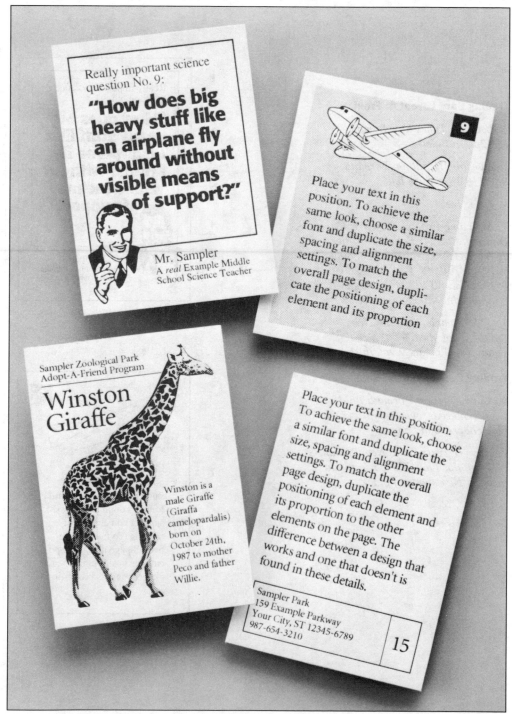

Really important science question No. 9:

"How does big heavy stuff like an airplane fly around without visible means of support?"

Mr. Sampler
A *real* Example Middle
School Science Teacher

9

Place your text in this position. To achieve the same look, choose a similar font and duplicate the size, spacing and alignment settings. To match the overall page design, duplicate the positioning of each element and its proportion

Sampler Zoological Park
Adopt-A-Friend Program

Winston Giraffe

Winston is a male Giraffe (Giraffa camelopardalis) born on October 24th, 1987 to mother Peco and father Willie.

Place your text in this position. To achieve the same look, choose a similar font and duplicate the size, spacing and alignment settings. To match the overall page design, duplicate the positioning of each element and its proportion to the other elements on the page. The difference between a design that works and one that doesn't is found in these details.

Sampler Park
159 Example Parkway
Your City, ST 12345-6789
987-654-3210

15

Trading Card Layout A: Front

1 · Lead In: Times New Roman, 12/12pt, flush left

2 · Question Headline: Formata Bold, 18/18pt, flush left

3 · Line: 1pt

4 · Man and Airplane Clip Art: From DigitArt, Vol. 21: Fabulous Fifties, by Image Club Graphics Inc., 800-387-9193, 10545 West Donges, Ct., Milwaukee, WI 53224 © Image Club Graphics Inc. All rights reserved

5 · "Mr. Sampler": Times New Roman, 12pt, flush left. "A real...": Times New Roman, 9/9pt, flush left

Trading Card Layout A: Back

6 · Card Number: Formata Bold, 14pt, centered, reverse (white) on a black background box

7 · Answer Text: Times New Roman, 12/14pt, flush left. The background box is a 10% shade of black.

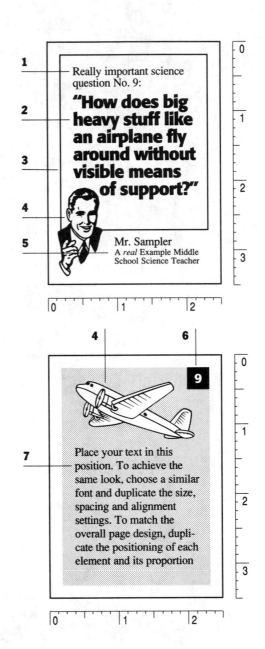

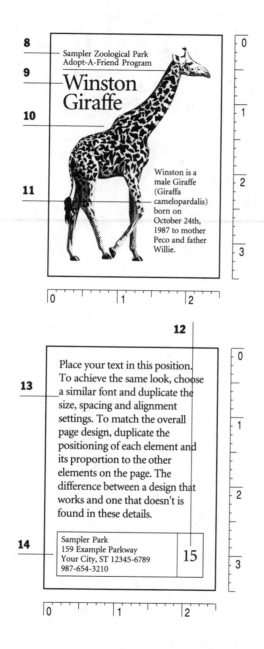

8 Sampler Zoological Park
Adopt-A-Friend Program

9 Winston
Giraffe

10

Winston is a
male Giraffe
(Giraffa
camelopardalis)
born on
October 24th,
1987 to mother
Peco and father
Willie.

11

0
1
2
3

0 1 2

12

Place your text in this position.
To achieve the same look, choose
a similar font and duplicate the
size, spacing and alignment
settings. To match the overall
page design, duplicate the
positioning of each element and
its proportion to the other
elements on the page. The
difference between a design that
works and one that doesn't is
found in these details.

13

Sampler Park
159 Example Parkway
Your City, ST 12345-6789
987-654-3210

15

14

0
1
2
3

0 1 2

Trading Card Layout B: Front

8 · Organization Name: Minion Regular, 9/9pt, flush left, .5pt line below

9 · Card Title: Minion Regular, 24/24pt, flush left

10 · Giraffe Clip Art: From ClickArt EPS Animals & Nature by T/Maker Company, 415-962-0195, 1390 Villa Street, Mountain View, CA 94041 © T/Maker Company. All rights reserved

11 · Cover Text: Minion Regular, 9/10pt, flush left

Trading Card Layout B: Back

12 · Card Number: Minion Regular, 15pt, centered

13 · Body Text: Minion Regular, 12/14pt, flush left

14 · Organization Name and Address: Minion Regular, 9/10pt, flush left, .5pt line around

127

CHAPTER 7
Correspondence Projects

Fax Cover Sheet

Transmit the most information in the least amount of space

One way to save on your phone bill and simplify communications is to rethink the standard fax message and cover sheet formats.

The Idea Book example shows how to compress the necessary details into a form that saves time and supplies.

To create your version, just substitute your name, address, and phone numbers. If you need more space, add lines to the "Message" section and expand it down the page.

Use sans serif typefaces similar to those on the example to minimize the deterioration in clarity that takes place during transmission.

Print the fax sheets three to a sheet, directly from your computer.

For an even more frugal approach (below) add a simple box with the basic listings to your standard memo form or letterhead and fax away!

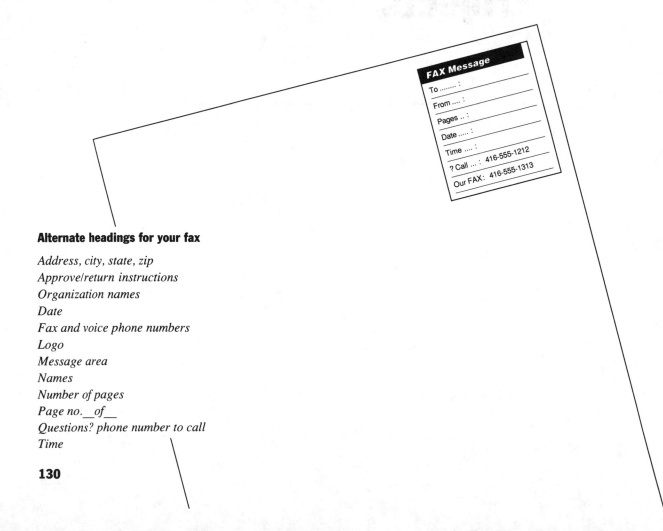

Alternate headings for your fax

Address, city, state, zip
Approve/return instructions
Organization names
Date
Fax and voice phone numbers
Logo
Message area
Names
Number of pages
Page no.__of__
Questions? phone number to call
Time

Fax Message Layout

1 · Title: Helvetica Black, 63pt, centered, all caps, extra-tight letter spacing

2 · Fill-In: Helvetica, 10pt, flush left, .5pt lines

3 · "MESSAGE": Helvetica Bold, 10pt, centered, all caps, reverse (white) on a black background box, add one space between characters

4 · Organization Name, Address, and Phone: Helvetica, 10/12pt, flush left

5 · Line: .5pt

6 · Add a dotted line to aid in lining up the first sheet. Instruction: Helvetica, 9/10pt, centered

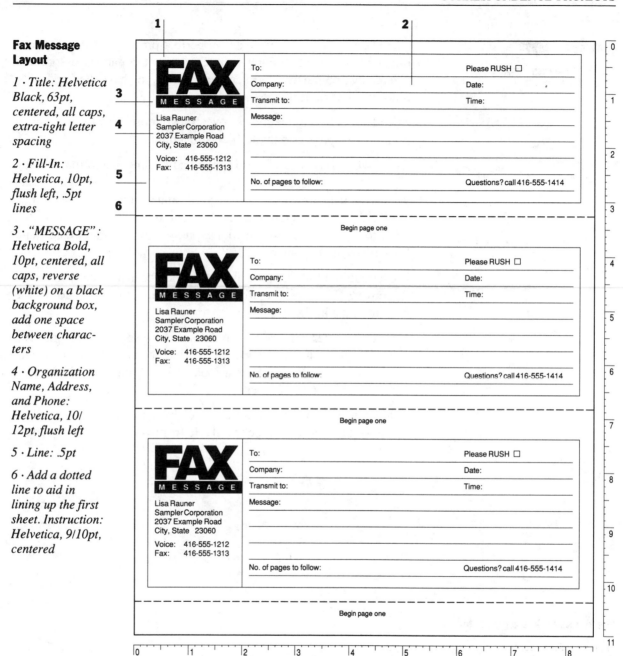

Invitation

Make it formal or fun

Invitations and announcements are perfect projects for desktop production. Instead of limiting your choice to the canned assortment offered by a commercial printer or card shop, you have the freedom to tailor the message and look.

The Idea Book example shows how an accounting service might use a humorous approach to invite clients to a picnic.

Begin with a ruse: use a formal sounding headline in a formal looking typeface. (*See* the layouts on pages 134-135.) Inside, reverse gears with an amusing payoff to your headline and an upbeat clip art image. Within the frame, include the details about times, dates, what to bring, what to wear, locations, directions, phone numbers, rain dates, and how and when to respond.

For a traditional version, use the same typeface inside that you use on the cover. Eliminate the clip art and center your message on the bottom of the inside page.

Print one master copy of the invitation and take it to a commercial printer to have it reproduced on 65 lb uncoated cover stock and machine folded. For the formal look and feel, have it printed on a cream colored or white stock.

Folded once, the invitation measures 6" by 4 1/2" and fits a standard A6 announcement envelope (available from your local office supply dealer).

Use the same basic layout for

Moving announcements
Thank you notes
Traditional wedding announcements
Holiday greeting cards

The Idea Book example shows how an accounting service might use a humorous approach to invite clients to a picnic.

Sampler Accounting Services respectfully requests the pleasure of your company at...

a July 4th Picnic that should forever dispell the myth of the stodgy accountant.

Bring your family for food, swimming and fireworks. 3 & 11 PM at the River Park Club, 1455 Example Ridge. For more information call 555-1212

Invitation Layout:
Back and Front Cover

1 · Cover Headline: Shelley Allegro, 36/34pt, centered

The dotted lines on the right and left edges represent folds.

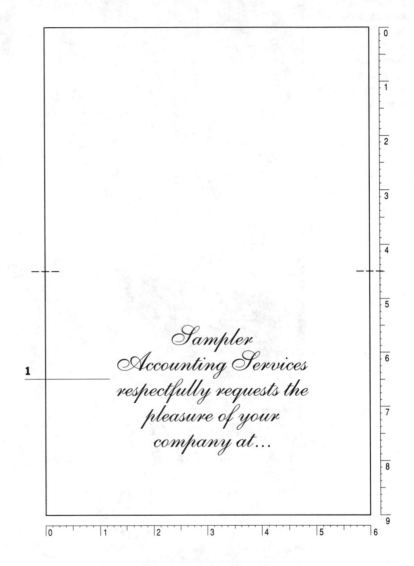

a July 4th Picnic that should forever dispell the myth of the stodgy accountant.

Bring your family for food, swimming and fireworks. 3 & 11 PM at the River Park Club, 1455 Example Ridge. For more information call 555-1212

Invitation Layout: Inside

2 · Fireworks Clip Art: From Electronic Clipper by Dynamic Graphics, 800-255-8800, 6000 N. Forest Park Dr., Peoria, IL 61614-3592 © Dynamic Graphics, Inc. All rights reserved

3 · Line: 2pt around a white background box

4 · Inside Headline: Formata Bold, 20/22pt, centered

5 · Invitation Details: Formata Light, 10/11pt, flush left

The dotted lines on the right and left edges represent folds.

Kid's Mail

An all-in-one mailer for your young writer

The *Kid's Mail* project makes a terrific gift for any youngster of writing age. You may even find that personalized stationery prompts your child to write more often. The layout is a standard 8 1/2" by 11" sheet that you fold in half, stamp, and drop in the mail.

Your version highlights the child's name and address on the inside page along with clip art that reflects his or her special interests. (*See* the layouts on pages 138-139.) On the outside, include the return address and a fill-in box for the name and address of the recipient. For younger children, add prompts for "To:, Street:, City:, Stamp!" etc.

Print one master copy of the mailer and take it to a commercial printer to have it reproduced in quantity. Although you can mail a lighter paper, 65 lb uncoated cover stock or heavier will have a better chance of surviving the mail. If you want to print directly from your computer, use as heavy a stock as the printer can handle. In either case, choose stock with a smooth, uncoated finish so it's easy to write on with pen, pencil, or crayon.

To top it off, include a package of brightly colored stickers to seal the bottom of the pages for mailing.

The layout is a standard 8 1/2" by 11" sheet that you fold in half, stamp, and drop in the mail.

Kid's Mail Layout: Outside

1 · Recipient's Address Fill-In: Formata Light, 12/36pt, flush left, .1pt line around

2 · Stamp Reminder: Formata Light, 12pt, centered

3 · Line: 1pt

4 · Return Address: Formata Light, 14/16pt, flush left

5 · Bicycle Cartoon Clip Art: From Presentation Task Force by New Vision Technologies, Inc., 613-727-8184, 38 Auriga Drive, Unit 13, Nepean, Ontario, Canada K2E 8A5 © New Vision Technologies, Inc. All rights reserved

The dotted lines on the left and right edges represent folds.

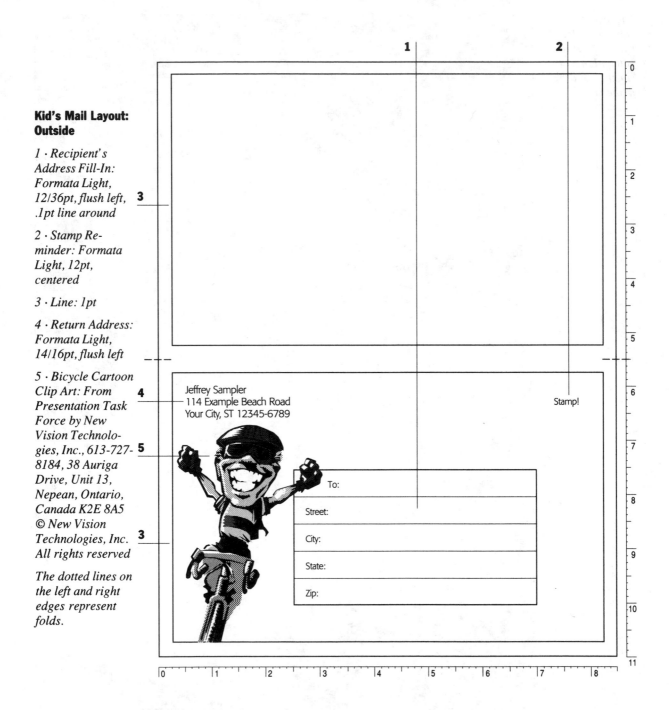

Jeffrey Sampler
114 Example Beach Road
Your City, ST 12345-6789

Stamp!

To:

Street:

City:

State:

Zip:

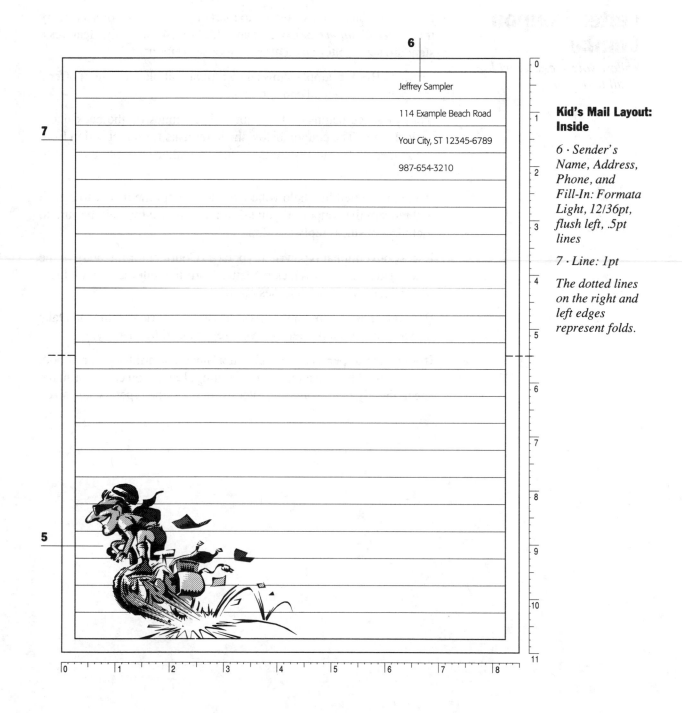

6

Jeffrey Sampler

114 Example Beach Road

Your City, ST 12345-6789

987-654-3210

7

5

Kid's Mail Layout: Inside

6 · Sender's Name, Address, Phone, and Fill-In: Formata Light, 12/36pt, flush left, .5pt lines

7 · Line: 1pt

The dotted lines on the right and left edges represent folds.

Letter/Coupon Combo

Follow your message with a call to action

Next time you compose a letter to market your product or service try this *Letter/Coupon Combo*. It is an 8 1/2" by 14" sheet that features a standard sized letter *and* a direct response coupon.

The Idea Book example shows how a financial planner might offer a free personal financial consultation.

Your message begins on the front and continues on the back like a typical letter. The coupon below the letter asks for direct action from the reader. Use it to restate the offer, to gather information, and to describe the details.

Position a dotted line below the letter to prompt the reader to detach and redeem the coupon. If you ask for a response by mail, be sure to include a business reply envelope.

Use a conventional typewriter typeface (Courier) for the body of the letter. This visually divides the letter from the letterhead, and direct mail experts swear it increases response.

Print one master copy of the artwork with a generic greeting and take it to a commercial printer to have it reproduced in quantity.

If you want to personalize each letter, have the printer preprint both sides with all but the address and greeting. Later, you can imprint the sheet directly from your computer using the same typeface and size.

Letter/Coupon Combo Layout

1 · Organization Name and Address: Century Old Style, 10/12pt, flush left

2 · Headline: Helvetica Black Italic, 14/13pt, flush left, .5pt rule below

3 · Body Text: Courier Bold, 10/14pt, flush left

4 · This dotted line prints.

5 · Offer Headline: Helvetica Black Italic, 14pt, flush left. "FREE Offer!" is reverse (white) on a black background box.

6 · "Yes!": Helvetica Black Italic, 14pt, flush left. Box Line: .5pt. Offer Text: Century Old Style, 10/12pt, flush left

7 · Fill-In: Century Old Style, 8/24pt, flush left, .5pt lines

8 · Details and Restrictions Text: Century Old Style, 8/10pt, flush left

The dotted lines on the right and left edges represent folds.

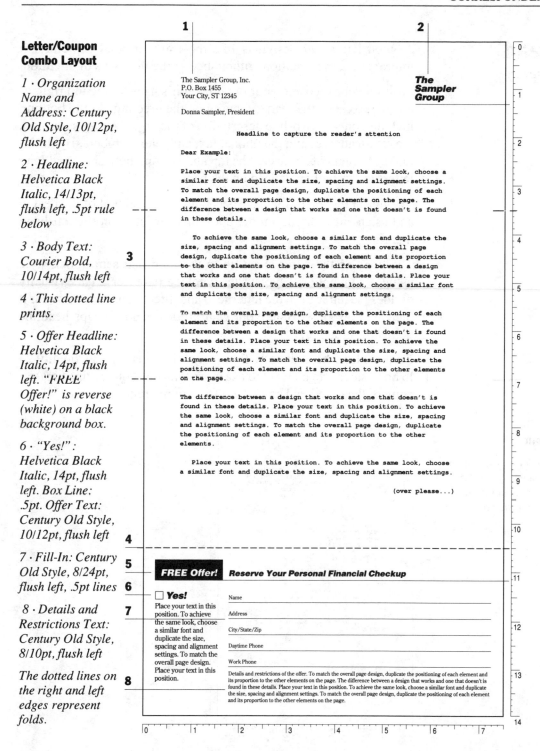

Letterhead

Frame your message

A good letterhead design is like the frame around a picture: it improves the presentation without becoming the focus of attention.

Position your logo and your organization's name at the top right of the page to keep the reader focused on the greeting. At the bottom, include a one- or two-line description of the organization's mission, the return address and the phone, fax, and telex numbers. By dividing these elements between the top and bottom, both short and long letters are visually balanced on the page.

The line at the top of the page acts both as an element of the design and as an aid to lining up the body of your letter on the left-hand margin.

The body of the letter is set up in the modified semi-block style using a conventional typewriter typeface (Courier). This visually divides the letter from the letterhead and direct mail experts swear it increases response. State your central idea in an all caps headline below the greeting.

Print the letterhead directly from your computer on high quality 24 lb bond stock. If you want to use more than one color, print a master copy of the letterhead and take it to a commercial printer.

Half-Sheet Layout

For extremely brief notes, use half-sheet size stationery. All of the typefaces and sizes remain the same; only the page size and margins change.

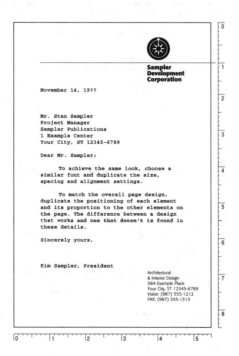

Letterhead Layout

1 · Compass Clip Art: From Logic Arts, 804-266-7996, 11475 Chickahominy Branch., Glen Allen, VA 23060 © Logic Arts Corp. All rights reserved

2 · Organization Name: Formata Bold, 12/12pt, flush left

3 · Line: .5pt

4 · Body Text: Courier Bold, 11/13pt, flush left

5 · Description of Services, Address, and Phones: Formata Light, 9/10pt, flush left, all caps

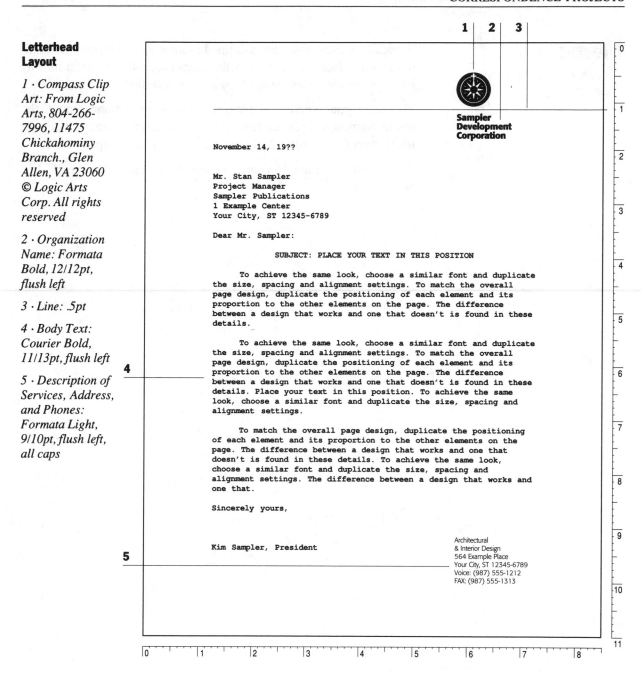

Sampler
Development
Corporation

November 14, 19??

Mr. Stan Sampler
Project Manager
Sampler Publications
1 Example Center
Your City, ST 12345-6789

Dear Mr. Sampler:

SUBJECT: PLACE YOUR TEXT IN THIS POSITION

To achieve the same look, choose a similar font and duplicate the size, spacing and alignment settings. To match the overall page design, duplicate the positioning of each element and its proportion to the other elements on the page. The difference between a design that works and one that doesn't is found in these details.

To achieve the same look, choose a similar font and duplicate the size, spacing and alignment settings. To match the overall page design, duplicate the positioning of each element and its proportion to the other elements on the page. The difference between a design that works and one that doesn't is found in these details. Place your text in this position. To achieve the same look, choose a similar font and duplicate the size, spacing and alignment settings.

To match the overall page design, duplicate the positioning of each element and its proportion to the other elements on the page. The difference between a design that works and one that doesn't is found in these details. To achieve the same look, choose a similar font and duplicate the size, spacing and alignment settings. The difference between a design that works and one that.

Sincerely yours,

Kim Sampler, President

Architectural
& Interior Design
564 Example Place
Your City, ST 12345-6789
Voice: (987) 555-1212
FAX: (987) 555-1313

Memo

Create the best possible impression

Typically, a memorandum is defined as an informal interoffice communication. But in recent years the memo format is making its way into the day-to-day exchange between organizations.

To create your version, substitute your organization's name, the return address and phone, fax, and telex numbers. Choose a clip art illustration for the bottom of the page or use your company logo.

Print the memo directly from your computer on high-quality 24 lb bond stock.

Memo Layout

1 · Title: Helvetica Black, 11/11pt, centered, all caps

2 · Organization Name and Address: Helvetica Light, 11pt, flush left

3 · Introduction: Helvetica Light, 12/16pt, flush left

4 · Body Text: Helvetica Light, 12/14pt, justified

5 · Line: .5pt

6 · Globe Clip Art: From ClickArt EPS Business Art by T/Maker Company, 415-962-0195, 1390 Villa Street, Mountain View, CA 94041 © T/Maker Company. All rights reserved

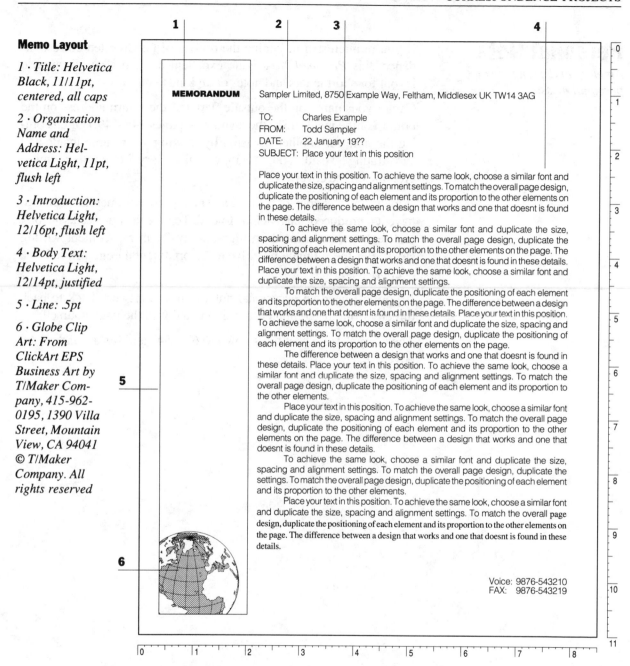

MEMORANDUM

Sampler Limited, 8750 Example Way, Feltham, Middlesex UK TW14 3AG

TO: Charles Example
FROM: Todd Sampler
DATE: 22 January 19??
SUBJECT: Place your text in this position

Place your text in this position. To achieve the same look, choose a similar font and duplicate the size, spacing and alignment settings. To match the overall page design, duplicate the positioning of each element and its proportion to the other elements on the page. The difference between a design that works and one that doesnt is found in these details.

To achieve the same look, choose a similar font and duplicate the size, spacing and alignment settings. To match the overall page design, duplicate the positioning of each element and its proportion to the other elements on the page. The difference between a design that works and one that doesnt is found in these details. Place your text in this position. To achieve the same look, choose a similar font and duplicate the size, spacing and alignment settings.

To match the overall page design, duplicate the positioning of each element and its proportion to the other elements on the page. The difference between a design that works and one that doesnt is found in these details. Place your text in this position. To achieve the same look, choose a similar font and duplicate the size, spacing and alignment settings. To match the overall page design, duplicate the positioning of each element and its proportion to the other elements on the page.

The difference between a design that works and one that doesnt is found in these details. Place your text in this position. To achieve the same look, choose a similar font and duplicate the size, spacing and alignment settings. To match the overall page design, duplicate the positioning of each element and its proportion to the other elements.

Place your text in this position. To achieve the same look, choose a similar font and duplicate the size, spacing and alignment settings. To match the overall page design, duplicate the positioning of each element and its proportion to the other elements on the page. The difference between a design that works and one that doesnt is found in these details.

To achieve the same look, choose a similar font and duplicate the size, spacing and alignment settings. To match the overall page design, duplicate the settings. To match the overall page design, duplicate the positioning of each element and its proportion to the other elements.

Place your text in this position. To achieve the same look, choose a similar font and duplicate the size, spacing and alignment settings. To match the overall page design, duplicate the positioning of each element and its proportion to the other elements on the page. The difference between a design that works and one that doesnt is found in these details.

Voice: 9876-543210
FAX: 9876-543219

145

Personal Note

An elegant design for your personal message

If you're interested in joining the revival of handwritten correspondence, this *Personal Note* is an excellent start. It's an all-purpose layout for short letters and notes of all kinds.

Center your name on the outside flap and the return address on the bottom of the inside. (*See* the layouts on pages 148-149.) Or customize the note for another occasion by moving your name inside and substituting "Thank You," "Happy Anniversary," or another similar greeting on the cover.

Print one master copy of the note and take it to a commercial printer to have it reproduced and machine folded. To give the note a classic look and feel, have it printed on high-quality 24 lb rag content writing stock. For the ultimate note, have the ornamental edge printed in a deep, rich color.

If you just need an occasional note, print the artwork back to back directly from the computer, trim it out and fold the page yourself.

The 6" by 8 1/2" sheet folds down to 6" by 4" and fits a standard A6 envelope.

Customize the note for another occasion by moving your name inside and substituting "Thank You," "Happy Anniversary," or another similar greeting on the cover.

Gwen H. Sampler

9206 Example Bridge Circle
Your City, State 12345

Personal Note Layout: Outside

1 · Name: Adobe Caslon Regular, 14pt, centered

2 · Ornament: Adobe Caslon Ornaments, 24pt, centered, reverse (white) on a black background box. The edge pattern is created by repeating the ornament. Note that the ornament faces down.

The dotted lines on the left and right edges represent folds.

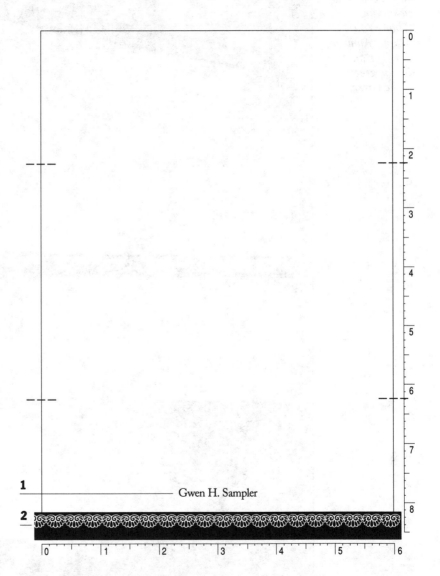

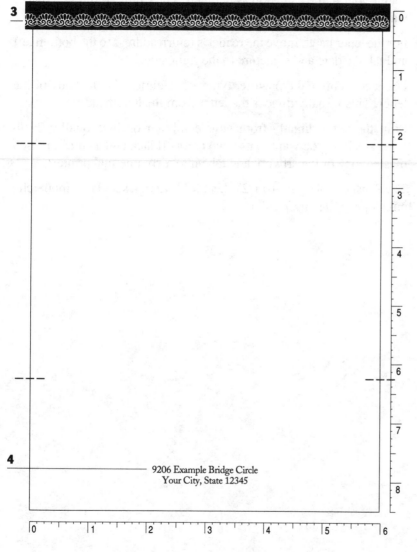

Personal Note Layout: Inside

3 · Substitute the face-up version of the ornament used on the outside layout.

4 · Address: Adobe Caslon Regular, 12/13pt, centered

The dotted lines on the right and left edges represent folds.

9206 Example Bridge Circle
Your City, State 12345

Personal Stationery

Express your personal style

There is nothing quite like a personal letter. An unexpected letter from a friend is one of life's simple pleasures. And a letter of praise or a well-worded protest carries ten times the weight of a phone call.

Choose a small ornament or personal logo for the top of the page and center your name and address below it. The example shows a maple leaf, the national symbol of Canada.

For the letter itself, move the reader's return address to the bottom left and tab the date and signature to the right side.

Use a conventional typewriter typeface (Courier) for the body of the letter. This visually divides the letter from the letterhead.

Print the letter directly from your computer on high-quality 24 lb bond stock. If you want to use two colors (black and a color), print a master copy of the artwork and take it to a commercial printer.

The finished 7 1/4" by 10 1/2" sheet folds to fit a standard "monarch" envelope (3 7/8" by 7 1/2").

Personal Stationery Layout

1 · Symbol: Adobe Carta, 48pt, centered

2 · Name and Address: Cochin, 14/18pt, centered

3 · Body Text: Courier Bold, 11/13pt, flush left

4 · Recipient's Address: Courier Bold, 11/13pt, flush left

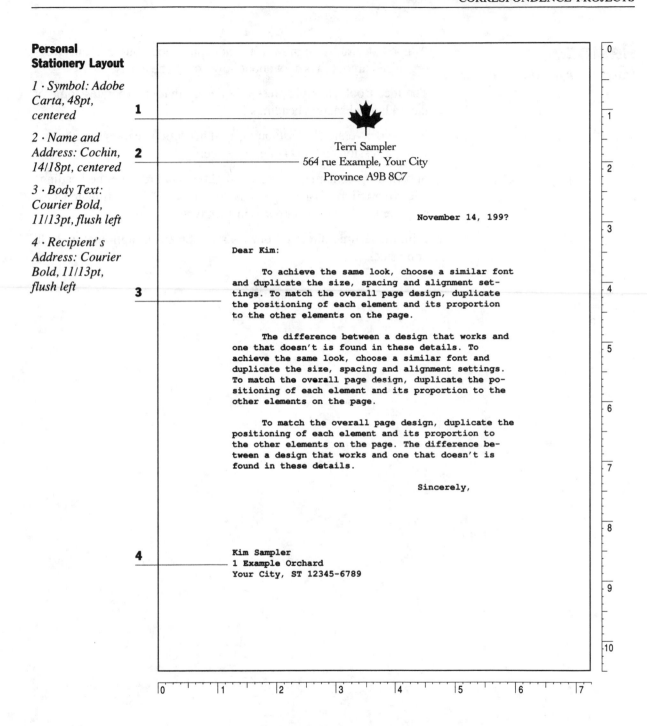

Terri Sampler
564 rue Example, Your City
Province A9B 8C7

November 14, 199?

Dear Kim:

To achieve the same look, choose a similar font and duplicate the size, spacing and alignment settings. To match the overall page design, duplicate the positioning of each element and its proportion to the other elements on the page.

The difference between a design that works and one that doesn't is found in these details. To achieve the same look, choose a similar font and duplicate the size, spacing and alignment settings. To match the overall page design, duplicate the positioning of each element and its proportion to the other elements on the page.

To match the overall page design, duplicate the positioning of each element and its proportion to the other elements on the page. The difference between a design that works and one that doesn't is found in these details.

Sincerely,

Kim Sampler
1 Example Orchard
Your City, ST 12345-6789

151

Resumé

Stand out in a crowd

A good resumé design won't land you a job, but a clear, well-organized layout says a lot about how you do business.

The Idea Book example presents a design that incorporates some of the traditional section headings.

Begin your version by fashioning a list of section headings that match your profession and level of experience.

Substitute your name, address, and phone, and replace the headings with your tailored list. If you consider the "RESUMÉ" title unnecessary, replace it with your name in 14pt type.

Print the resume directly from your computer on high-quality 24 lb bond stock.

Resumé Layout

1 · Title: Formata Bold, 18pt, flush left, all caps

2 · Line: The resumé lines are a series of periods, Times New Roman, 8pt, flush left

3 · Body Text: Times New Roman, 12/14pt, flush left

4 · Section Headings: Formata Bold, 11pt, flush left

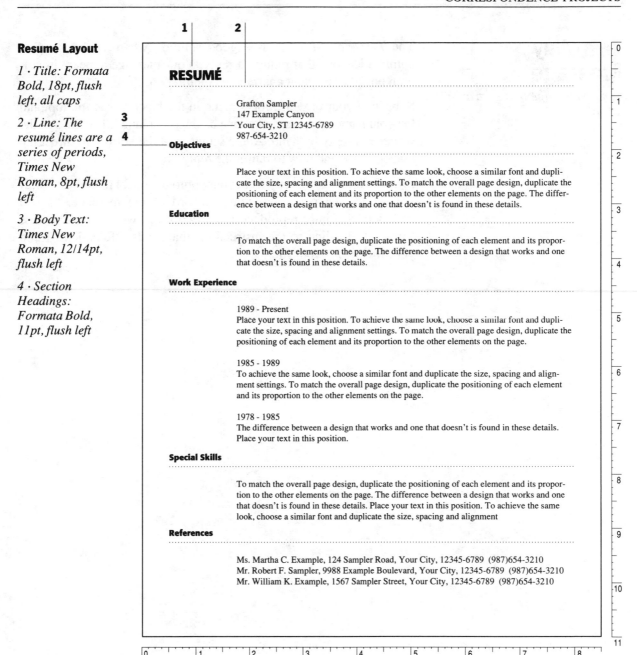

RESUMÉ

Grafton Sampler
147 Example Canyon
Your City, ST 12345-6789
987-654-3210

Objectives

Place your text in this position. To achieve the same look, choose a similar font and duplicate the size, spacing and alignment settings. To match the overall page design, duplicate the positioning of each element and its proportion to the other elements on the page. The difference between a design that works and one that doesn't is found in these details.

Education

To match the overall page design, duplicate the positioning of each element and its proportion to the other elements on the page. The difference between a design that works and one that doesn't is found in these details.

Work Experience

1989 - Present
Place your text in this position. To achieve the same look, choose a similar font and duplicate the size, spacing and alignment settings. To match the overall page design, duplicate the positioning of each element and its proportion to the other elements on the page.

1985 - 1989
To achieve the same look, choose a similar font and duplicate the size, spacing and alignment settings. To match the overall page design, duplicate the positioning of each element and its proportion to the other elements on the page.

1978 - 1985
The difference between a design that works and one that doesn't is found in these details. Place your text in this position.

Special Skills

To match the overall page design, duplicate the positioning of each element and its proportion to the other elements on the page. The difference between a design that works and one that doesn't is found in these details. Place your text in this position. To achieve the same look, choose a similar font and duplicate the size, spacing and alignment

References

Ms. Martha C. Example, 124 Sampler Road, Your City, 12345-6789 (987)654-3210
Mr. Robert F. Sampler, 9988 Example Boulevard, Your City, 12345-6789 (987)654-3210
Mr. William K. Example, 1567 Sampler Street, Your City, 12345-6789 (987)654-3210

Two-Way Message

Send a message that guarantees a reply

The *Two-Way Message* is a good solution when you're sending communications that require a reply. Your message appears in column one; the recipient answers in column two.

Substitute your organization's name in the black bar at the top, and list your name, address, and phone below it. Include fill-in lines so the reader can reply by hand. Add a sentence at the bottom to direct the reader where and how to return the reply.

Print the message directly from your computer on 24 lb bond stock. If you want each party to retain a record of the message, have a commercial printer reproduce the artwork on two-page carbonless forms. Add a line to the instructions that reads: "Recipient: Keep yellow copy for your file."

Two-Way Message Layout

1 · Organization Name: Gill Sans Bold, 12pt, centered, all caps, reverse (white) on a black background box. Add one space between characters.

2 · Headings: Gill Sans, 9pt, flush left, all caps

3 · Sender's Information: Gill Sans, 12/14pt, centered

4 · Organization Name: Gill Sans Bold, 10pt, centered, all caps, reverse (white) on a black background box. Add one space between characters.

5 · Fill-In: All fill-in lines and boxes are .5pt.

6 · Instructions: Gill Sans, 11pt, centered

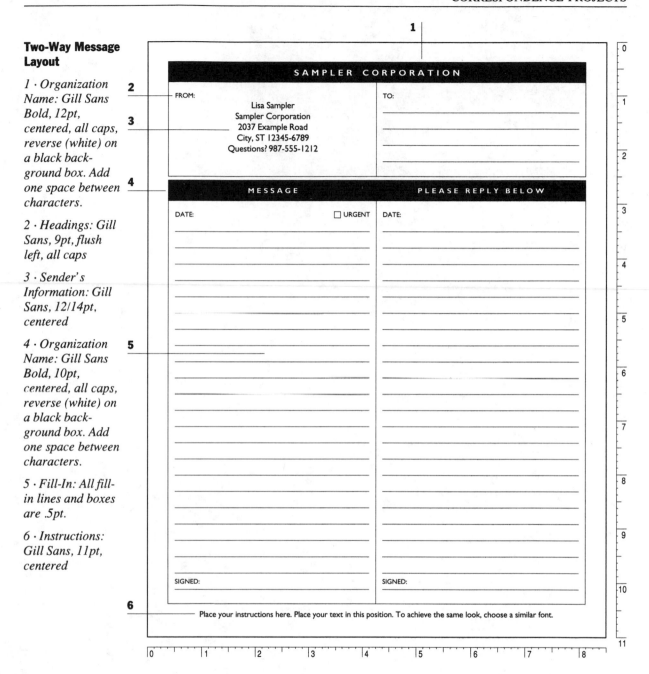

1

SAMPLER CORPORATION

2 FROM:

Lisa Sampler
Sampler Corporation
2037 Example Road
City, ST 12345-6789
Questions? 987-555-1212

3

TO:

4 MESSAGE

PLEASE REPLY BELOW

DATE: ☐ URGENT

DATE:

5

SIGNED:

SIGNED:

6 Place your instructions here. Place your text in this position. To achieve the same look, choose a similar font.

155

CHAPTER 8
Envelope Projects

Envelope Billboard

Maximize valuable message space

Every time you mail a letter, you could be mailing your own miniature billboard. In a few moments on your desktop system you can customize your envelope with a message that grabs the reader's attention and previews the contents.

Your version of the billboard needs a provocative headline for the face of the envelope and a subhead or quotation for the back flap. (*See* the layouts on page 160.) Keep the headline well above the address, no lower than 1 3/8" from the top edge on a #10 business envelope. Printing type and graphics on envelopes is tricky, so keep all text and lines at least 1/4" from the edges.

If you prefer not to print a message on the front of the envelope, consider using the back flap alone. (*See* the layouts on page 161.) The examples include a version (5) that previews the envelope's contents, a version (6) that prompts the reader to call with questions, and an alternative layout (7) for your name and return address.

Print the artwork directly from your computer on #10 business envelopes or have the envelopes preprinted in quantity by a commercial printer.

More envelope headlines

Here's the information you requested
This news will be of special interest to:
Questions about _____? Call 987-654-3210
We moved. Please note our new address.
Please RUSH this letter to:
Thank you for your order!
Don't forget, _____ is just one month away!

The Idea Book example shows how a small business association might piggyback a message on a general letter to members.

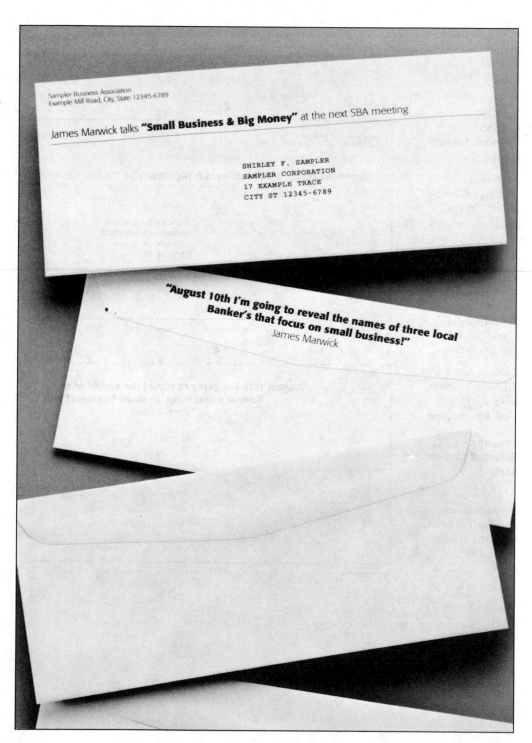

Sampler Business Association
Example Mill Road, City, State 12345-6789

James Marwick talks **"Small Business & Big Money"** at the next SBA meeting

SHIRLEY F. SAMPLER
SAMPLER CORPORATION
17 EXAMPLE TRACE
CITY ST 12345-6789

"August 10th I'm going to reveal the names of three local Banker's that focus on small business!"
James Marwick

Envelope Billboard Layout: Front

1 · Return Address: Formata Light, 10/12pt, flush left

2 · Headline: "James...": Formata Light, 16pt, flush left. "Small...": Formata Bold, 16pt, flush left, .5pt line below

3 · Recipient's Address: Courier Bold, 12/16pt, flush left, all caps

Envelope Billboard Layout: Back

4 · Headline: Formata Bold, 16/18pt, centered. Credit: Formata Light, 16pt, centered

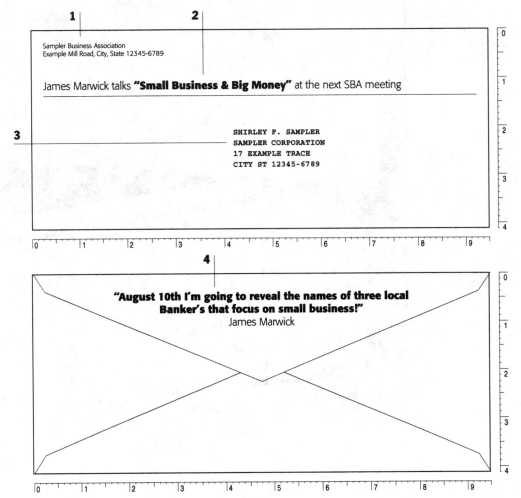

1 **2**

Sampler Business Association
Example Mill Road, City, State 12345-6789

James Marwick talks **"Small Business & Big Money"** at the next SBA meeting

3

SHIRLEY F. SAMPLER
SAMPLER CORPORATION
17 EXAMPLE TRACE
CITY ST 12345-6789

4

"August 10th I'm going to reveal the names of three local Banker's that focus on small business!"
James Marwick

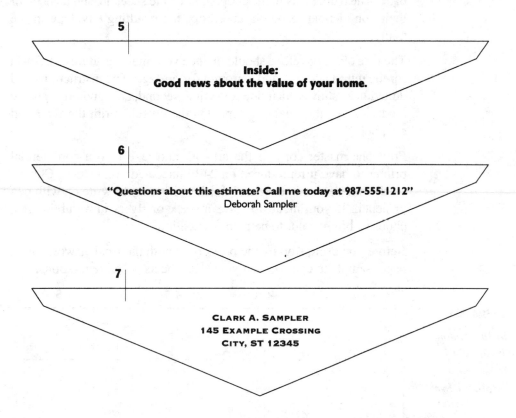

5

Inside:
Good news about the value of your home.

6

"Questions about this estimate? Call me today at 987-555-1212"
Deborah Sampler

7

CLARK A. SAMPLER
145 EXAMPLE CROSSING
CITY, ST 12345

**Envelope
Billboard Layout:
Flap Options**

*5 · Headline:
Formata Bold,
16/18pt, centered*

*6 · Headline: Gill
Sans Bold,
16/18pt, centered.
Credit: Gill Sans,
16pt, centered*

*7 · Name and
Address: Copper-
plate 33BC,
16/18pt, centered,
all caps*

Flyer Envelope

Add a free envelope to your flyer

If your flyer requires a sealed response, but you don't have the budget for a return envelope, this *Flyer Envelope* will solve the problem. Your flyer and coupon go on side one; the envelope is printed on the back. The reader fills in the coupon, folds the sheet around a check or their confidential response, and drops the resulting envelope in the mail.

The face of the envelope should include your mailing address, a fill-in for the return address, and a prompt for postage. The instructions and dotted lines show which line folds first, second, etc., and prompts the reader to tape the final envelope. On the outside, print the flyer and coupon.

Print one master copy of the artwork and take it to a commercial printer to have it reproduced on 24 lb uncoated bond stock. Choose stock with a smooth, uncoated finish so it's easy to write on with pen or pencil. If you intend to leave a stack of flyers in a public area, choose a bright color to help draw attention.

Before you print, stop by the post office with the final artwork and a paper sample to confirm that your flyer meets postal regulations.

Flyer Envelope Layout: Outside

1 · Return Address Fill-In: Minion Regular, 8pt, flush left, .5pt lines

2 · Reader Clip Art: From ARTSOURCE Vol. 2: Borders, Symbols, Holidays, & Attention Getters, by The Church Art Works, available from Youth Specialties Order Center, 800-776-8008, PO Box 4406, Spartanburg, SC 29305-9976 © Youth Specialties Inc. All rights reserved

3 · Instruction Text: Minion Regular, 8pt, centered

4 · Organization Address: Minion Regular, 14/18pt, flush left

5 · Stamp Reminder: Minion Regular, 8/10pt, centered, .5pt line around

6 · Dotted lines are printed to aid the reader in folding the envelope for mailing.

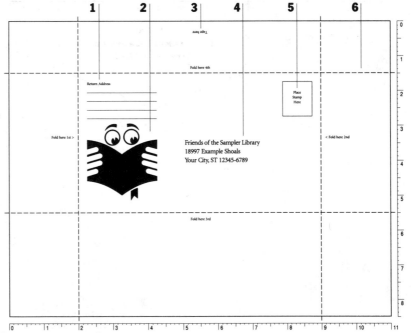

The Idea Book example shows how a charitable organization might use the layout to solicit new members and donations.

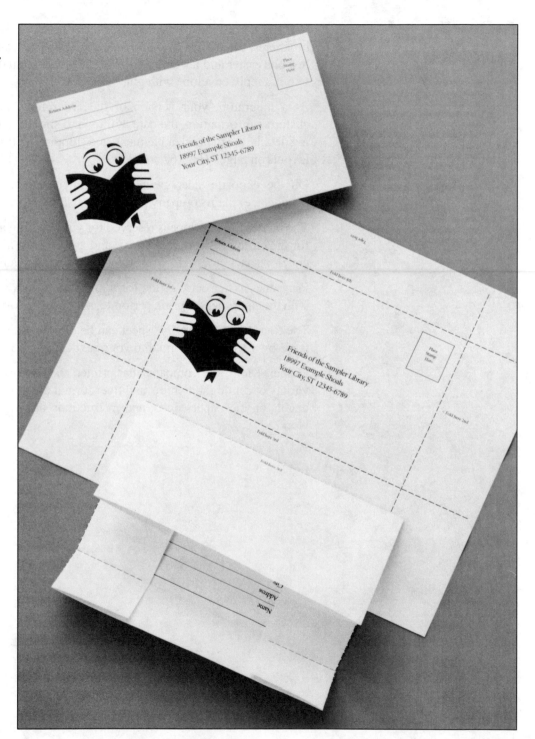

Order Form/ Envelope

Include an order form that speeds response

If you send out lots of catalogs, product sheets, and direct response brochures, this *Order Form/Envelope* will enable your customers to respond easier and faster. Part one of the layout is an order form; part two is a reply envelope with glue flap.

At a minimum, your version of the order form needs space for customer information, the date, bill to: and ship to: addresses, ordering details, the method of payment, and shipping instructions. (*See* the layouts on pages 166-167.)

On the opposite side, greet the customer with a letter from the president, explain company policies, or list more products.

The face of the envelope is reserved for your mailing address, a fill-in for the customer's return address, and a prompt to add postage. The envelope back is a perfect space for a marketing headline.

Print one master copy of the form and send it to a specialty printer with the equipment to print, perforate, and glue the form (*see* Source:).

The final 10 1/2" by 8 1/4" sheet can be distributed as is or folded to 6 1/2 by 8 1/4" and bound into your next catalog.

Dinner+Klein, the company that printed the example, also prints a variety of catalog, brochure, and flyer formats. Their catalog includes details on the papers, inks, and instructions on preparing your artwork.

The Idea Book example shows how a marine supply company might use the layout to process orders and do some selling.

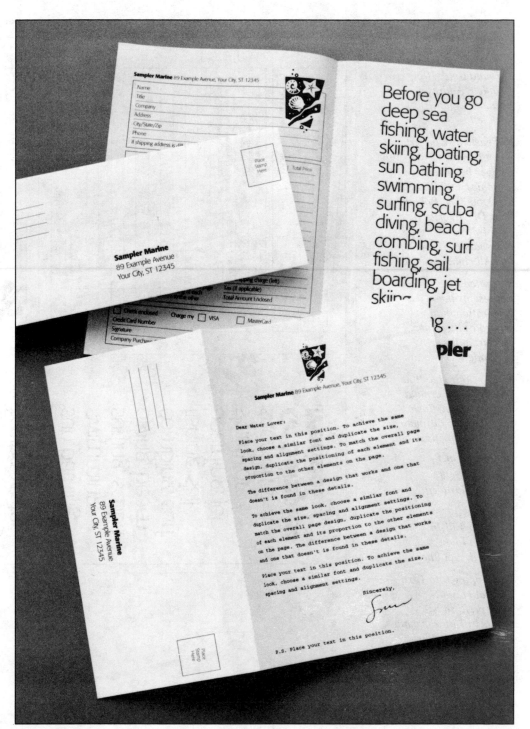

Source: Custom Reply Envelopes

The "REPLY-VELOPE" insert order form was printed by Dinner+Klein 800-234-6637, P.O. Box 3814, 600 S. Spokane Street, Seattle, WA 98124

Order Form/Envelope Layout: Side One

1 · Organization Name: Formata Bold, 10pt, flush left. Address: Formata Light, 10pt, flush left

2 · Seashells Clip Art: From Electronic Clipper by Dynamic Graphics, 800-255-8800, 6000 N. Forest Park Dr., Peoria, IL 61614-3592 © Dynamic Graphics, Inc. All rights reserved

3 · Dotted Line: Represents the perforation that separates the order form from the reply envelope.

4 · Envelope Headline: "Before..." : Formata Light, 36/36pt, flush left. "Go..." : Formata Bold, 36/36pt, flush left

5 · Buyer Fill-In: Formata Light, 10/18pt, flush left, .5pt lines

6 · Order Fill-In: Formata Light, 9pt, centered, .5pt lines

7 · Shipping Info Text: Formata Light, 10/11pt, flush left. Totals Fill-In: Formata Light, 10/18pt, flush left, .5pt lines

8 · Method of Payment Fill-In: Formata Light, 10/18pt, flush left, .5pt lines

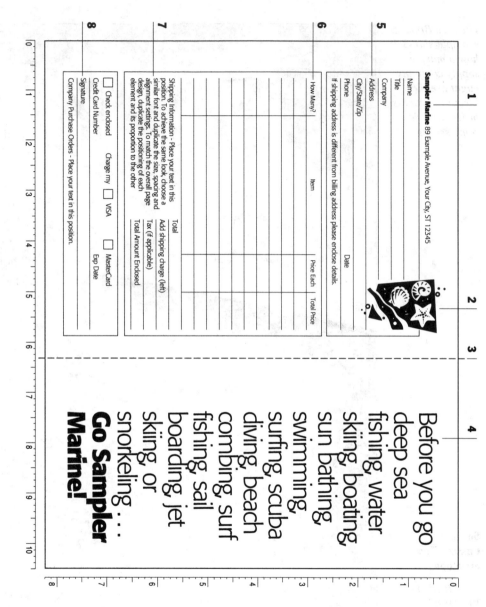

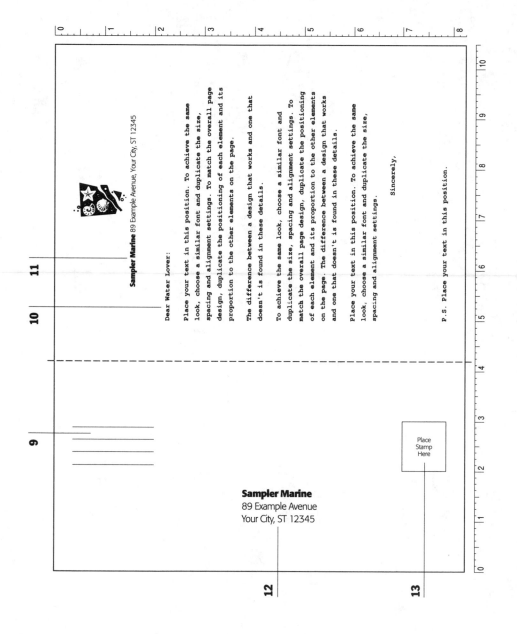

*9 · Return Address
Fill-In: .5pt lines*

*10 · Letter Text:
Courier Bold,
10/16pt, flush left*

*11 · Organization
Name: Formata Bold,
10pt. Address:
Formata Light, 10pt,
centered*

*12 · Organization
Name: Formata Bold,
14pt, flush left.
Address: Formata
Light, 14/18pt,
flush left*

*13 · Stamp Reminder:
Formata Light,
9/10pt, centered,
.5pt line*

CHAPTER 9
Flyer Projects

In-Store Flyer

Promote in-store sales

Typically, you distribute flyers with the hope of luring customers into the store. This flyer layout is used to generate interest *after* the customer arrives.

The Idea Book example shows how a retailer might use the flyer to offer unannounced discounts.

Begin your version with a headline that emphasizes "in-store exclusive." If it looks like a typical flyer, few customers will give it a second look.

Use each of the boxes around the headline to highlight a product, description, and the normal and discount prices.

Print one master copy and take it to a commercial printer to have it reproduced on brightly colored 24 lb uncoated bond stock.

Use the same basic layout to

Advertise the brands you stock
Define terms used in your business
Explain guarantees, policies, and perks
List product features
Map out the store
Survey customers

In-Store Flyer Layout

1

1 · Item Heading: Century Old Style, 12pt, centered. Item Text: Century Old Style, 11/12pt, flush left. Price Text: Century Old Style, 11/13pt, flush left

2

2 · Line: .5pt

3 · Organization Name: Century Old Style, 16pt, centered, all caps

3

4

4 · Headline: Futura Condensed Extra Bold, 105/90pt, centered

5 · Tag Line: Century Old Style Italic, 20/20pt, centered

5

Sampler Product

Product description and where the products are located in-store. Description and where the products are locate din-store.

Everyday price $29.50
In-store special $24.95

Sampler Product

Product description and where the products are located in-store. Description and where the products are locate din-store.

Everyday price $29.50
In-store special $24.95

Sampler Product

Product description and where the products are located in-store. Description and where the products are locate din-store.

Everyday price $29.50
In-store special $24.95

Sampler Product

Product description and where the products are located in-store. Description and where the products are locate din-store.

Everyday price $29.50
In-store special $24.95

Sampler Product

Product description and where the products are located in-store. Description and where the products are locate din-store.

Everyday price $29.50
In-store special $24.95

SAMPLER SUPPLY

Sampler Product

Product description and where the products are located in-store. Description and where the products are locate din-store.

Everyday price $29.50
In-store special $24.95

NOW THAT YOU'RE HERE!

Sampler Product

Product description and where the products are located in-store. Description and where the products are locate din-store.

Everyday price $29.50
In-store special $24.95

Sampler Product

Product description and where the products are located in-store. Description and where the products are locate din-store.

Everyday price $29.50
In-store special $24.95

These un-advertised specials will make you glad you came in!

Sampler Product

Product description and where the products are located in-store. Description and where the products are locate din-store.

Everyday price $29.50
In-store special $24.95

Sampler Product

Product description and where the products are located in-store. Description and where the products are locate din-store.

Everyday price $29.50
In-store special $24.95

Sampler Product

Product description and where the products are located in-store. Description and where the products are locate din-store.

Everyday price $29.50
In-store special $24.95

Sampler Product

Product description and where the products are located in-store. Description and where the products are locate din-store.

Everyday price $29.50
In-store special $24.95

Sampler Product

Product description and where the products are located in-store. Description and where the products are locate din-store.

Everyday price $29.50
In-store special $24.95

Map Flyer

Steer customers to your door

When you need to lead people to your door, make a map the focus of your flyer. You don't need a sophisticated drawing program or a degree in geography. You can do it with nothing more than the basic boxes and lines available in most desktop publishing programs.

The Idea Book example shows how a realtor might use a map to market a business center and steer potential customers to the site.

Your version should include enough of the surrounding territory to orient the reader. Add an arrow pointing north, symbols for schools, churches, traffic signals, and other landmarks to help lead the way. The box at the right frames your headline and marketing message.

Print one master copy of the artwork and take it to a commercial printer to have it reproduced on 24 lb uncoated bond stock.

Map Layout

1 · Street Lines: 2pt. The background box is a 20% screen of black.

2 · Street Headings: Formata Bold, 12/12pt, flush left

3 · Focus Point: Formata Bold, 18/18pt, centered, reverse (white) on a black background box

4 · Symbol: Adobe Carta, 24pt

5 · Subhead: Century Old Style, 14pt, flush left. Headline: Formata Bold, 30/28pt, flush left. Body Text: Century Old Style, 14/15pt, flush left, overprints a white background box

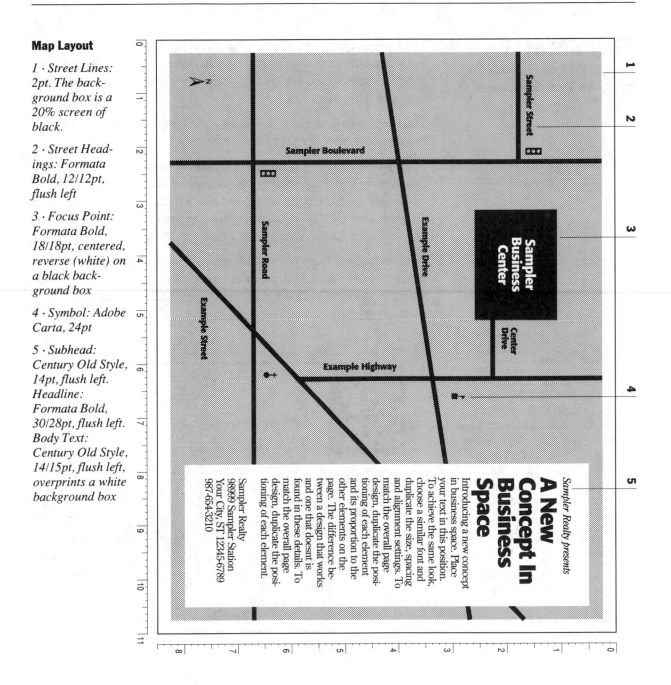

Play Sheet

Occupy little hands while you meet with Mom and Dad

Most parents agree that capturing a child's attention for fifteen or twenty minutes is no small feat. If you meet often with parents and their children or entertain young visitors, this *Play Sheet* should win you some new friends.

The Idea Book example shows how a retailer might add another twist by offering a prize for the best coloring job.

Start your version with a headline that names your organization, followed by text that explains the rules of the contest. Use a full-page clip art image as the coloring subject or compose a story using several different illustrations. Most major clip art companies offer collections of cartoons and animals ideal for a coloring sheet.

Print one master copy of the sheet and take it to a commercial printer to have it reproduced on 24 lb uncoated bond stock. Choose stock with a smooth, uncoated finish so it's easy to color with crayons or colored pencils.

Play Sheet Layout

1 · Jungle Clip Art: From Electronic Clipper by Dynamic Graphics, 800-255-8800, 6000 N. Forest Park Dr., Peoria, IL 61614-3592 © Dynamic Graphics, Inc. All rights reserved

2 · Line: 4pt

3 · Headline: Formata Bold, 36/34, flush left, reverse (white) on a black background box

4 · Instructions Text: Minion Regular, 16/18pt, flush left

5 · Artist Fill-In: Minion Regular, 16/18pt, flush left, .5pt lines

Sampler Lighting Center Coloring Contest

Once every 3 months we choose the very best coloring job and award the winner a special lamp designed just for kids! Color this picture while you're here or take it home and mail the finished picture to: Sampler Lighting Center, PO Box 6789, Your City, ST 12345 Good Luck!

Artist:
Age:
Phone:

The Idea Book example shows how a retailer might add another twist by offering a prize for the best coloring job.

Product Sheet

Answer all the customer's questions

To manufacturers and resellers, a well-designed, information-packed *Product Sheet* is not a nicety, it's a necessity. It is one of the primary tools used by distributors and dealers to resell a product or service. They typically add their names to the sheet as a source and pass it on to potential buyers.

The Idea Book example shows how a manufacturer might use the sheet to provide everything from the marketing highlights to the technical details.

The focus of the product sheet is a large illustration or photograph of your product. The tab-like title down the right side will help the customer find the sheet in a file or binder.

Compose a provocative headline for the left-hand column and follow it with the formal name of the product. The text below makes the marketing pitch; and the list details item numbers, sizes, and other technical tidbits.

There is space at the bottom for your organization's name, address, and phone. The reseller adds its name and contact information in the white box at the bottom of the photo area.

Print one master copy of the sheet and take it to a commercial printer to have it reproduced and hole punched. Request 80 lb coated text stock to maximize the reproduction quality of the photographs.

Product Sheet Layout

1 · Headline: Minion Regular, 48/40pt, flush left

2 · Photo Area

3 · Tab Headline: Minion Bold, 18pt, centered, reverse (white) on a black background box

4 · Subhead: Minion Regular, 18/18pt, flush left

5 · Body Text: Minion Regular, 12/14pt, flush left

6 · Hole Punch

7 · Listing: Minion Regular, 10/16pt, flush left, .5pt lines

8 · Organization Name: Minion Regular, 16/15pt, flush left, all caps. Address and Phone: Minion Regular, 12/14pt, flush left

9 · Dealer Imprint Area: Minion Regular, 12/14pt, flush left, on a white background box

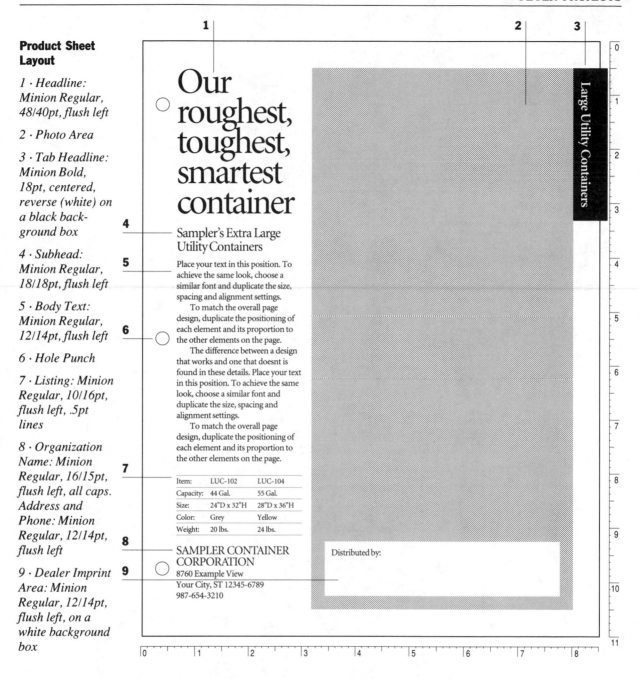

1　**2**　**3**

Large Utility Containers

Our roughest, toughest, smartest container

4

Sampler's Extra Large Utility Containers

5

Place your text in this position. To achieve the same look, choose a similar font and duplicate the size, spacing and alignment settings.

To match the overall page design, duplicate the positioning of each element and its proportion to the other elements on the page.

The difference between a design that works and one that doesnt is found in these details. Place your text in this position. To achieve the same look, choose a similar font and duplicate the size, spacing and alignment settings.

To match the overall page design, duplicate the positioning of each element and its proportion to the other elements on the page.

6

7

Item:	LUC-102	LUC-104
Capacity:	44 Gal.	55 Gal.
Size:	24"D x 32"H	28"D x 36"H
Color:	Grey	Yellow
Weight:	20 lbs.	24 lbs.

8

SAMPLER CONTAINER
CORPORATION
8760 Example View
Your City, ST 12345-6789
987-654-3210

9

Distributed by:

CHAPTER 10
Form Projects

Computer Files Record

Never lose a file again

If you don't have your own scheme for naming, organizing, and finding files, this may turn out to be the most valuable idea in the book. The *Computer Files Record* is a plain little form that does a big job.

The key lies in naming your files (*see* the example below). Number the first four characters beginning with 0001. The fifth character represents the software program you used to create the file. Use the next three characters to represent the type of document, i.e., a letter=LTR, a spreadsheet=SPR, a proposal=PRO, etc. The last three characters identify the type of file; typically, the default file name your software adds when you save the file.

Next time you create a new file, add it to your record. Include blank listings at the bottom of the form and fill them in by hand. Once every week or two enter the new files and print an updated list.

The form lists the file name, the date you created it, a brief description of the file and the name of anyone associated with it.

Next time you're searching for one file in a mountain of names, scan a printout of the list. Or use the Search or Find feature of your software to search the file for any of the file name parts, dates, descriptions, or names.

Use the Courier typeface; it spaces all characters equally and makes your listing much easier to read.

```
   A    B   C      D
0121 A L T R . E X T
```

File Naming Scheme

A · Sequential number of the file

B · The software program used to create the file

C · The type of document

D · The natural extension of the file

**Computer Files
Record Layout**

*1 · Header:
Courier Bold,
10/14pt, flush left*

*2 · Column
Headings:
Courier Bold,
10/14pt, flush left,
.5pt line below*

*3 · Listings:
Courier Bold,
10/14pt, flush left*

4 · Hole Punch

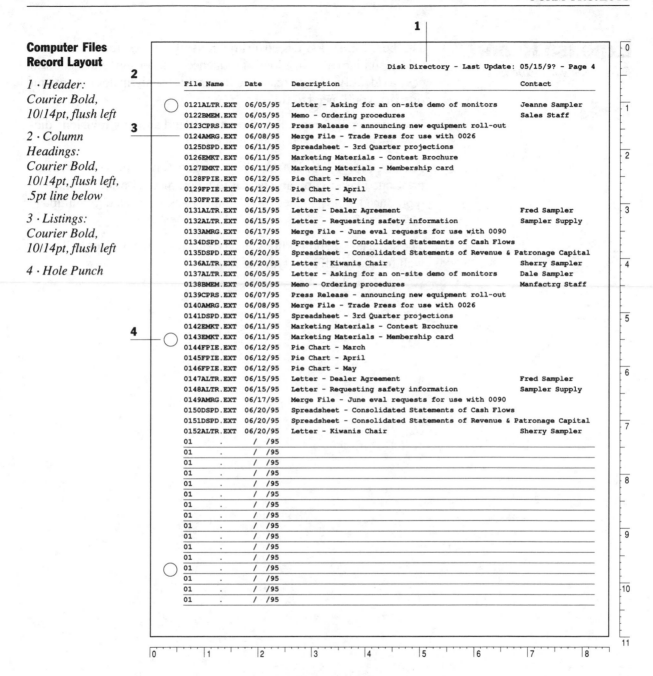

```
                                    Disk Directory - Last Update: 05/15/9? - Page 4

File Name    Date      Description                                         Contact

0121ALTR.EXT 06/05/95  Letter - Asking for an on-site demo of monitors     Jeanne Sampler
0122BMEM.EXT 06/05/95  Memo - Ordering procedures                          Sales Staff
0123CPRS.EXT 06/07/95  Press Release - announcing new equipment roll-out
0124AMRG.EXT 06/08/95  Merge File - Trade Press for use with 0026
0125DSPD.EXT 06/11/95  Spreadsheet - 3rd Quarter projections
0126EMKT.EXT 06/11/95  Marketing Materials - Contest Brochure
0127EMKT.EXT 06/11/95  Marketing Materials - Membership card
0128FPIE.EXT 06/12/95  Pie Chart - March
0129FPIE.EXT 06/12/95  Pie Chart - April
0130FPIE.EXT 06/12/95  Pie Chart - May
0131ALTR.EXT 06/15/95  Letter - Dealer Agreement                           Fred Sampler
0132ALTR.EXT 06/15/95  Letter - Requesting safety information              Sampler Supply
0133AMRG.EXT 06/17/95  Merge File - June eval requests for use with 0090
0134DSPD.EXT 06/20/95  Spreadsheet - Consolidated Statements of Cash Flows
0135DSPD.EXT 06/20/95  Spreadsheet - Consolidated Statements of Revenue & Patronage Capital
0136ALTR.EXT 06/20/95  Letter - Kiwanis Chair                              Sherry Sampler
0137ALTR.EXT 06/05/95  Letter - Asking for an on-site demo of monitors     Dale Sampler
0138BMEM.EXT 06/05/95  Memo - Ordering procedures                          Manfactrg Staff
0139CPRS.EXT 06/07/95  Press Release - announcing new equipment roll-out
0140AMRG.EXT 06/08/95  Merge File - Trade Press for use with 0026
0141DSPD.EXT 06/11/95  Spreadsheet - 3rd Quarter projections
0142EMKT.EXT 06/11/95  Marketing Materials - Contest Brochure
0143EMKT.EXT 06/11/95  Marketing Materials - Membership card
0144FPIE.EXT 06/12/95  Pie Chart - March
0145FPIE.EXT 06/12/95  Pie Chart - April
0146FPIE.EXT 06/12/95  Pie Chart - May
0147ALTR.EXT 06/15/95  Letter - Dealer Agreement                           Fred Sampler
0148ALTR.EXT 06/15/95  Letter - Requesting safety information              Sampler Supply
0149AMRG.EXT 06/17/95  Merge File - June eval requests for use with 0090
0150DSPD.EXT 06/20/95  Spreadsheet - Consolidated Statements of Cash Flows
0151DSPD.EXT 06/20/95  Spreadsheet - Consolidated Statements of Revenue & Patronage Capital
0152ALTR.EXT 06/20/95  Letter - Kiwanis Chair                              Sherry Sampler
01        .    /  /95
01        .    /  /95
01        .    /  /95
01        .    /  /95
01        .    /  /95
01        .    /  /95
01        .    /  /95
01        .    /  /95
01        .    /  /95
01        .    /  /95
01        .    /  /95
01        .    /  /95
01        .    /  /95
01        .    /  /95
```

Expense Report

Fast-track your expenses

The best forms don't need instructions. They ask for information using familiar terms in a logical sequence. This design makes a form easy to identify, easy to read, and it accurately anticipates the amount of space you'll need to fill it in.

For your version, reproduce the artwork and add any revisions dictated by your organization's policies.

Print the report directly from your computer on 24 lb bond stock. Or print one master copy and take it to a commercial printer to have it reproduced, hole punched, divided into pads, or printed in multipage carbonless form.

The same layout, proportions, and typeface styles and sizes will work well for many different types of forms.

Expense Report Layout

1 · Form Title: Adobe Caslon Regular, 18pt, flush left

2 · Column Headings: Adobe Caslon Regular, 8/18pt, flush left, all caps, .5pt lines

3 · Item Listing: Adobe Caslon Regular, 10/18pt, flush left, .5pt lines

4 · Signature and Total Fill-Ins: Adobe Caslon Regular, 8/18pt, flush left, all caps, .5pt lines

1

2

3

4

Weekly Expense Report

EXPENSES	SUN	MON	TUE	WED	THU	FRI	SAT	TOTAL
Airfare								
Breakfast								
Lunch								
Dinner								
Lodging								
Parking/Tolls								
Postage								
Supplies								
Copies								
Tips								
Telephone								
Transportation								
Other								
TOTAL								

ENTERTAINMENT

DATE	PERSON & COMPANY	PLACE	BUSINESS PURPOSE	AMOUNT
			TOTAL	

OTHER EXPENSES

DATE	REMARKS	AMOUNT
	TOTAL	

	TOTAL FROM ABOVE
EMPLOYEE SIGNATURE	ADJUSTMENTS
	MINUS ADVANCE
APPROVED BY	TOTAL DUE EMPLOYEE (DUE COMPANY)

Itinerary

Solve your travel headaches

Traveling to faraway destinations is enough of a challenge when you're well-organized. But, if you don't know the who, what, where and when, that challenge can turn to disaster. This *Itinerary* is a pocket-sized organizer that details everything from the time you depart until the time you touch down.

To create your version, add the name of the traveler you're scheduling and list each event in the order it takes place. Number and date the finished pages at the bottom right.

Print the artwork directly from your computer on 24 lb bond stock and trim it to size.

Itinerary Layout

1 · Title: Helvetica Narrow Bold, 10pt, flush left, reverse (white) on a black background box

2 · Lines: The lines are actually a series of periods, Helvetica Narrow, 10pt, flush left

3 · Heading: Helvetica Narrow Bold, 10pt, flush left

4 · Listing Text: Helvetica Narrow, 10/11pt, flush left

5 · Page Number and Date: Helvetica Narrow, 10pt, flush right

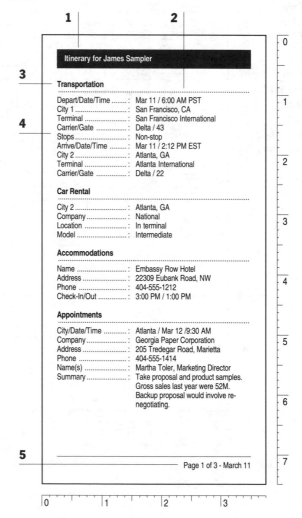

This Itinerary is a pocket-sized organizer that lists everything from the time you depart until the time you touch down.

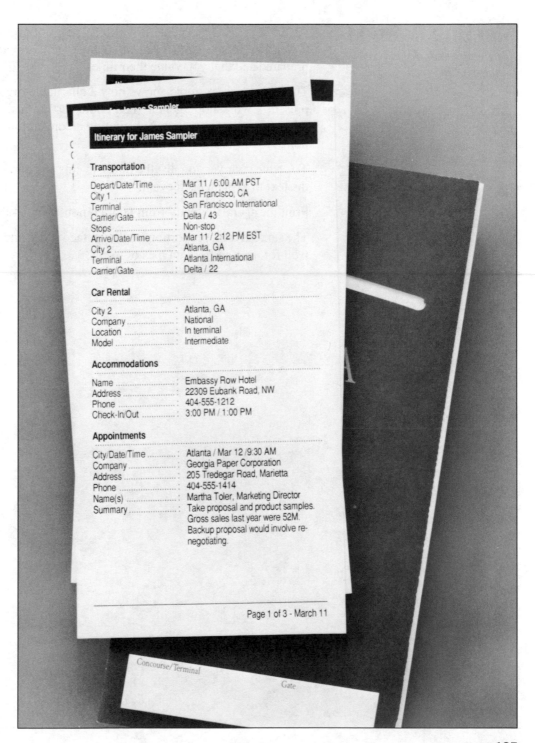

Itinerary for James Sampler

Transportation

Depart/Date/Time	: Mar 11 / 6:00 AM PST
City 1	: San Francisco, CA
Terminal	: San Francisco International
Carrier/Gate	: Delta / 43
Stops	: Non-stop
Arrive/Date/Time	: Mar 11 / 2:12 PM EST
City 2	: Atlanta, GA
Terminal	: Atlanta International
Carrier/Gate	: Delta / 22

Car Rental

City 2	: Atlanta, GA
Company	: National
Location	: In terminal
Model	: Intermediate

Accommodations

Name	: Embassy Row Hotel
Address	: 22309 Eubank Road, NW
Phone	: 404-555-1212
Check-In/Out	: 3:00 PM / 1:00 PM

Appointments

City/Date/Time	: Atlanta / Mar 12 /9:30 AM
Company	: Georgia Paper Corporation
Address	: 205 Tredegar Road, Marietta
Phone	: 404-555-1414
Name(s)	: Martha Toler, Marketing Director
Summary	: Take proposal and product samples. Gross sales last year were 52M. Backup proposal would involve re-negotiating.

Page 1 of 3 - March 11

Concourse/Terminal

Gate

Meeting Agenda

*Start your meeting with a
winning plan*

On the surface, an agenda is just a glorified list of events or topics. But a well-designed agenda, sent in advance, tells the audience you're prepared and that you value their time.

The Idea Book example shows how a charitable organization might present a workshop agenda. You could just as easily set it up as a formal meeting agenda by substituting a conventional list of agenda items.

To create your version, list the times, events and participants, and use the text to explain each event.

Print the agenda directly from your computer on 24 lb bond stock.

The same layout, proportions, and typeface styles and sizes will work well for many different types of forms.

A formal meeting version might include

Call to order
Approval of minutes
Report of treasurer
Report of board
Report of officers
Report of committees
Unfinished business
New business
Appointments
Nominations and elections
Program
Announcements
Adjournment

Meeting Agenda Layout

1 · Title: Copperplate 33BC, 18pt, centered, all caps, reverse (white) on a black background box

2 · Event: Copperplate 33BC, 14pt, centered, all caps. Location and Date: Times New Roman, 12/14pt, centered

3 · Time: Copperplate 33BC, 12/14pt, flush left, all caps, 5pt line above

4 · Meeting Description Title: Copperplate 33BC, 12/14pt, flush left, all caps. Meeting Description Text: New Times Roman, 12/14pt, flush left. Location: New Times Roman, 10/12pt, flush left

5 · Line: .5pt

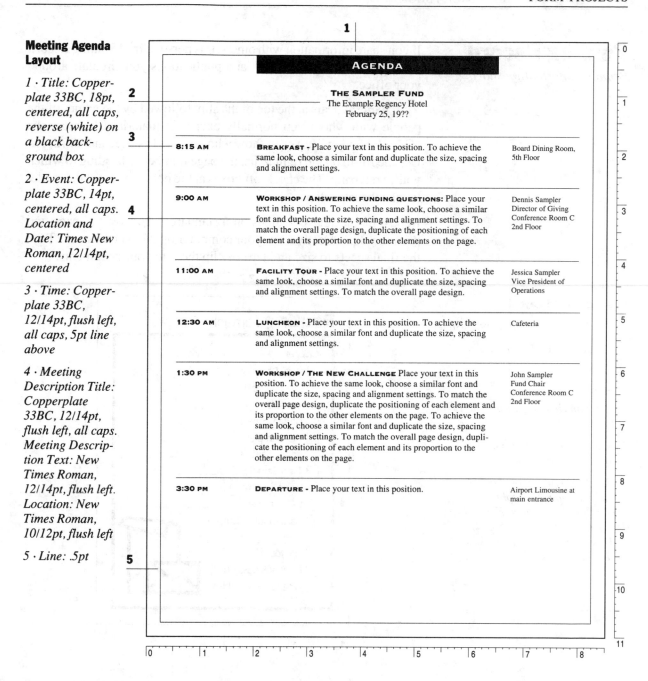

Routing Record

Promote information sharing

If you share information with others, this personalized *Routing Record* will help track the files, mail, and publications you circulate around your office.

Your name appears at the top of the slip, followed by the names of the people with whom you normally exchange materials. Number the "Order of review" boxes to show who reviews first, second, third, etc. Use the fill-in on the right to list the page number or heading to which you're referring. The check-off boxes at the bottom prompt the reader to take the next step.

Repeat the design four times on a standard 8 1/2" by 11" page and print the slips directly from your computer on 24 lb bond stock. Trim the final sheets to size and tape or clip them to your documents.

Routing Record Layout

1 · Title: Formata Bold, 24pt, flush left

2 · Sender Name: Formata Light, 18pt, flush left

3 · Line: 4pt

4 · Column Headings: Formata Light 12pt, flush left

5 · Listings: Formata Light 14/20pt, flush left, .5pt lines

6 · Mail Clip Art: From Designer's Club by Dynamic Graphics, 800-255-8800, 6000 N. Forest Park Dr., Peoria, IL 61614-3592 © Dynamic Graphics, Inc. All rights reserved

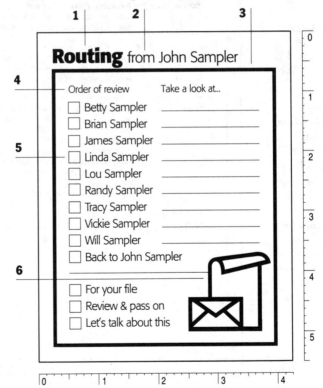

The Idea Book example shows how a manager might use the form to route publications.

Six-Month Planner

Plan the big picture

Most off-the-shelf calendars show familiar holidays on the day they take place. Once you know that New Year's Day falls on Wednesday you can do some advance planning. Why not apply the same idea to your group's planning calendar by adding upcoming business events?

The Idea Book example shows how a corporate marketing department might use the planner to remind the staff of upcoming events.

Lead off your version by centering the name of your organization at the top of the page. Just below, fashion a subtitle that tells who prepared the form and where to call with questions.

Add a description of each event next to the date on which it falls. Leave the remaining dates blank so each member of the group can fill in their own schedule.

Recreating the page is easier than it looks. By listing the days in a single column, you eliminate the need for six different layouts. Once you complete the first month, copy and paste the other five.

Print one master copy of the planner and take it to a commercial printer to have it reproduced on 24 lb bond stock. Hole punch the finished sheets and distribute them to your group.

Six-Month Planner Layout

1 · Title: Copperplate 33BC, 14pt, centered, all caps, reverse (white) on a black background box

2 · Questions?: Helvetica, 9pt, centered

3 · Day-By-Day Listing: Copperplate 33BC, 8/10pt, flush left, all caps, .5pt lines

4 · Month Headings: Copperplate 33BC, 11pt, centered, all caps

5 · Hole Punch

6 · Lines: .5pt

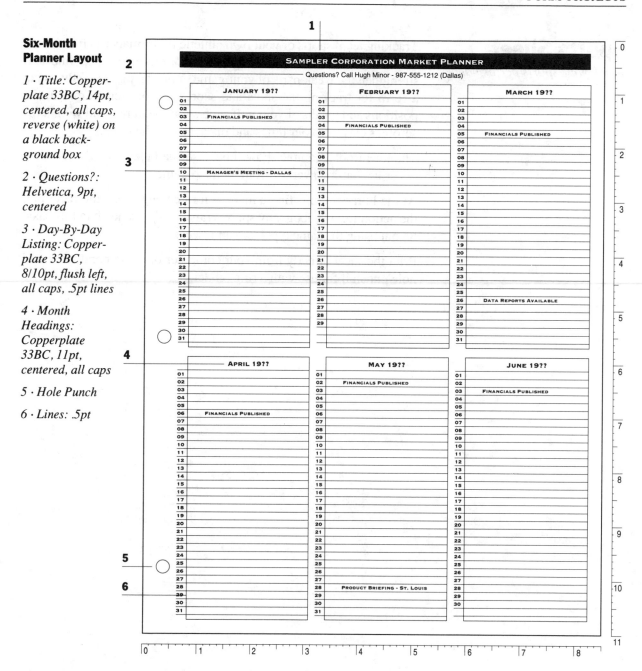

SAMPLER CORPORATION MARKET PLANNER

Questions? Call Hugh Minor - 987-555-1212 (Dallas)

JANUARY 19??
- 03 FINANCIALS PUBLISHED
- 10 MANAGER'S MEETING - DALLAS

FEBRUARY 19??
- 04 FINANCIALS PUBLISHED

MARCH 19??
- 05 FINANCIALS PUBLISHED
- 26 DATA REPORTS AVAILABLE

APRIL 19??
- 06 FINANCIALS PUBLISHED

MAY 19??
- 02 FINANCIALS PUBLISHED
- 28 PRODUCT BRIEFING - ST. LOUIS

JUNE 19??
- 03 FINANCIALS PUBLISHED

Sports Sheet

Track your sports performance

Tracking team sports or your own athletic performance is fun. It may surprise you how documenting your progress helps you find and strengthen the weak parts of your game. You can just as easily create a form for tracking the shots and scores of your tennis match, the positions and results of your golf shots, your heart rate and weight for aerobics class, or your times and distances on the track.

The Idea Book example shows how a softball player might calculate his or her batting average from game to game.

At the library, you'll find a method for keeping score and recording the action for just about any sport. Translate that scheme to this basic layout using the same typefaces and sizes.

Print the sheet directly from your computer on 24 lb bond stock and hole punch it for use with a ring binder.

Sports Sheet Layout

1 · Title: Formata Bold, 10pt, flush left, reverse (white) on a black background box

2 · Listings: Formata Light, 8/19pt, flush left, .5pt line above

3 · Hole Punch

4 · Line: .5pt

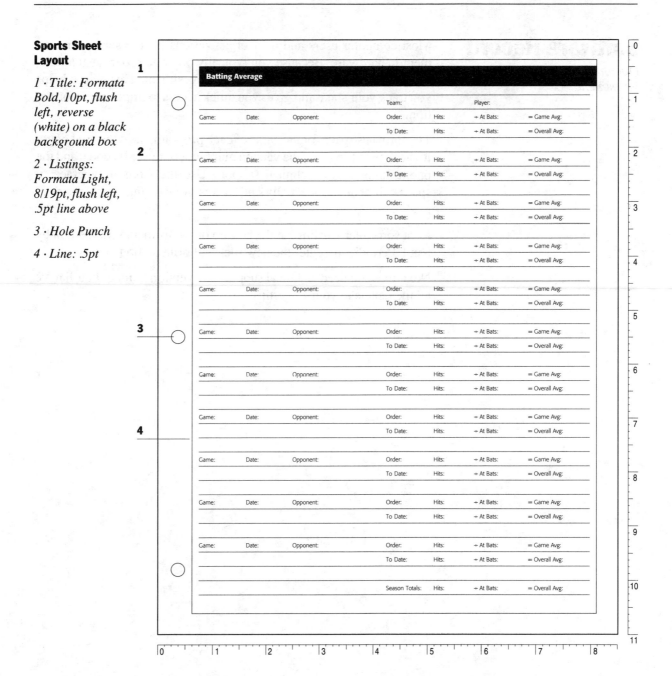

1

2

3

4

Software Record

Document your software investment

Most computer users and their organizations have a serious investment in hardware. Because you typically buy one program at a time, it's easy to lose sight of your software investment. This record helps you track your stake and gives you quick access to important information.

The form has space for the name of each program, the date you bought it, the type of program, the version number, your user ID code, and the phone number for technical support. Use the Courier typeface; it spaces all characters equally and makes your listing much easier to read.

Print some blank listings at the bottom of the form and fill them in by hand. Periodically enter the new files and print an updated list.

Next time you need technical support or a version number you'll have all the details at your fingertips.

Software Record Layout

1 · Header: Courier Bold, 10pt, flush left

2 · Column Headings: Courier Bold, 10pt, flush left, .5pt line below

3 · Listings: Courier Bold, 10/14pt, flush left

4 · Hole Punch

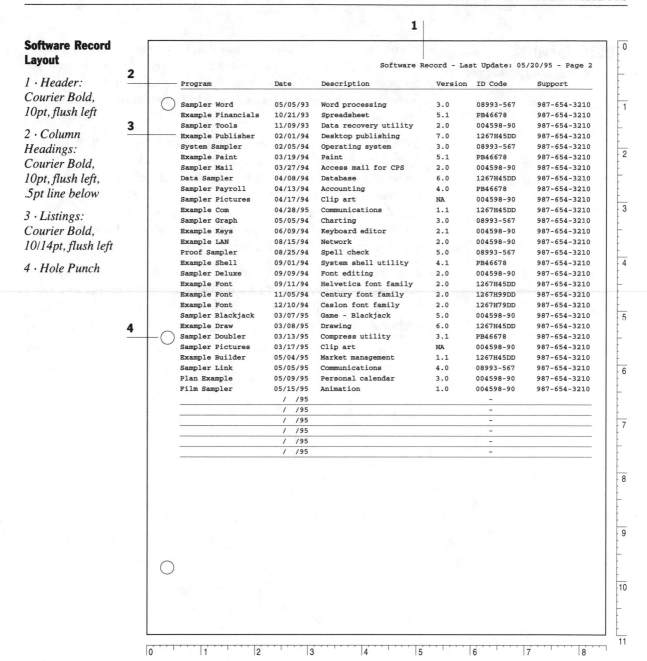

Software Record - Last Update: 05/20/95 - Page 2

Program	Date	Description	Version	ID Code	Support
Sampler Word	05/05/93	Word processing	3.0	08993-567	987-654-3210
Example Financials	10/21/93	Spreadsheet	5.1	PB46678	987-654-3210
Sampler Tools	11/09/93	Data recovery utility	2.0	004598-90	987-654-3210
Example Publisher	02/01/94	Desktop publishing	7.0	1267H45DD	987-654-3210
System Sampler	02/05/94	Operating system	3.0	08993-567	987-654-3210
Example Paint	03/19/94	Paint	5.1	PB46678	987-654-3210
Sampler Mail	03/27/94	Access mail for CPS	2.0	004598-90	987-654-3210
Data Sampler	04/08/94	Database	6.0	1267H45DD	987-654-3210
Sampler Payroll	04/13/94	Accounting	4.0	PB46678	987-654-3210
Sampler Pictures	04/17/94	Clip art	NA	004598-90	987-654-3210
Example Com	04/28/95	Communications	1.1	1267H45DD	987-654-3210
Sampler Graph	05/05/94	Charting	3.0	08993-567	987-654-3210
Example Keys	06/09/94	Keyboard editor	2.1	004598-90	987-654-3210
Example LAN	08/15/94	Network	2.0	004598-90	987-654-3210
Proof Sampler	08/25/94	Spell check	5.0	08993-567	987-654-3210
Example Shell	09/01/94	System shell utility	4.1	PB46678	987-654-3210
Sampler Deluxe	09/09/94	Font editing	2.0	004598-90	987-654-3210
Example Font	09/11/94	Helvetica font family	2.0	1267H45DD	987-654-3210
Example Font	11/05/94	Century font family	2.0	1267H99DD	987-654-3210
Example Font	12/10/94	Caslon font family	2.0	1267H79DD	987-654-3210
Sampler Blackjack	03/07/95	Game - Blackjack	5.0	004598-90	987-654-3210
Example Draw	03/08/95	Drawing	6.0	1267H45DD	987-654-3210
Sampler Doubler	03/13/95	Compress utility	3.1	PB46678	987-654-3210
Sampler Pictures	03/17/95	Clip art	NA	004598-90	987-654-3210
Example Builder	05/04/95	Market management	1.1	1267H45DD	987-654-3210
Sampler Link	05/05/95	Communications	4.0	08993-567	987-654-3210
Plan Example	05/09/95	Personal calendar	3.0	004598-90	987-654-3210
Film Sampler	05/15/95	Animation	1.0	004598-90	987-654-3210
	/ /95			-	
	/ /95			-	
	/ /95			-	
	/ /95			-	
	/ /95			-	
	/ /95			-	

195

Time Sheet

Reclaim lost hours and income

If you charge by the hour but you don't use a form, or you merely want to improve your time estimates, this layout could be an eye-opener. Like so many other forms, the hidden value of this *Time Sheet* is that its mere presence prompts you to keep records you otherwise might not.

You can substitute your own time management method or use this example: Beginning at the left, enter the date and describe the task or name the client. In column three, enter the number of hours you estimate it will take to complete the job. Next, list the time you started and the time you finished. In the last column, calculate the actual number of hours. Compare the estimated and actual hours to gauge the accuracy of your estimates.

Print the record directly from your computer on 24 lb bond stock. Or print one master copy and take it to a commercial printer to have it reproduced, hole punched, divided into pads, or printed in multipage carbonless form.

The same layout, proportions, and typeface styles and sizes will work well for many different types of forms.

Time Sheet Layout

1 · Title: Helvetica Narrow Bold, 12pt, flush left, reverse (white) on a black background box

2 · Column Headings and Totals: Helvetica Narrow, 9pt, flush left

3 · Line: .5pt

4 · Fill-In Lines: .5pt

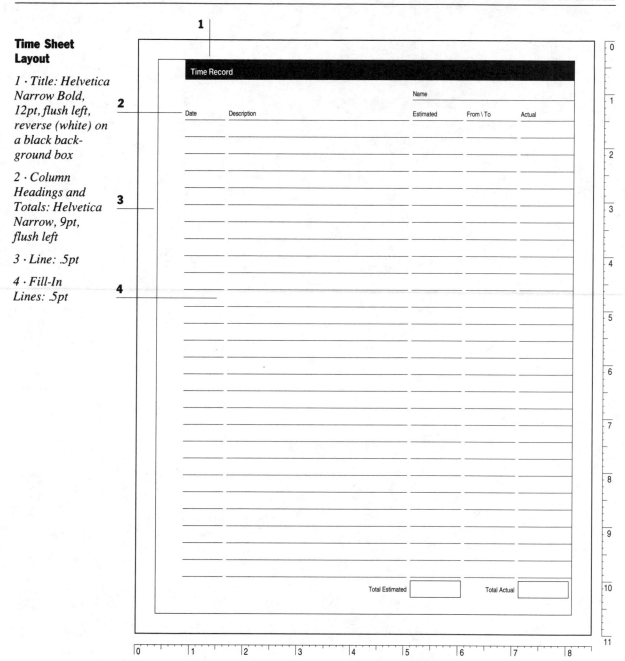

CHAPTER 11
News Projects

Birth Announcement

Report the ultimate news event

This personalized *Birth Announcement* is a project your family will appreciate now and cherish later.

To create your version, begin by centering your family name on the miniature album cover. (*See* the layouts on pages 202-203.) On the inside-left page, list the baby's name, the time and date of birth, the name of the doctor, the hospital, his or her weight and length, and mom's and dad's names.

The four black squares on the inside-right page simulate old-fashioned photo corners. Space the squares to fit the size of photograph you're using. Cut a 45 degree slot through the center of each square with a sharp art knife and tuck the corners of the photograph into the slots.

Print one master copy of the artwork and take it to a commercial printer to have it reproduced in quantity and machine folded. Have it printed on 80 lb uncoated cover stock in the appropriate pink or blue.

The 6" by 9" sheet folds down to 6" by 4 1/2" and fits a standard A6 envelope.

Use the same layout to send

Anniversary portraits
Baby pictures
Bar Mitzvah portraits
Baptism portraits
Confirmation portraits
Holiday greeting pictures
Family portraits
Graduation portraits
Kid's school pictures
Military service portraits
Wedding portraits

The four black squares on the inside-right page of the Birth Announcement simulate old-fashioned photo corners.

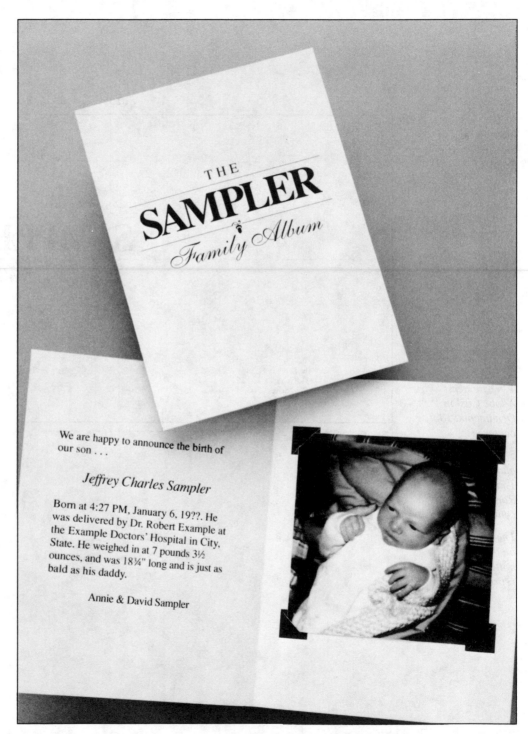

Birth Announcement Layout: Back and Front Covers

1 · Family Name: Times New Roman Bold, 55pt, centered, all caps

2 · "THE": Times New Roman, 18pt, centered, all caps, .5pt line below

3 · Title: Shelley Allegro, 36pt, centered, .5pt line below

4 · Ornament: Adobe Caslon Ornaments, 18pt, centered

5 · Family Name and Address: Times New Roman, 12/14pt, centered

The dotted lines on the top and bottom edges represent folds.

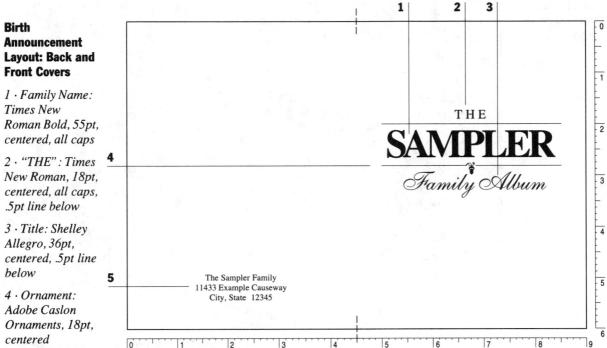

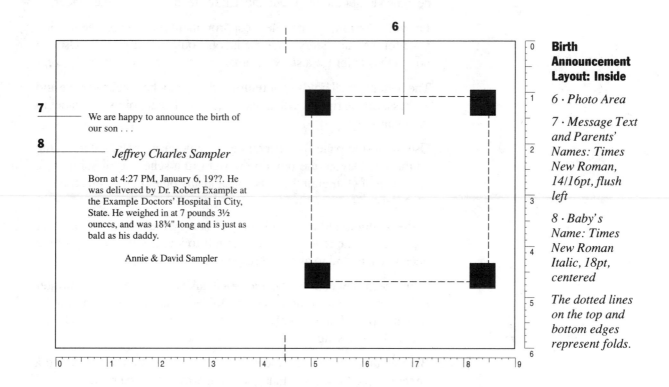

6

7

8

We are happy to announce the birth of
our son . . .

Jeffrey Charles Sampler

Born at 4:27 PM, January 6, 19??. He
was delivered by Dr. Robert Example at
the Example Doctors' Hospital in City,
State. He weighed in at 7 pounds 3½
ounces, and was 18¾" long and is just as
bald as his daddy.

Annie & David Sampler

**Birth
Announcement
Layout: Inside**

6 · Photo Area

*7 · Message Text
and Parents'
Names: Times
New Roman,
14/16pt, flush
left*

*8 · Baby's
Name: Times
New Roman
Italic, 18pt,
centered*

*The dotted lines
on the top and
bottom edges
represent folds.*

Church News

Inspire positive communication

Do you know of a church or synagogue that *doesn't* publish a newsletter? In this portable age, a weekly or monthly publication is one way for your religious family to stay in touch. This layout is designed to get the word out and ask for feedback from the reader.

For your version, reserve the most prominent position on the outside page for the main story. (*See* the layouts on pages 206-207.) Use the box in the center for a story summary the reader can "clip and save."

The bottom panel holds your return address and the reader's name and address. On the right is a headline or quotation that points the reader to the main story.

Use the inside page for general news, announcements, letters to the editor, etc. Devote the box on the right to a schedule of services, a statement of your church's mission, and any other items you repeat in each issue.

At the bottom, add a questionnaire to survey the reader on topics of the day. Use the reverse box on the left to identify the subject of the questionnaire and to ask for a response.

Print one master copy of the mailer and take it to a commercial printer to have it reproduced and machine folded. Although you can mail a lighter paper, 60 lb uncoated cover stock or heavier will have a better chance of surviving the mail.

Before you print, stop by the post office with the final artwork and a paper sample to confirm that your mailer meets postal regulations.

In this portable age, a weekly or monthly publication is one way for your religious family to stay in touch.

Church Bulletin Layout: Outside

1 · Subhead: Adobe Caslon Regular Italic, 12pt, centered, 8pt line above

2 · Headline: Charlemagne, 24/28pt, centered, all caps. Headline Credit: Adobe Caslon Regular, 11pt, flush left

3 · Body Text: Adobe Caslon Regular Italic, 11/12pt, flush left

4 · Clip and Save Text: Adobe Caslon Regular Bold, 11pt, centered (list is flush left), reverse (white) on a black background. Add a dotted line around the text and center the words "CLIP AND SAVE" below.

5 · Line: .5pt

6 · Envelope Headline: Charlemagne, 30/36pt, flush left, all caps. Return Address and Headline Credit: Adobe Caslon Regular, 11/12pt, flush left. Recipient's Address: Courier Bold, 11/12pt, flush left

The dotted lines on the top and bottom edges represent folds.

January Focus: Everyday Ethics

I WOULD RATHER BE THE MAN THAT BOUGHT THE BROOKLYN BRIDGE THAN THE MAN WHO SOLD IT. –Will Rodgers

Place your text in this position. To achieve the same look, choose a similar font and duplicate the size, spacing and alignment settings. To match the overall page design, duplicate the positioning of each element and its proportion to the other elements on the page. The difference between a design that works and one that doesn't is found in these details.

To achieve the same look, choose a similar font and duplicate the size, spacing and alignment settings. To match the overall page design, duplicate the positioning of each element and its proportion to the other elements on the page. The difference between a design that works and one that doesn't is found in these details. Place your text in this position. To achieve the same look, choose a similar font and duplicate the size, spacing and alignment settings.

To match the overall page design, duplicate the positioning of each element and its proportion to the other elements on the page. The difference between a design that works and one that doesn't is found in these details. Place your text in this position. To achieve the same look, choose a similar font and duplicate the size, spacing and alignment settings. To match the overall page design, duplicate the positioning of each element and its proportion to the other elements on the page.

The difference between a design that works and one that doesn't is found in these details. Place your text in this position. To achieve the same look, choose a similar font and duplicate the size, spacing and alignment settings. To

match the overall page design, duplicate the positioning of each element and its proportion to the other elements.

Place your text in this position. To achieve the same look, choose a similar font and duplicate the size, spacing and alignment settings. To match the overall page design, duplicate the positioning of each element and its proportion to the

Everyday Ethics

1. First key point to remember.

2. Second key point to remember.

3. Third key point to remember.

4. Fourth key point to remember.

5. Fifth key point to remember.

CLIP AND SAVE

other elements on the page. The difference between a design that works and one that doesn't is found in these details.

To achieve the same look, choose a similar font and duplicate the size, spacing and alignment settings. To match the overall page design, duplicate the positioning of each element and its proportion to the other elements on the page. The difference between a design that works and one that doesn't is found in these details. Place your text in this position. To achieve the same look, choose a similar font and duplicate the

size, spacing and alignment settings.

To match the overall page design, duplicate the positioning of each element and its proportion to the other elements on the page. The difference between a design that works and one that doesn't is found in these details. Place your text in this position. To achieve the same look, choose a similar font and duplicate the size, spacing and alignment settings. To match the overall page design, duplicate the positioning of each element and its proportion to the other elements.

The difference between a design that works and one that doesn't is found in these details. Place your text in this position. To achieve the same look, choose a similar font and duplicate the size, spacing and alignment settings. To match the overall page design, duplicate the positioning of each element and its proportion to the other elements.

Place your text in this position. To achieve the same look, choose a similar font and duplicate the size, spacing and alignment settings. To match the overall page design, duplicate the positioning of each element and its proportion to the other elements on the page. The difference between a design that works and one that doesn't is found in these details.

To achieve the same look, choose a similar font and duplicate the size, spacing and alignment settings. To match the overall page design, duplicate the positioning of each element and its proportion to the other elements on the page. Choose a similar font and duplicate the size, spacing and alignment settings.

To match the overall page design,

The Sampler Church
1233 Example Boulevard West
City, State 12345-6789

THERE IS NO RIGHT WAY TO DO A WRONG THING

–From *The Power of Ethical Management*, by Kenneth Blanchard and Norman Vincent Peale

The Sampler Family
14475 Example Avenue
City, State 12345

7

8

ANNOUNCEMENTS

Place your text in this position. To achieve the same look, choose a similar font and duplicate the size, spacing and alignment settings.

To achieve the same look, choose a similar font and duplicate the size, spacing and alignment settings. To match the overall page design, duplicate the positioning of each element and its proportion to the other elements on the page.

To match the overall page design, duplicate the positioning of each element and its proportion to the other elements on the page.

LETTERS

Dear Name:

To match the overall page design, duplicate the positioning of each element and its proportion to the other elements on the page. The difference between a design that works and one that doesn't is found in these details. Place your text in this position. To achieve the same look, choose a similar font and duplicate the size, spacing and alignment settings. –Name

Dear Name:

To match the overall page design, duplicate the positioning of each element and its proportion to the other elements on the page. The difference between a design that works and one that doesn't is found in these details. Place your text in this position. To achieve the same look, choose a similar font and duplicate the size, spacing and alignment settings. To match the overall page design, duplicate the positioning of each element and its proportion to the other elements on the page. To match the overall page design, duplicate the positioning of each element and its proportion to the other elements on the page. To match the overall page design, duplicate the positioning of each

element and its proportion to the other elements on the page. The difference between a design that works and one that doesn't is found in these details. Place your text in this position. To achieve the same look, choose a similar font and duplicate the size, spacing and alignment settings. –Name

PEOPLE

Place your text in this position. To achieve the same look, choose a similar font and duplicate the size, spacing and alignment settings. To match the overall page design, duplicate the positioning of each element and its proportion to the other elements on the page. The difference between a design that works and one that doesn't is found in these details.

To achieve the same look, choose a similar font and duplicate the size, spacing and alignment settings. To match the overall page design, duplicate the positioning of each element and its proportion to the other elements on the page. The difference between a design that works and one that doesn't is found in these details. Place your text in this position. To achieve the same look, choose a similar font and duplicate the size, spacing and alignment settings.

To match the overall page design, duplicate the positioning of each element and its proportion to the other elements on the page. The difference between a design that works and one that doesn't is found in these details. To achieve the same look, choose a similar font and duplicate the size, spacing and alignment settings. To match the overall page design, duplicate the positioning of each element and its proportion to the other elements on the page.

To achieve the same look, choose a similar font and duplicate the size, spacing and alignment settings. To match the overall page design, duplicate the positioning of each element and its proportion to the other elements.

CALENDAR

Event, Date, Time, Description - place your text in this position. To achieve the same look, choose a similar font and duplicate the size, spacing and alignment settings.

Event, Date, Time, Description - place your text in this position. To achieve the same look, choose a similar font and duplicate the size, spacing and alignment settings.

Event, Date, Time, Description - place your text in this position. To achieve the same look, choose a similar font and duplicate the size, spacing and alignment settings.

Event, Date, Time, Description - place your text in this position. To achieve the same look, choose a similar font and duplicate the size, spacing and alignment settings.

Event, Date, Time, Description - place your text in this position. To achieve the same look, choose a similar font and duplicate the size, spacing and alignment settings.

Event, Date, Time, Description - place your text in this position. To achieve the same look, choose a similar font and duplicate the size, spacing and alignment settings.

OUR MISSION

Place your text in this position. To achieve the same look, choose a similar font and duplicate the size, spacing and alignment settings.

SERVICES

First type of service .... Time
Second type of service .... Time
Third type of service .... Time
Fourth type of service .... Time
Fifth type of service .... Time

9

Next month's focus:

SPEAK OUT: DRUG ABUSE & THE AMERICAN FAMILY

Clip and return your questionnaire to:
Monthly Focus
The Sampler Church
1233 Example Boulevard West
City, State 12345-6789

Question 1: Place your text in this position.

Question 2: To achieve the same look, choose a similar font and duplicate the size.

Question 3: To match the overall page design, duplicate the positioning.

Question 4: To match the overall page design, duplicate the positioning.

Name (optional): _____

Church Bulletin Layout: Inside

7 · Story Headings: Charlemagne, 12pt, flush left, all caps, .5pt below

8 · Response Fill-In: Adobe Caslon Regular Italic, 11pt, flush left, .5pt lines

9 · Response Headline: Charlemagne, 24/28pt, flush left, all caps. Return Address: Adobe Caslon Bold, 11/12pt, flush left. Both are reverse (white) on a black background box.

Add a dotted line around the response panel to prompt the reader to remove and return it.

The dotted lines on the right and left edges represent folds.

News Release

Beat the best advertisement

Just about any organization could issue a release from time to time, but surprisingly few do. That's an unfortunate fact, because many public relations experts consider it the world's best and least expensive advertising.

Any good public relations book can tell you what to say and how to say it, but when you get around to the layout, this *News Release* should get you noticed.

Size and position the "NEWS RELEASE" title and your organization's name and address to capture attention without crowding the headline.

Use a conventional typewriter typeface (Courier) for the body of the release. This visually divides the message from the design of the form, plus direct mail experts swear it increases response.

Print the telegram directly from your computer on a high-quality 24 lb bond stock.

News Release Layout

1 · "NEWS": Formata Bold, 25pt, flush left, all caps. "RELEASE" is Formata Light, 25pt, flush left, all caps

2 · Line: .5pt

3 · Contact Information: Courier Bold, 12/16pt, flush left

4 · Organization Name and Address Formata Light, 10/12pt, flush left

5 · Headline: Courier Bold, 12pt centered, all caps

6 · Body Text: Courier Bold, 12/24pt, flush left

7 · Footer: Courier Bold, 12pt, centered

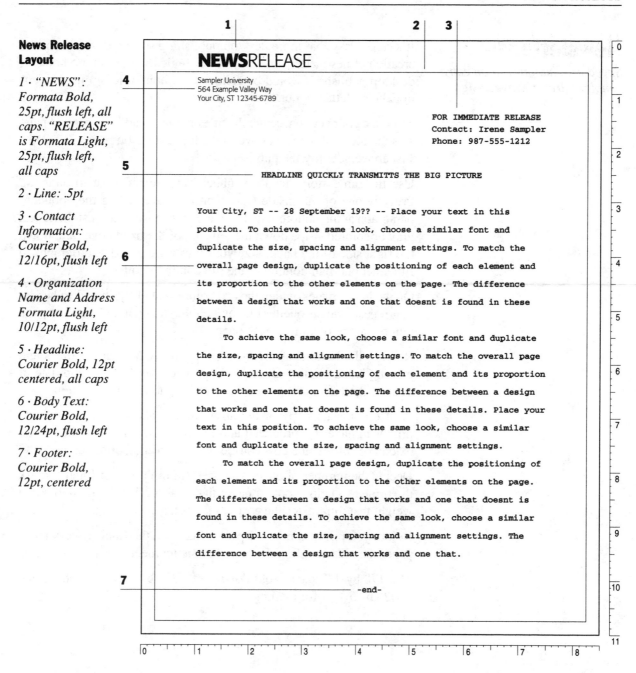

NEWSRELEASE

Sampler University
564 Example Valley Way
Your City, ST 12345-6789

FOR IMMEDIATE RELEASE
Contact: Irene Sampler
Phone: 987-555-1212

HEADLINE QUICKLY TRANSMITTS THE BIG PICTURE

Your City, ST -- 28 September 19?? -- Place your text in this position. To achieve the same look, choose a similar font and duplicate the size, spacing and alignment settings. To match the overall page design, duplicate the positioning of each element and its proportion to the other elements on the page. The difference between a design that works and one that doesnt is found in these details.

To achieve the same look, choose a similar font and duplicate the size, spacing and alignment settings. To match the overall page design, duplicate the positioning of each element and its proportion to the other elements on the page. The difference between a design that works and one that doesnt is found in these details. Place your text in this position. To achieve the same look, choose a similar font and duplicate the size, spacing and alignment settings.

To match the overall page design, duplicate the positioning of each element and its proportion to the other elements on the page. The difference between a design that works and one that doesnt is found in these details. To achieve the same look, choose a similar font and duplicate the size, spacing and alignment settings. The difference between a design that works and one that.

-end-

Newsletter

Speed production with an extra-simple, extra-effective design

It's safe to say that more desktop publishing software is sold for the creation of newsletters than any other single project. So, no book on desktop publishing would be complete without at least one conventional newsletter layout.

To create your version, center the title or "masthead" at the top of page 1 as the focus of the front cover. (*See* the layouts on pages 211-213.) Just above, identify the publisher.

Use the same story headline/subhead and text format throughout. Preview one of the inside stories on the cover using the "pointer" paragraph at the bottom left. To create some visual interest, include a gray or colored stripe down the left side of the front cover and down the right side of the back. Size your illustrations and photographs to fill either one-half column or the full column width.

On the inside pages, widen the text columns slightly and add a header that repeats the newsletter title and publication date. Center the page number at the bottom of each page.

Reserve the bottom of the back cover for your return address and mailing label. On the bottom-right is space for the time and date of your next meeting or a statement of the organization's mission.

Print one master copy of the artwork and take it to a commercial printer to have it reproduced and machine folded. Have the printer extend or "bleed" the cover stripe off the top and bottom edge.

Decide the number of pages you need (in multiples of four) and ask the printer to help choose a paper that will survive the mail, but in a weight that minimizes the cost of the postage.

Before you print, stop by the post office with the final artwork and a paper sample to confirm that your newsletter meets postal regulations.

The 17" by 11" pages fold down to 8 1/2" by 11" for reading and 8 1/2" by 5 1/2" for mailing.

Newsletter Layout: Front Cover

1 · Masthead: Times New Roman, 60pt, centered, .5pt line below

2 · Masthead Subtitle: Times New Roman, 10pt, centered, all caps

3 · "Inside...": Times New Roman, 11/18pt, flush left, .5pt lines

4 · Color Strip

5 · Headline: Times New Roman, 24/24pt, centered. Subhead: Times New Roman Italic, 11pt, centered

6 · Photo Area

7 · Body Text: Times New Roman, 12/14pt, flush left

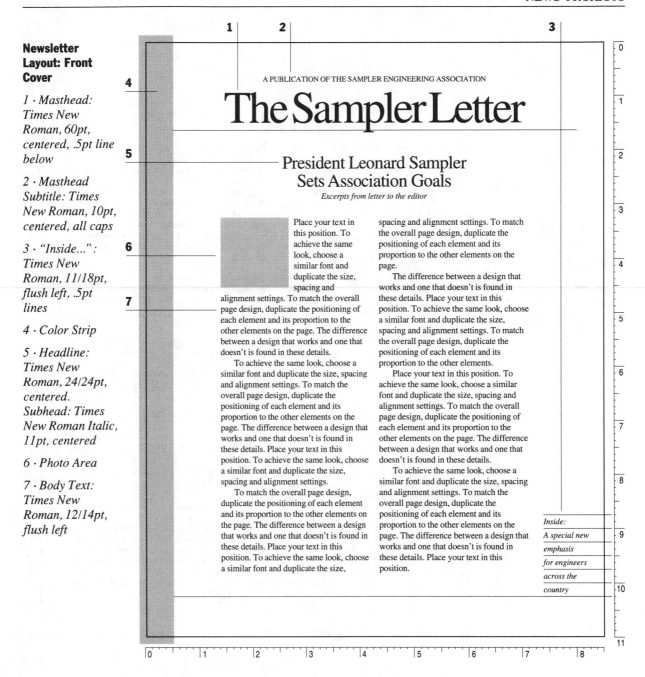

A PUBLICATION OF THE SAMPLER ENGINEERING ASSOCIATION

The Sampler Letter

President Leonard Sampler Sets Association Goals

Excerpts from letter to the editor

Place your text in this position. To achieve the same look, choose a similar font and duplicate the size, spacing and alignment settings. To match the overall page design, duplicate the positioning of each element and its proportion to the other elements on the page. The difference between a design that works and one that doesn't is found in these details.

To achieve the same look, choose a similar font and duplicate the size, spacing and alignment settings. To match the overall page design, duplicate the positioning of each element and its proportion to the other elements on the page. The difference between a design that works and one that doesn't is found in these details. Place your text in this position. To achieve the same look, choose a similar font and duplicate the size, spacing and alignment settings.

To match the overall page design, duplicate the positioning of each element and its proportion to the other elements on the page. The difference between a design that works and one that doesn't is found in these details. Place your text in this position. To achieve the same look, choose a similar font and duplicate the size,

spacing and alignment settings. To match the overall page design, duplicate the positioning of each element and its proportion to the other elements on the page.

The difference between a design that works and one that doesn't is found in these details. Place your text in this position. To achieve the same look, choose a similar font and duplicate the size, spacing and alignment settings. To match the overall page design, duplicate the positioning of each element and its proportion to the other elements.

Place your text in this position. To achieve the same look, choose a similar font and duplicate the size, spacing and alignment settings. To match the overall page design, duplicate the positioning of each element and its proportion to the other elements on the page. The difference between a design that works and one that doesn't is found in these details.

To achieve the same look, choose a similar font and duplicate the size, spacing and alignment settings. To match the overall page design, duplicate the positioning of each element and its proportion to the other elements on the page. The difference between a design that works and one that doesn't is found in these details. Place your text in this position.

Inside:

A special new

emphasis

for engineers

across the

country

211

8

Data Yield Questions, Few Answers

Banks and other lenders on the hot seat

Place your text in this position. To achieve the same look, choose a similar font and duplicate the size, spacing and alignment settings. To match the overall page design, duplicate the positioning of each element and its proportion to the other elements on the page. The difference between a design that works and one that doesn't is found in these details.

To achieve the same look, choose a similar font and duplicate the size, spacing and alignment settings. To match the overall page design, duplicate the positioning of each element and its proportion to the other elements on the page. The difference between a design that works and one that doesn't is found in these details. Place your text in this position. To achieve the same look, choose a similar font and duplicate the size, spacing and

alignment settings.

To match the overall page design, duplicate the positioning of each element and its proportion to the other elements on the page. The difference between a design that works and one that doesn't is found in these details. Place your text in this position. To achieve the same look, choose a similar font and duplicate the size, spacing and alignment settings.
the overall page design, duplicate the positioning of each element and its proportion to the other elements on the page.

The difference between a design that works and one that doesn't is found in these details. Place your text in this position. To achieve the same look, choose a similar font and duplicate the size, spacing and alignment

Findings Reignite Debate

A new point of contention

Place your text in this position. To achieve the same look, choose a similar font and duplicate the size, spacing and alignment settings. To match the overall page design, duplicate the positioning of each element and its proportion to the other elements on the page. The difference between a design that works and one that doesn't is found in these details.

To achieve the same look, choose a similar font and duplicate the size, spacing and alignment settings. To match the overall page design, duplicate the positioning of each element and its proportion to the other elements on the page. The difference between a design that works and one that doesn't is found in these details. Place your text in this position. To achieve the same look, choose a similar font and duplicate the size, spacing and alignment settings.

To match the overall page design, duplicate the positioning of each element and its proportion to the other elements on the page. The difference between a design that works and one that doesn't is found in these details. Place your text in this position. To achieve the

same look, choose a similar font and duplicate the size, spacing and alignment settings.
To achieve the same look, choose a similar font and duplicate the size, spacing and alignment settings. To match the overall page design, duplicate the positioning of each element and its proportion to the other elements on the page. The difference between a design that works and one that doesn't is found in these details. Place your text in this position.

2

Newsletter Layout: Inside Pages

8 · Header: Times New Roman, 10pt, centered, all caps, .5pt line below

9 · Photo Area

10 · Page Number: Times New Roman, 11pt, centered

9

10

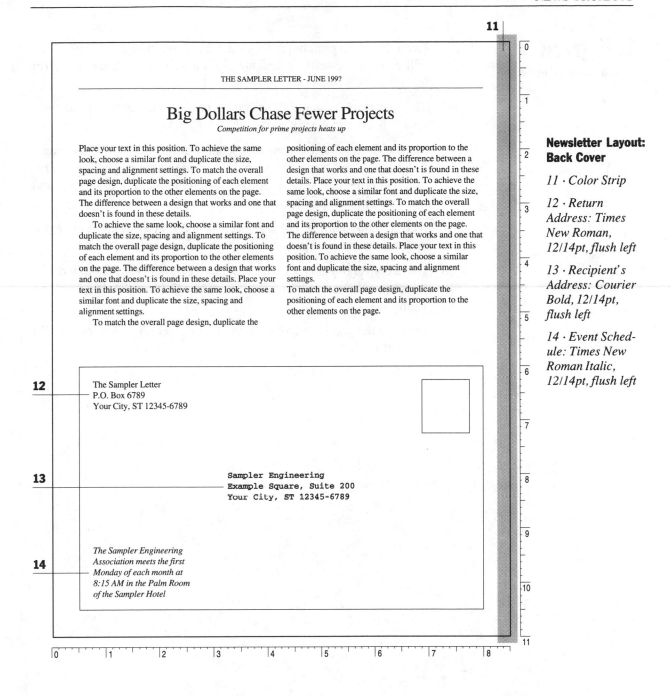

THE SAMPLER LETTER - JUNE 199?

Big Dollars Chase Fewer Projects

Competition for prime projects heats up

Place your text in this position. To achieve the same look, choose a similar font and duplicate the size, spacing and alignment settings. To match the overall page design, duplicate the positioning of each element and its proportion to the other elements on the page. The difference between a design that works and one that doesn't is found in these details.

To achieve the same look, choose a similar font and duplicate the size, spacing and alignment settings. To match the overall page design, duplicate the positioning of each element and its proportion to the other elements on the page. The difference between a design that works and one that doesn't is found in these details. Place your text in this position. To achieve the same look, choose a similar font and duplicate the size, spacing and alignment settings.

To match the overall page design, duplicate the

positioning of each element and its proportion to the other elements on the page. The difference between a design that works and one that doesn't is found in these details. Place your text in this position. To achieve the same look, choose a similar font and duplicate the size, spacing and alignment settings. To match the overall page design, duplicate the positioning of each element and its proportion to the other elements on the page. The difference between a design that works and one that doesn't is found in these details. Place your text in this position. To achieve the same look, choose a similar font and duplicate the size, spacing and alignment settings.

To match the overall page design, duplicate the positioning of each element and its proportion to the other elements on the page.

The Sampler Letter
P.O. Box 6789
Your City, ST 12345-6789

Sampler Engineering
Example Square, Suite 200
Your City, ST 12345-6789

The Sampler Engineering Association meets the first Monday of each month at 8:15 AM in the Palm Room of the Sampler Hotel

Newsletter Layout: Back Cover

11 · Color Strip

12 · Return Address: Times New Roman, 12/14pt, flush left

13 · Recipient's Address: Courier Bold, 12/14pt, flush left

14 · Event Schedule: Times New Roman Italic, 12/14pt, flush left

Telegram

Add a sense of urgency

Even though overnight packages are now commonplace, most of us still associate a sense of urgency with a yellow sheet and the term telegram.

The Idea Book example shows how a tax service might alert customers to changes in the tax code.

Start your version by centering your title at the top of the page. Subtitle it with "News from" and insert the name of your organization. Describe the purpose of the message in the box to the left and show the time and issue date to the right.

Add a phone number for questions at the bottom-right, and center your organization's name, address, and fax number below it.

Use a conventional typewriter typeface (Courier) for the body of the telegram. This visually divides the message from the design of the form.

Print the telegram directly from your computer on yellow or gold 24 lb bond stock.

Telegram Layout

1 · Masthead Message: Formata Light, 11/12pt, centered, all caps

2 · Title: Formata Bold, 24pt, centered, all caps. Subtitle: Formata Light, 11pt, centered

3 · Line: .5pt

4 · Body Text: Courier Bold, 12/14, flush left

5 · Phone: Formata Light, 11/12pt, centered. Phone Clip Art: From Presentation Task Force by New Vision Technologies, Inc., 613-727-8184, 38 Auriga Drive, Unit 13, Nepean, Ontario, Canada K2E 8A5 © New Vision Technologies, Inc. All rights reserved

6 · Organization Name, Address, and Fax: Formata Light, 11pt, centered, .5pt line below

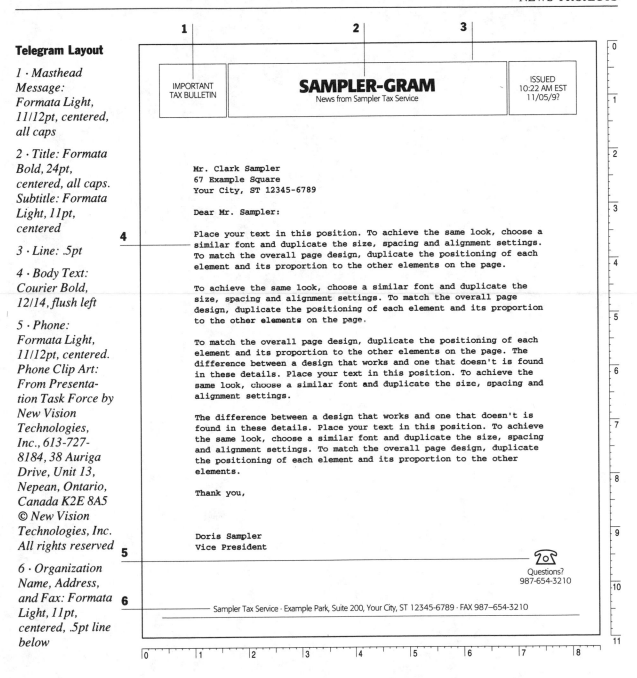

1

2

3

IMPORTANT
TAX BULLETIN

SAMPLER-GRAM
News from Sampler Tax Service

ISSUED
10:22 AM EST
11/05/9?

4

Mr. Clark Sampler
67 Example Square
Your City, ST 12345-6789

Dear Mr. Sampler:

Place your text in this position. To achieve the same look, choose a similar font and duplicate the size, spacing and alignment settings. To match the overall page design, duplicate the positioning of each element and its proportion to the other elements on the page.

To achieve the same look, choose a similar font and duplicate the size, spacing and alignment settings. To match the overall page design, duplicate the positioning of each element and its proportion to the other elements on the page.

To match the overall page design, duplicate the positioning of each element and its proportion to the other elements on the page. The difference between a design that works and one that doesn't is found in these details. Place your text in this position. To achieve the same look, choose a similar font and duplicate the size, spacing and alignment settings.

The difference between a design that works and one that doesn't is found in these details. Place your text in this position. To achieve the same look, choose a similar font and duplicate the size, spacing and alignment settings. To match the overall page design, duplicate the positioning of each element and its proportion to the other elements.

Thank you,

Doris Sampler
Vice President

5

Questions?
987-654-3210

6

Sampler Tax Service · Example Park, Suite 200, Your City, ST 12345-6789 · FAX 987–654-3210

CHAPTER 12
Packaging Projects

Billboard Box

Grab attention and gather information

Finding the places your target group frequents is the key to a *Billboard Box* campaign. Once you find it, the box does the work.

The Idea Book example shows how a hiking club might use the box to attract new members. Likely locations for the box would be a sporting goods shop, a health club, or even a shoe store with a big display of hiking boots.

Your version features a big bold headline and a clip art image to draw attention. Below the headline, add a simple sentence or two to prompt the reader to take action. Keep your coupon short by asking for only the details you need to make the next contact.

Print the sign directly from your computer and use spray adhesive to mount it to the "hi-back" panel of the contest box (*see* Source:).

Billboard Box Layout

1 · Headline: Formata Bold, 82/70pt, centered

2 · Subhead: Formata Light, 46/46pt, centered

3 · Line: 1pt

4 · Deer Cartoon Clip Art: From ARTSOURCE Vol. 2: Borders, Symbols, Holidays & Attention Getters, by The Church Art Works, available from Youth Specialties Order Center, 800-776-8008, PO Box 4406, Spartanburg, SC 29305-9976 © Youth Specialties Inc. All rights reserved

More headlines for your billboard box

Enter our contest
Make a donation
Drop your business card
Add your name to our list
Join our club
Make a suggestion
Answer our survey
Win our trade show giveaway

The Idea Book example shows how a hiking club might use the box to attract new members.

Meet other nature lovers. Join the Sampler Hikers Club. Fill in a coupon and we'll send details!

Source: Billboard Box

The "Contest Box" is from R&M, 800-231-9600, P.O. Box 2152, Sante Fe Springs, CA 90670

219

Box Mailer

Send a mailer that <u>must</u> be opened

If you have a good list of potential customers and your goal is to get product samples in their hands, this *Box Mailer* can work magic.

The Idea Book example begins with a provocative headline: "You're going to save three-hundred dollars in the next sixty seconds." Inside is a message card attached to a product sample. The message explains how buying a quantity of the product saves the buyer $300 (read the layout text for the full effect).

The result? A potential customer sits with the product in hand, focused on your advertising message. Mission accomplished.

Print the box headline for your mailer directly from your computer on a colored sheet. (*See* the layouts on pages 222-223.) Use spray adhesive to mount it on a white corrugated box (*see* Source:).

Print one master copy of the message card artwork and take it to a commercial printer to have it reproduced and machine folded. Request 65 lb uncoated cover stock in the same color as the box headline label. Hole punch the finished card and attach it to the product with a length of string.

Ship your mailer wrapped in brown paper, packaged in a larger box, or in a padded mailing envelope.

The Idea Book example shows how an organization might distribute sample products to corporate buyers.

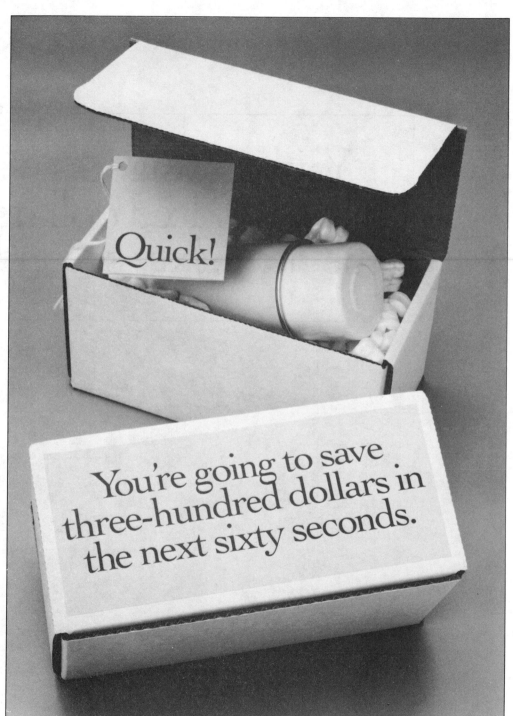

**Source:
Mailing Boxes**

The "Super Structure Mailer" (4" by 4" by 8") is from BrownCor International, 800-327-2278, 770 South 70th St., PO Box 14770, Milwaukee, WI 53214

**Box Mailer
Layout**

*1 · Headline:
Cochin, 64/56pt
centered*

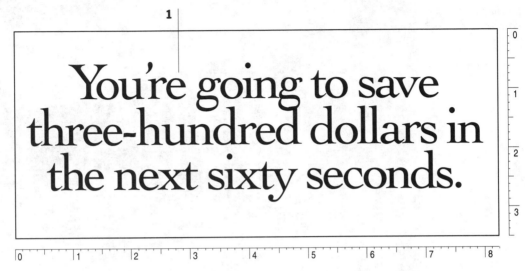

You're going to save three-hundred dollars in the next sixty seconds.

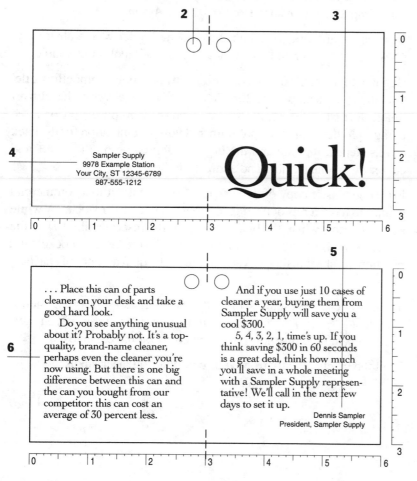

Sampler Supply
9978 Example Station
Your City, ST 12345-6789
987-555-1212

Quick!

Message Card Layout: Back and Front Covers

2 · Hole Punch

3 · Message: Cochin, 72pt, centered

4 · Organization Name, Address, and Phone: Helvetica, 9/11pt, centered

Message Card Layout: Inside

5 · Sender's Name and Title: Helvetica, 9/11pt, flush right

6 · Message Text: Cochin, 14/14pt, flush left

The dotted lines on the top and bottom edges represent folds.

. . . Place this can of parts cleaner on your desk and take a good hard look.

Do you see anything unusual about it? Probably not. It's a top-quality, brand-name cleaner, perhaps even the cleaner you're now using. But there is one big difference between this can and the can you bought from our competitor: this can cost an average of 30 percent less.

And if you use just 10 cases of cleaner a year, buying them from Sampler Supply will save you a cool $300.

5, 4, 3, 2, 1, time's up. If you think saving $300 in 60 seconds is a great deal, think how much you'll save in a whole meeting with a Sampler Supply representative! We'll call in the next few days to set it up.

Dennis Sampler
President, Sampler Supply

223

Cassette Album

Package your best audio show

A professional quality recording of your resident expert giving a workshop, or a top spokesperson explaining your organization can be a powerful persuader. You can sell the tapes for a profit or give them away to attract business. But before you send them out the door, add some impact with this handsome *Cassette Album*.

Besides the artwork, you'll need a cassette binder with a clear vinyl pocket on the cover and a set of audio cassette labels (*see* Source:).

Begin with the name of your organization and a bold, compelling title. (*See* the layouts on pages 226-227.) Illustrate the cover with a clip art image to match the topic of the program. Compose two or three paragraphs describing the program and your organization for the back cover. Repeat the title and the organization name on the spine, and center the phone number and address on the back.

Print one master copy of the cover insert and take it to a commercial printer to have it reproduced on 65 lb uncoated cover stock. (A white sheet conceals where the binder ends and the insert begins.) Trim the final insert 1/4" smaller than the overall size of the pocket and position the sheet in the pocket so there is an equal amount of space on all sides.

The cassette labels establish the subject of each tape, the order (side 1, side 2, side 3 . . .), and contain any necessary legalese. If you have room, repeat the illustration from the cover on the cassettes.

Print the labels directly from your computer on laser labels.

Other ready-made packages you can customize

Videotapes
Film strips
35mm slides
Computer disks
CDs
Videodiscs

The Idea Book example shows how a personnel company might use audio tapes to demonstrate their knowledge of the field.

**Source:
Cassette Album**

The Clear Overlay Cassette Album is from Vulcan Binder & Cover, 800-633-4526, One Looseleaf Lane, Vincent, AL 35178

**Source:
Audio Tape Laser Labels**

The Cassette Labels are from Avery Dennison, 800-252-8379, 818 Oak Park Road, Covina, CA 91724

Cassette Album Layout

1 · Line: 2pt

2 · Spine Header: Helvetica Black Italic, 12pt, centered

3 · Front Cover Subtitle: Helvetica Black Italic, 12/13pt, flush left

4 · Title: Cochin, 72/62pt, flush left

5 · Hanging Man Clip Art: From Metro ImageBase, Business Graphics, by Metro Creative Graphics, Inc., 800-223-1600, 33 West 34th St., New York, NY 10001 © Metro Creative Graphics, Inc. All rights reserved

6 · Lead In: Helvetica Black Italic, 12pt, flush left

7 · Body Text: Cochin, 14/16pt, flush left

8 · Spine Title: Cochin, 26pt, flush left, rotated

9 · Organization Phone, Name, and Address: Cochin, 14/16pt, centered

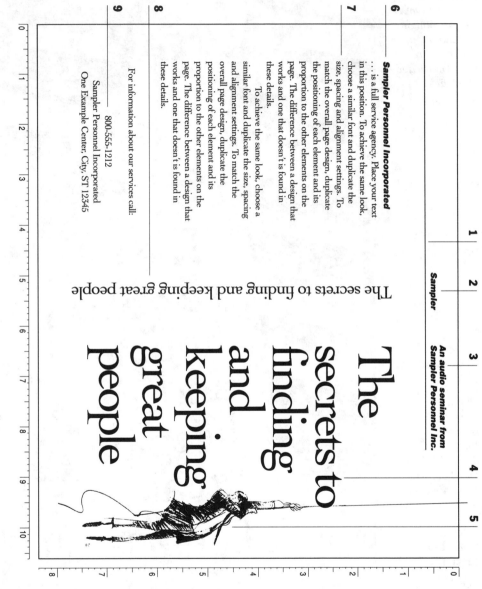

Sampler Personnel Incorporated
. . . is a full service agency. Place your text in this position. To achieve the same look, choose a similar font and duplicate the size, spacing and alignment settings. To match the overall page design, duplicate the positioning of each element and its proportion to the other elements on the page. The difference between a design that works and one that doesn't is found in these details.

To achieve the same look, choose a similar font and duplicate the size, spacing and alignment settings. To match the overall page design, duplicate the positioning of each element and its proportion to the other elements on the page. The difference between a design that works and one that doesn't is found in these details.

For information about our services call:

—————
800-555-1212
Sampler Personnel Incorporated
One Example Center, City, ST 12345

Sampler

An audio seminar from Sampler Personnel Inc.

The secrets to finding and keeping great people

The secrets to finding and keeping great people

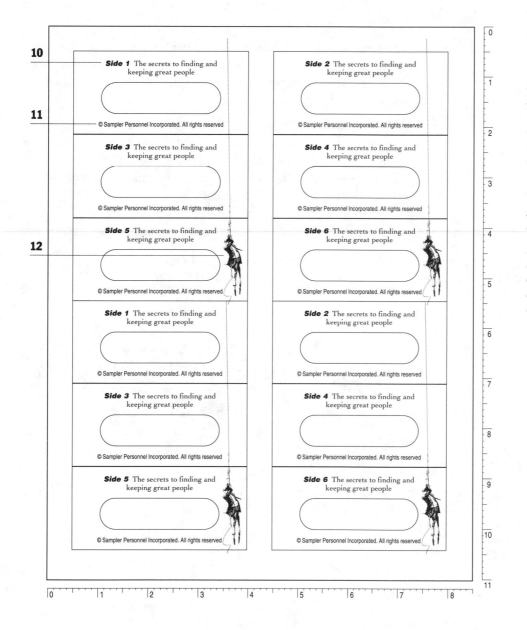

10

11

12

Cassette Label Layout

10 · "Side 1" : Helvetica Black Italic, 10pt, centered. "The secrets...": Cochin, 11/12pt, centered

11 · Copyright Text: Helvetica Narrow, 9pt, centered

12 · The illustration used on the cover is reduced and re-used here.

Coin Bank

Promote saving and giving

Have you have ever fantasized about owning your own bank? Even if this isn't what you had in mind, the *Coin Bank* can be an effective way to promote your organization.

The Idea Book example shows how a bank might use this concept to teach children the benefits of saving. The title reads "The Magic Bank" and the text explains how depositing small amounts at an early age can reap big rewards later in life.

To create your *Coin Bank*, you'll need your version of the layout and a supply of coin cans (*see* Source:). Print the sheet directly from your computer, trim it to fit, and wrap it around the can. Secure the wrap with tape or spray adhesive. A metal plug on the bottom of the bank gives you easy access to the contents.

Coin Bank Layout

1 · "The" : Times New Roman, 48pt, centered. "Magic Bank" : Times New Roman, 66/50pt, centered

2 · Organization Name: Times New Roman, 18pt, centered. Address and Phone: Times New Roman, 12/14pt, centered

3 · Instruction Text: Times New Roman, 18/18pt, flush left. Details: Times New Roman, 12/14pt, flush left

4 · Pot-of-Gold Clip Art: The illustration is of a single pot of coins repeated in various sizes. From Presentation Task Force by New Vision Technologies, Inc., 613-727-8184, 38 Auriga Drive, Unit 13, Nepean, Ontario, Canada K2E 8A5 © New Vision Technologies, Inc. All rights reserved

Start saving when you're young; the magic is called "compound interest". . . Place your text in this position. To achieve the same look, choose a similar font and duplicate the size, spacing and alignment settings.

The Magic Bank

Sampler Federal
One Sampler Plaza
Your City, ST 12345-6789
987-654-3210

**More Coin
Bank ideas**

*Collect donations
Teacher's aid
Decorate as a gift*

**Source:
Coin Can**

*The "Coin
Collection Can"
is from Freund
Can Company,
773-224-4230,
155 West 84th
Street, Chicago,
IL 60620*

Jar & Label

Do it yourself with jars, cans, and bottles

From your desktop you can easily label jars, cans, bottles, and containers of every imaginable shape and size.

The first Idea Book example shows how a gardener might prepare a jar of herbs as a gift for friends. The second shows how a jar of sweets might be used as a New Year's greeting to clients.

Personalize these basic layouts or use your imagination to create your own. Print the artwork directly from your computer on 4" by 1 1/2" or 4" by 3 1/3" laser labels and apply them to the jars (*see* Source:).

Jar Label Layout: Small

1 · Ornament: Adobe Caslon Ornaments, 16pt, centered

2 · Organization Name: Times New Roman, 14pt, centered, .5pt line above and below

3 · Product Name: Charlemagne, 24pt, centered, all caps

4 · Tag Line: Times New Roman, 9pt, centered

Jar Label Layout: Large

5 · Greeting and Organization Name: Formata Light, 13/15pt, flush left

6 · "THANK" : Arcadia, 100pt, centered, all caps. "YOU" : Arcadia, 100pt, centered, all caps, reverse (white) on a black background box

7 · Services Listing: Formata Light, 13/15pt, flush left

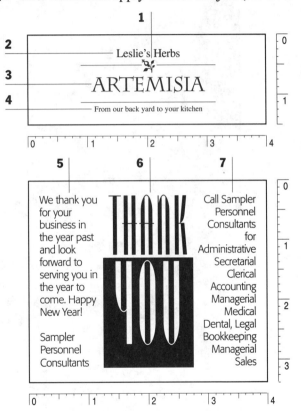

The first Idea Book example shows how a gardener might prepare a jar of herbs as a gift for friends. The second shows how a jar of sweets might be used as a New Year's greeting to clients.

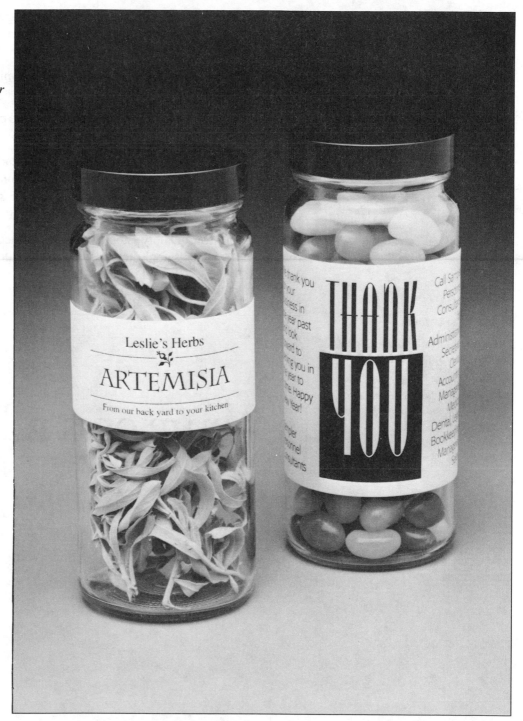

Source: Jars

The "Glass Jars" are from Freund Can Company, 773-224-4230, 155 West 84th Street, Chicago, IL 60620

Source: Laser Labels

The "Laser Labels" are from Avery Dennison, 800-252-8379, 818 Oak Park Road, Covina, CA 91724

Mailing Tube

Get your documents through the mail in one piece

Savvy marketers print headlines on mailing tubes and boxes to grab the reader's attention. You can achieve the same results with a simple sheet from your desktop system.

The Idea Book example shows how an association might distribute a new roster of members.

Compose a headline for your tube and center it on the page. The return address appears in the top-left corner.

Print the wrap directly from your computer on a standard 14" by 11" sheet of paper. Trim the sheet to size and wrap it around a 12" mailing tube (*see* Source:). Secure the wrap with tape or spray adhesive. Attach the mailing label, the postage and drop it in the mail.

Before you print in quantity, stop by the post office with the final artwork and a paper sample to confirm your mailer meets postal regulations.

Mailing Tube Layout

1 · Return Address: Adobe Caslon Regular, 11/13pt, flush left

2 · Recipient's Address: Courier Bold, 10/12pt, flush left. The line represents the position of the address label.

3 · Headline: Adobe Caslon Regular, 120pt, centered

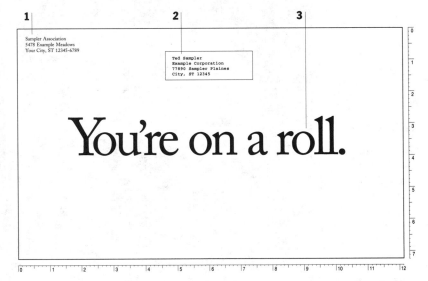

232

The Idea Book example shows how an association might distribute a new roster of members.

Source: Mailing Tubes

The "Mailing Tube" (12" length by 2" diameter, with Plastic End Caps) is from BrownCor International, 800-327-2278, 770 South 70th St., PO Box 14770, Milwaukee, WI 53214

Poly Bag Pack

Create <u>the</u> most frugal package

Polyethylene bags are made from a plastic particularly well-suited to packaging. They range in size from 2" by 3" to well over 3' by 5' (*see* Source:). By attaching a simple tent top label, you can create the world's most frugal package.

The Idea Book example shows how one organization might package bird seed for a fundraiser.

Reserve the front of your tent top for the product name and an illustration. The back contains the organization's name and address, your marketing text, and a list of ingredients.

Print one master copy of the artwork, then take it to a commercial printer to have it reproduced on 65 lb uncoated cover stock and machine folded.

Seal the bag one inch below the top and staple the tent to the unsealed area. Hole punch the final package so it can be hung on a display.

Polybag Tent Top

1 · Product Description and Ingredients: Times New Roman, 10/12pt, flush left

2 · Organization Name and Address: Times New Roman, 9/9pt, centered

3 · "Sampler's" : Times New Roman, 10pt, centered, reverse (white) on a black background box. "Gourmet" : Franklin Gothic Condensed, 36pt, centered. "BIRD FEED" : Copperplate 33BC, 22pt, centered, all caps

4 · Hole Punch

5 · The illustration is positioned over a box filled with a 20% screen of black. Bird Clip Art: From Presentation Task Force by New Vision Technologies, Inc., 613-727-8184, 38 Auriga Drive, Unit 13, Nepean, Ontario, Canada K2E 8A5 © New Vision Technologies, Inc. All rights reserved

6 · "Sampler's" : Times New Roman, 14pt, centered, reverse (white) on a black background box. "Gourmet" : Franklin Gothic Condensed, 52pt, centered. "BIRD FEED" : Copperplate 33BC, 32pt, centered, all caps. Weight: Times New Roman, 9/9pt, centered, all caps

7 · Line: .5pt

The dotted lines on the top and bottom edges represent folds.

Or use the Poly Bag Pack to package

Crafts
Food
Hardware
Parts
Rubber stamps
Samples
Toys
Trading cards

Source: Heavy Duty Plastic Bags

The "Poly Bag" (5" by 7", 4 Mil) is from National Bag, 800-247-6000, 2233 Old Mill Road, Hudson, OH 44236

Videotape Proposal

Add action to your next proposal

A proposal supported by a videotape of your people and products in action allows customers to witness your organization firsthand. One effective way to package the proposal and tape requires nothing more than a ring binder fitted with a videotape loose-leaf page (*see* Source:).

The Idea Book example shows how a home inspection company might use the package to attract high-ticket home buyers.

Present the text of the proposal with your version of the *Instant Binder* (*see* page 28). Your videotape provides the backup evidence to seal the deal.

The label for the face of the videotape includes the program title, your organization's name, and any necessary legalese. The spine label repeats the title. Choose a clip art symbol for the overall proposal and repeat it on the binder cover and the tape. Print the final artwork directly from your computer on videotape laser labels (*see* Source).

Videotape Label Layout: Face

1 · Title: Cochin, 24/28pt, flush left, on a background box filled with a 20% shade of black

2 · Key Clip Art: From ProArt, Business Collection by Multi-Ad Services Inc., 309-692-1530, 1720 W. Detweiller Drive, Peoria, IL 61615-1695 © Multi-Ad Services Inc. All rights reserved

3 · Organization Name and Address: Cochin, 11/11pt, flush left

4 · Tape Size and Running Time: Cochin, 8pt, flush left

Videotape Label Layout: Spine

5 · Title: Cochin, 30pt, flush left, on a background box filled with a 20% shade of black

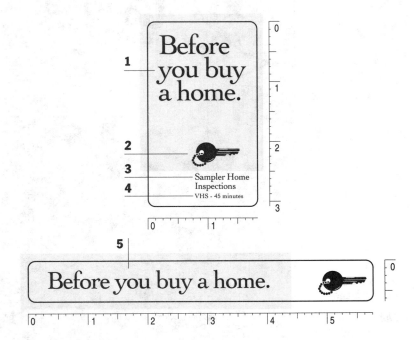

236

The Idea Book example shows how a home inspection company might use the package to attract high-ticket home buyers.

Source: Videotape Loose-Leaf Page

The "Video Cassette Loose-Leaf Page" (VHS) is from Vinaseal Company, Inc., 201-589-0850, 25 Prospect St., Newark, NJ, 07105

Source: Videotape Laser Labels

The "Videotape Laser Labels" are from Avery Dennison, 800-252-8379, 818 Oak Park Road, Covina, CA 91724

CHAPTER 13
Pad Projects

Custom Post-it™ Notes

Get the max from this new medium

Post-it™Notes, those terrific self-stick notes by 3M, are available blank or preprinted with stock messages. There are notes for faxing, phone messages, routing, and more. But now there's a specialty printer that enables you to reproduce your custom layout in this patented format (*see* Source:).

For your version, personalize these designs or dream up your own. Print one master copy of the note and send it to a specialty printer (*see* Source:). Or print the notes on traditional pads and tape or staple them to the article you're sending.

Custom Post-it™ Notes Pad Layout: Small Pad

1 · Headline: Formata Bold, 15/15pt, flush left

2 · From: Formata Light, 10/12pt, centered

3 · Arrow and Artist's Tools Clip Art: From Presentation Task Force by New Vision Technologies, Inc., 613-727-8184, 38 Auriga Drive, Unit 13, Nepean, Ontario, Canada K2E 8A5 © New Vision Technologies, Inc. All rights reserved

Custom Post-it™ Notes Pad Layout: Large Pad

4 · Lead In: Minion Regular, 10pt, flush left

5 · Instructions: Minion Regular, 10pt, flush right

6 · Organization Name, Address, and Phone: Formata Bold, 11/12pt, flush left

More custom Post-it™ ideas:

Check-off listing ship, copy, file, etc. "Don't forget" with fill-in lines
Fax form
Reprint your business card
Routing form

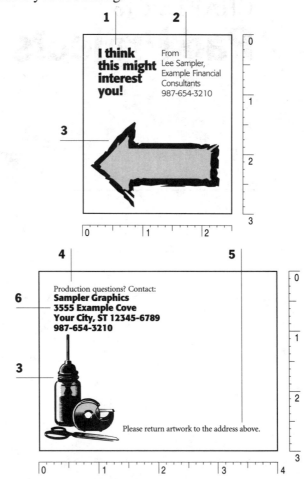

The first Idea Book example shows how a financial consultant might use the notes to pass on articles of interest to her clients. The second example shows how a graphics studio might use the notes to send instructions to its commercial printer.

**Source:
Custom Printed
Post-it™ Notes**

Custom Post-it™ Notes can be purchased from HA-LO Marketing & Promotions, 800-474-4256, 1001 E. Main St., #917, Richmond, VA 23219

Shopping List Pad

Promote your next sale

Many organizations distribute scratch pads with their name, address, and advertising message. The hope is that customers will use the pads around their home or office and see the message again and again. This version adds another dimension by including a check-off shopping list.

To create your's, use the "Don't Forget" or a similar headline to establish the purpose of the pad. Leave plenty of writing room. Substitute a list of specific products or your general product categories.

Print one master copy of the shopping list and take it to a commercial printer to have it reproduced on 20 lb uncoated bond stock and bound as pads.

Shopping List Pad Layout

1 · Headline: Adobe Caslon Regular, 38/32pt, flush left, reverse (white) on a black background box

2 · Reminder List: Adobe Caslon Regular, 11/12pt, flush left. Check-Off Box Symbol: Adobe Carta Font, 10/12, flush left

3 · Line: .5pt

4 · Organization Name, Address, and Phone: Adobe Caslon Regular, 11/12pt, flush left

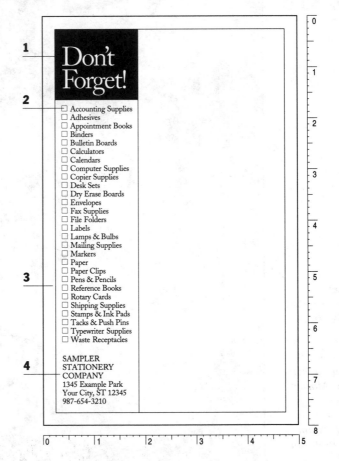

The Idea Book example shows how a retailer might use the layout to prompt and prepare customers to place an order.

Don't Forget!

☐ Accounting Supplies
☐ Adhesives
☐ Appointment Books
☐ Binders
☐ Bulletin Boards
☐ Calculators
☐ Calendars
☐ Computer Supplies
☐ Copier Supplies
☐ Desk Sets
☐ Dry Erase Boards
☐ Envelopes
☐ Fax Supplies
☐ File Folders
☐ Labels
☐ Lamps & Bulbs
☐ Mailing Supplies
☐ Markers
☐ Paper
☐ Paper Clips
☐ Pens & Pencils
☐ Reference Books
☐ Rotary Cards
☐ Shipping Supplies
☐ Stamps & Ink Pads
☐ Tacks & Push Pins
☐ Typewriter Supplies
☐ Waste Receptacles

SAMPLER
STATIONERY
COMPANY
1345 Example Park
Your City, ST 12345
987-654-3210

Sign Pad

Build a double-duty display

Countertop signs ask the questions salespeople sometimes forget or don't have the time to ask. This double-duty *Sign Pad* even asks for feedback.

For your version, start with a headline that grabs the reader's attention. Once you have it, use the subhead at the top to describe the action you want them to take. Keep your coupon short by asking for only the details you need to make the next contact. Include a prompt at the bottom directing the reader to return the filled-in version to a salesperson or to mail it in later.

Print the sign directly from your computer on a brightly colored stock and use spray adhesive to mount it to a sheet of rigid board. Attach the easel to the back of the board with glue (*see* Source:).

Print one master copy of the coupon and take it to a commercial printer to have it reproduced on 20 lb uncoated bond stock and to have the sheets bound as pads. Glue the final pad to the face of the sign.

Sign Pad Layout

1 · Subhead: Times New Roman, 24pt, centered

2 · Headline: Times New Roman, 130/100pt, centered

3 · Take One: Helvetica, 10pt, centered

4 · Dotted Line: 4pt

Coupon Layout

5 · "Yes,": Times New Roman, 36/18pt, flush left. Lead In: Times New Roman, 18/18pt, flush left

6 · Fill-In: Times New Roman, 10/12pt, flush left, all caps

7 · Instructions: Helvetica, 8/9pt, flush left

The Idea Book example shows how retailers might invite customers to join their mailing lists.

Source: Easels

The Easel Back is from Modernistic, 800-641-4610, 169 East Jenks Avenue, St. Paul, MN 55117

CHAPTER 14
Presentation
Projects

Certificate

Make a memory

With a single sheet of paper and a few inexpensive embellishments you can present an unforgettable award.

Position the award title at the top of the page followed by the name of the recipient. Next, compose a paragraph describing the details of the award. At the bottom include space for signatures of the appropriate officers. In the left-hand column, add an appropriate verse, quotation, or your organization's slogan.

Print the certificate directly from your computer on a high-quality 24 lb uncoated bond stock.

A seal, a ribbon, and a handsome presentation folder will make your certificate one of a kind (*see* Source:).

Certificate Layout: Left

1 · Title: Shelley Allegro, 65pt, centered

2 · "Presented To:" : Times New Roman, 16pt, centered. Recipient's Name: Times New Roman, 24pt, centered. Message Text: Times New Roman, 16/18pt, flush left

3 · Signature Fill-In: Times New Roman, 11pt, flush left, .5pt line above

4 · Line: 1pt

5 · Quotation: Times New Roman, 16/18pt, flush left, reverse (white) on a black background box.

6 · Seal Area

More certificate ideas:

Workplace anniversary
Contest or show winner
Dealer of the year
Meritorious service
Outstanding player
Public service
Retirement
Salesperson of the month
Service as an officer or chairperson

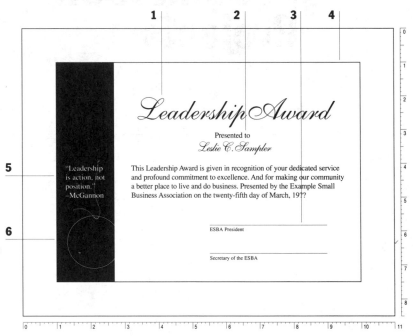

The Idea Book example shows how a group might use the layout for a leadership award.

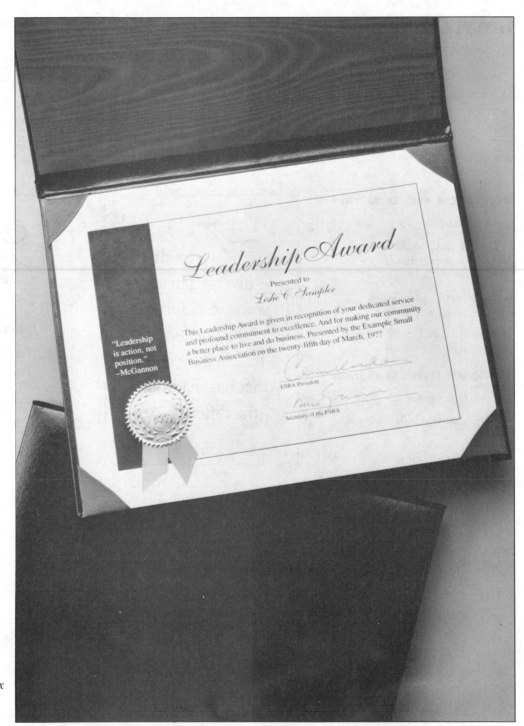

Source: Certificate Supplies

The "Deluxe Certificate Presentation Folder" and the "Official Seal of Merit" are from G. Neil Companies, 800-999-9111, 720 International Parkway, PO Box 450939, Sunrise, FL 33345-9111

Great Quotes

Motivate with words of wisdom

Most of us pick up bits of wisdom as we travel through life. Your favorite quote might be the revered words of a world leader or your uncle's favorite quip. This *Great Quotes* project is a way to share those thoughts with others or to preserve them for yourself.

Use a large delicate typeface and surround the quotation with a simple border. Print the sheet directly from your computer on a high-quality 24 lb uncoated bond stock. Trim the sheet to fit a mat or frame (*see Source:*).

Great Quotes Layout: Large Frame

1 · Line: Hairline

2 · Large Initial: Shelley Allegro, 110pt, on a background box filled with a 20% shade of black

3 · Body Text: Adobe Caslon Regular, 36/45pt, centered

4 · Credit: Adobe Caslon Regular, 12pt, flush right, all caps

Great Quotes Layout: Small Frame

5 · Line: Double .5pt

6 · Large Initial: Shelley Allegro, 100pt

7 · Body Text: Adobe Caslon Regular Italic, 36/42pt, centered

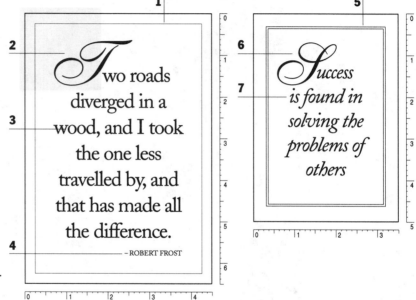

This Great Quotes project is a way to share favorite thoughts with others or to preserve them for yourself.

Two roads diverged in a wood, and I took the one less travelled by, and that has made all the difference.

–ROBERT FROST

Success is found in solving the problems of others

Source: Picture Frames and Mats

The frames and mats pictured are off-the-shelf items from a craft store. If you don't have a local source, call for the Dick Blick Art Materials catalog, 800-933-2542, P.O. Box 1267, Galesburg, IL 61401

Overhead Transparency

Produce fast, easy, understandable overheads

Though tens of millions of dollars have been spent pushing the latest and greatest presentation gimmicks, an enormous number of presenters still prefer the versatility and ease of overheads. And overheads are faster to produce and easier to edit than ever before from your desktop system.

To create a successful design, use a bold title and text large enough to read from the back row. Repeat your organization's name and logo in the same position on each transparency. Keep your transparency headings short, and fill in details with your words.

At the bottom right, label each frame with a number and any other notes you need to organize your presentation.

Print the transparencies directly from your computer on film with a built-in border; or, use blank film and mount them on conventional overhead frames (*see* Source).

Overhead Transparency Layout

1 · Title: Minion Bold, 48pt, flush left

2 · Organization Name: Minion Display, 30/25pt, flush right

3 · Microscope Clip Art: From DigitArt, Vol. 24, Science & Medicine, by Image Club Graphics Inc., 800-661-9410, Suite 5, 1902 Eleventh St. SE, Calgary, Alberta, Canada T2G 3G2 © Image Club Graphics Inc. All rights reserved

4 · Body Text: Minion Display, 44/48pt, flush left

5 · Frame Index: Minion Display, 20pt, flush right

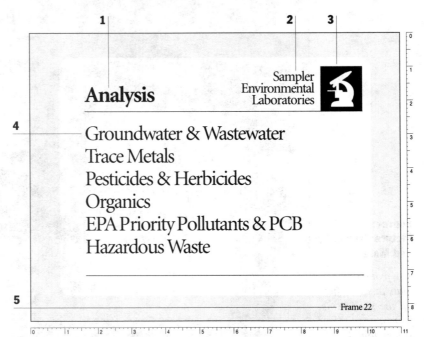

Analysis

Sampler Environmental Laboratories

Groundwater & Wastewater
Trace Metals
Pesticides & Herbicides
Organics
EPA Priority Pollutants & PCB
Hazardous Waste

Frame 22

The Idea Book example shows how a laboratory might adapt the layout.

Source: Laser Transparancy Film

The "Color Frames Laser Transparencies" are from Avery Dennison, 800-252-8379, 818 Oak Park Road, Covina, CA 91724

253

Presentation Summary

Guarantee they get your message

Did the audience get the point? Pass along this *Presentation Summary* at the end of your talk as insurance that they did. It also serves as an excellent brief for those who didn't attend.

The Idea Book example shows how an executive director might leave behind a summary of ideas for her audience.

Begin your summary with the title and an introductory paragraph. Use the first subhead to state the problem, the second to state the solution, and the third to explain the action you want the audience to take.

Position your organization's name at the top of the sheet and your name, title, address, and phone number at the bottom.

Print the summary directly from your computer on 24 lb bond stock.

Presentation Summary Layout

1 · Organization Name: Century Old Style, 9pt, centered

2 · Line .5pt

3 · Headline: Century Old Style Italic, 20pt, centered

4 · Body Text: Century Old Style, 12/14pt, flush left

5 · Major Point Subheads: Century Old Style and Italic, 14pt, centered

6 · Presenter Information: Century Old Style, 10/12pt, centered

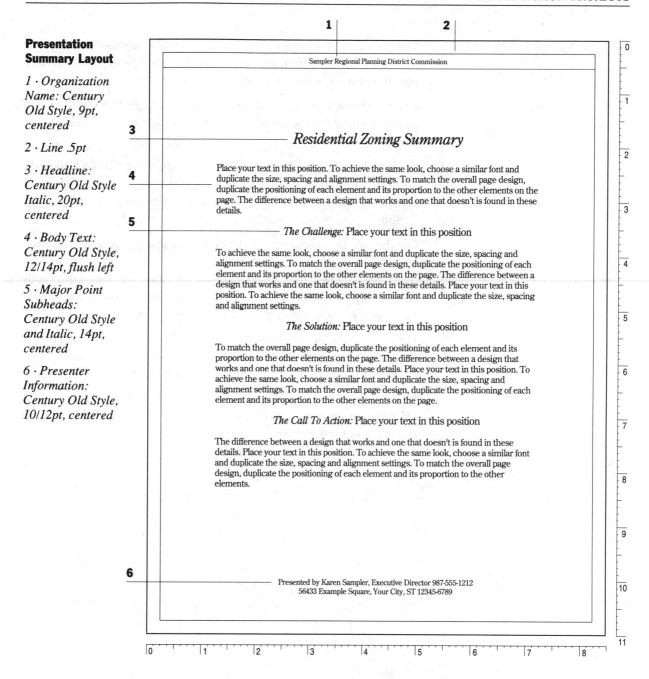

Sampler Regional Planning District Commission

Residential Zoning Summary

Place your text in this position. To achieve the same look, choose a similar font and duplicate the size, spacing and alignment settings. To match the overall page design, duplicate the positioning of each element and its proportion to the other elements on the page. The difference between a design that works and one that doesn't is found in these details.

The Challenge: Place your text in this position

To achieve the same look, choose a similar font and duplicate the size, spacing and alignment settings. To match the overall page design, duplicate the positioning of each element and its proportion to the other elements on the page. The difference between a design that works and one that doesn't is found in these details. Place your text in this position. To achieve the same look, choose a similar font and duplicate the size, spacing and alignment settings.

The Solution: Place your text in this position

To match the overall page design, duplicate the positioning of each element and its proportion to the other elements on the page. The difference between a design that works and one that doesn't is found in these details. Place your text in this position. To achieve the same look, choose a similar font and duplicate the size, spacing and alignment settings. To match the overall page design, duplicate the positioning of each element and its proportion to the other elements on the page.

The Call To Action: Place your text in this position

The difference between a design that works and one that doesn't is found in these details. Place your text in this position. To achieve the same look, choose a similar font and duplicate the size, spacing and alignment settings. To match the overall page design, duplicate the positioning of each element and its proportion to the other elements.

Presented by Karen Sampler, Executive Director 987-555-1212
56433 Example Square, Your City, ST 12345-6789

Proposal

Set your ideas in motion

There are countless ways to organize a proposal. Some require a tight verbal and visual structure, but this layout is designed with the sole purpose of communicating your ideas.

The inside and back cover of the proposal are standard 8 1/2" by 11" pages, but the cover is just 6" wide to reveal the right 2 1/2" of the title page.

Besides the title, your version of the title page should include the date and the name of the person and organization to which you are presenting the proposal. (*See* the layouts on pages 258-259.) At the bottom is your organization's name, address, and phone number.

On the inside pages, repeat the title and add a subhead for each section: "Introduction," "Project Profile," etc. Begin each new subhead on a new page. Under the subhead add the date, your organization's name, and the page number. Position the proposal text in a single column starting at the top of each page.

Have the proposal bound with plastic strip bindings (*see* Source:). Because the cover is not printed, you are free to select literally any type of cover stock. The example was covered with 80 lb Curtis Flannel.

Print the inside pages directly from the computer on 24 lb uncoated stock in a complementary color.

The Idea Book example shows how a computer systems company might present its proposal to a potential client.

**Source:
Quick Binding**

The "DUOBIND" binding (thick plastic strip) does not require a binding machine. It's from Duo-Tang Inc., 800-852-0039, 828 Duo-Tang Road, PO Box 208, Paw Paw, MI 49079

The "Velobind" binding (thin plastic strip) requires a binding machine, available from Southern Binding & Supply, 800-331-5295, PO Box 21489, Hot Springs, AR 71903

**Proposal Layout:
Title Page**

*1 · Title:
Charlemagne,
24/24pt, flush left,
all caps, .5pt line
below*

*2 · Date and
Presenter: Times
New Roman,
11/12pt, flush left*

3 · Hole Punch

*4 · Organization
Name, Address,
and Phone: Times
New Roman,
11/12pt, flush left*

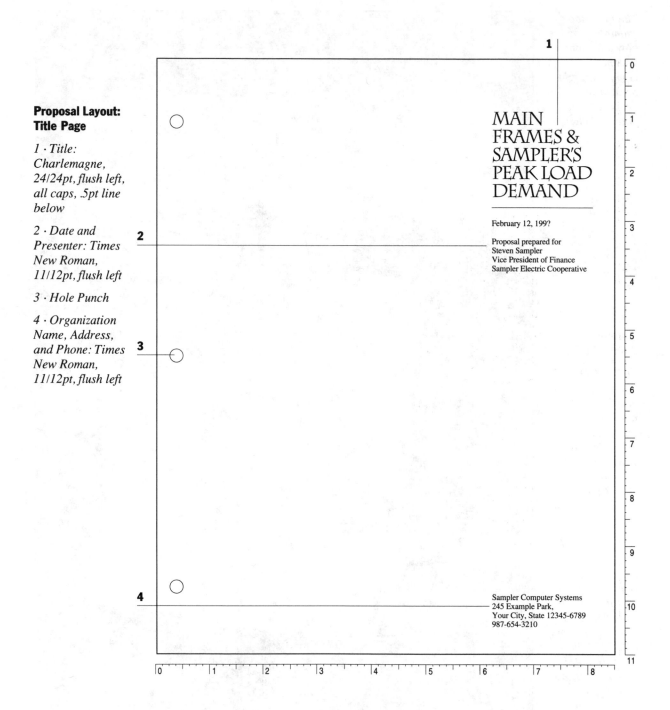

MAIN
FRAMES &
SAMPLER'S
PEAK LOAD
DEMAND

February 12, 199?

Proposal prepared for
Steven Sampler
Vice President of Finance
Sampler Electric Cooperative

Sampler Computer Systems
245 Example Park,
Your City, State 12345-6789
987-654-3210

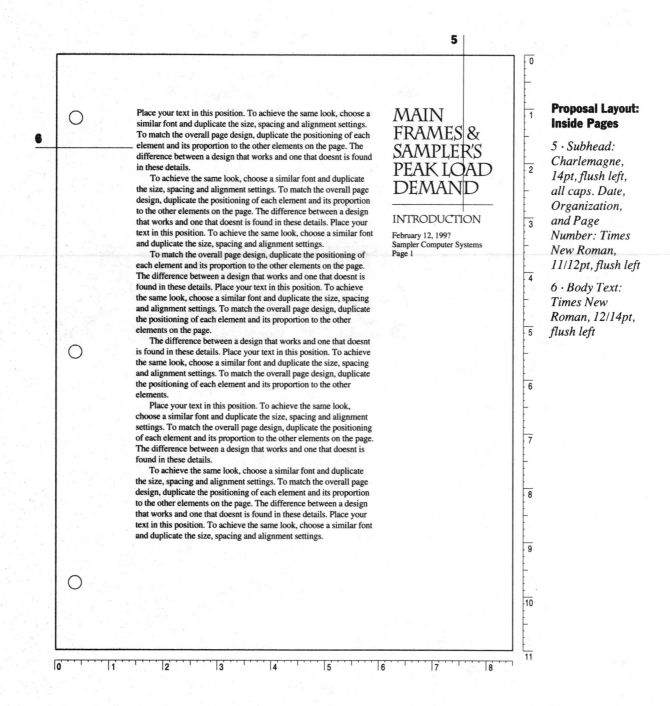

Place your text in this position. To achieve the same look, choose a similar font and duplicate the size, spacing and alignment settings. To match the overall page design, duplicate the positioning of each element and its proportion to the other elements on the page. The difference between a design that works and one that doesnt is found in these details.

To achieve the same look, choose a similar font and duplicate the size, spacing and alignment settings. To match the overall page design, duplicate the positioning of each element and its proportion to the other elements on the page. The difference between a design that works and one that doesnt is found in these details. Place your text in this position. To achieve the same look, choose a similar font and duplicate the size, spacing and alignment settings.

To match the overall page design, duplicate the positioning of each element and its proportion to the other elements on the page. The difference between a design that works and one that doesnt is found in these details. Place your text in this position. To achieve the same look, choose a similar font and duplicate the size, spacing and alignment settings. To match the overall page design, duplicate the positioning of each element and its proportion to the other elements on the page.

The difference between a design that works and one that doesnt is found in these details. Place your text in this position. To achieve the same look, choose a similar font and duplicate the size, spacing and alignment settings. To match the overall page design, duplicate the positioning of each element and its proportion to the other elements.

Place your text in this position. To achieve the same look, choose a similar font and duplicate the size, spacing and alignment settings. To match the overall page design, duplicate the positioning of each element and its proportion to the other elements on the page. The difference between a design that works and one that doesnt is found in these details.

To achieve the same look, choose a similar font and duplicate the size, spacing and alignment settings. To match the overall page design, duplicate the positioning of each element and its proportion to the other elements on the page. The difference between a design that works and one that doesnt is found in these details. Place your text in this position. To achieve the same look, choose a similar font and duplicate the size, spacing and alignment settings.

MAIN FRAMES & SAMPLER'S PEAK LOAD DEMAND

INTRODUCTION

February 12, 199?
Sampler Computer Systems
Page 1

Proposal Layout: Inside Pages

5 · Subhead: Charlemagne, 14pt, flush left, all caps. Date, Organization, and Page Number: Times New Roman, 11/12pt, flush left

6 · Body Text: Times New Roman, 12/14pt, flush left

259

Slides

*Create a slide show in
one hour or less*

Yes, with your desktop system, a few sheets of transparency film and some slide mounts, you can transform your ideas into 35mm slides in less than an hour.

Reserve the lead slide of your presentation for the name of the organization and the date. Use the second slide to title the program, and the third to establish the layout for the body of the presentation and the summary.

Print the slides directly from your computer on transparency film with a clear or solid black background (*see* Source:). Trim the slides and mount them in the slide mounts. Add a colored gel to add some visual interest and cut down on glare.

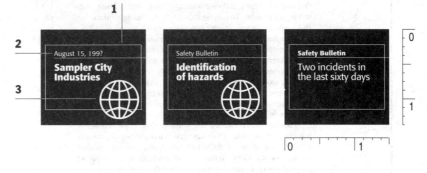

Slide Layout

1 · The area that projects is this size. The overall size fits the slide mount.

2 · Subhead: Formata Regular, 7pt, flush left, .5pt line below, reverse (white) on a black background. Headline: Formata Bold, 10/10, flush left, reverse (white) on a black background.

3 · Symbol: Adobe Carta Font, 60pt, flush right

The Idea Book example shows how a corporation might assemble a safety presentation in record time.

**Source:
Slide Film**

The slides are printed on "Laser Transparencies" from Avery Dennison, 800-252-8379, 818 Oak Park Road, Covina, CA 91724

CHAPTER 15
Sign Projects

Camera Card

Add a professional touch to your videotape presentations

Before the era of computer-generated titles, television stations used camera cards like these. They were used for advertisements, titles, credits, and as transitions between scenes or shows. You can use the same idea to create professional quality camera cards for your videotapes. Spotlight the finished card with a bright light, videotape it in high contrast, and edit it in the final tape.

For your version, center the titles in a 7" by 5 1/4" black box (video proportion is 4 by 3). Print the sheets directly from your computer on 24 lb bond stock and trim them out so that no white shows around the edges. Mount the final sheet on a 12" by 9" black card so you have plenty of dense black around the outside. Add color to the finished cards with markers or pencils.

Camera Card Layout: Title Card

1 · "THE": Copperplate 33BC, 70pt, centered, all caps, reverse (white) on a black background

2 · Program Title: Copperplate 33BC, 100/65pt, centered, all caps, reverse (white) on a black background

3 · Date: Helvetica Black, 35pt, centered, reverse (white) on a black background

Camera Card Layout: Scene Card

4 · Time: Helvetica Black, 35pt, centered, reverse (white) on a black background

5 · Dotted line reverse (white) on a black background

6 · Scene Title: Copperplate 33BC, 75/55pt, centered, all caps, reverse (white) on a black background

The Idea Book example shows how you might title a home video of a family reunion.

Doorknob Hanger

Use this medium for guaranteed contact

There is virtually no chance your audience will miss this message. That's a claim few marketing mediums can make. But if you have a highly targeted audience this simple *Doorknob Hanger* can deliver big results. The hanger uses a flyer sized to fit a disposable plastic bag (*see* Source:). You distribute the flyer by hooking the bag to the door of potential customers.

To create your version, keep the headline focused on what you are promising the reader. Like most advertising mediums, you have a few short seconds to win or lose their interest. The text that follows should clearly describe the next step you want the reader to take.

Print one master copy of the flyer and take it to a commercial printer to have it reproduced on 24 lb uncoated bond stock. You can also have your artwork printed on the precut doorknob hangers available through your commercial printer.

Doorknob Hanger Layout: Bag Insert

1 · Ornament: Adobe Caslon Ornaments Font, 30pt, centered

2 · Headline: Charlemagne, 90/85pt, centered, all caps

3 · "E" : Charlemagne, 30/16pt. Body Text: Times New Roman, 14/16pt, flush left

4 · Signature Fill-In and Phone: Times New Roman, 14pt, centered, .5pt line above

The Idea Book example shows how realtors might use the hanger to drum up business. When they spot a particularly attractive house, they leave the message: "YOU HAVE A LOVELY HOME." The text offers the realtor's services when the owner decides to sell (read the layout text for the full effect).

Source: Doorknob Bags

The "Doorknob Bag" (7" by 12") is from Associated Bag Company, 800-926-6100, 400 West Boden Street, Milwaukee, WI 53207-7120

YOU HAVE A LOVELY HOME.

Every so often we see a home we think is particularly attractive—the kind of house we like to represent. If you decide to put your home on the market we'd like the opportunity to show you how Sampler Realty can make the experience both profitable *and* pleasurable. If not, please accept our complements on your lovely home and the hard work it took to make it that way.

987-555-1212

Dry Erase Board

Organize your group with a custom message board

Dry erase or "white" boards are the modern-day version of the blackboard. You can write on the bright white surface in a rainbow of colors and wipe it clean in an instant. And, with a few simple sheets from your desktop system you can create a custom version.

Create your's by dividing each 8 1/2" by 11" page into two vertical rectangles. Use the first rectangle for general messages and follow it with one rectangle for each family member.

Print the sheets directly from your computer on 24 lb bond stock. Butt the sheets edge to edge and use spray adhesive to mount them on a rigid white posterboard.

Have the finished board laminated with a 10 mil gloss film (lamination is the process that applies a plastic coating to both sides of the paper) (*see* Source:). Markers and erasers for dry erase boards are available through any office supply dealer.

Dry Erase Board Layout

1 · Organization Name: Formata Bold, 40pt, flush left. Purpose: Formata Light, 36pt, flush left

2 · Name: Formata Light, 36pt, flush left

3 · Line: 1pt

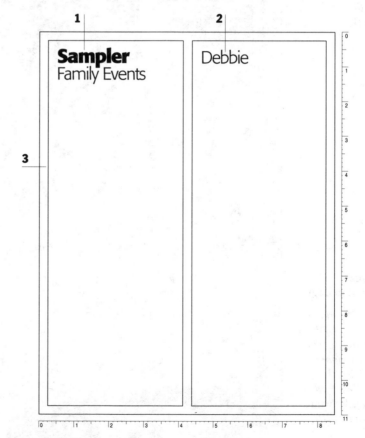

The Idea Book example shows how a family might use the board for messages.

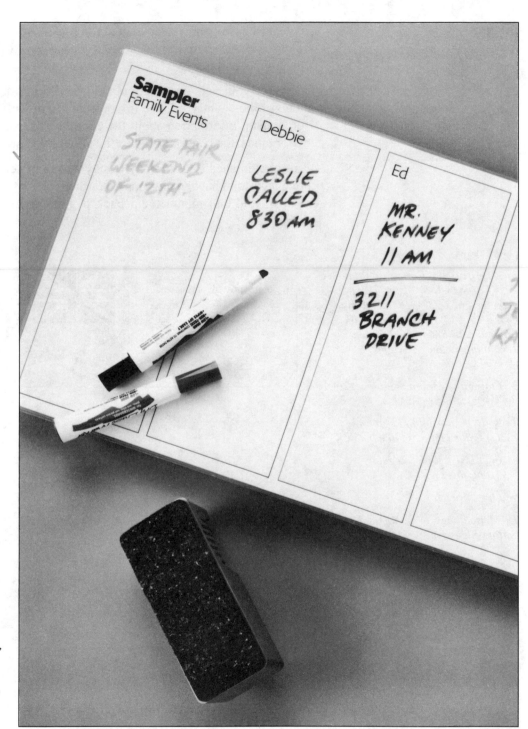

Source: Laminating

The dry erase board was laminated by SLAM-LAM Inc., 800-331-7526, 652 West Randolph Street, Chicago, IL 60606-2114

Flag

A unique flag you can print

If you teach geography, lead a scout troop, or have one or more pairs of busy hands around your house, this kid-tested project is both educational and fun.

To create your version, position a clip art flag to the right and the name of the country or state it represents to the left. You can also add general information about the country and list details like the major cities, the chief languages, the geographic area, etc.

Print the finished flags directly from your computer on 24 lb white bond stock and have your group color them. Trim the finished flags to size; fold and mount them back to back around a thin wood dowel.

Flag Layout

1 · Flag Clip Art: From Presentation Task Force by New Vision Technologies, Inc., 613-727-8184, 38 Auriga Drive, Unit 13, Nepean, Ontario, Canada K2E 8A5 © New Vision Technologies, Inc. All rights reserved

2 · Flag Title: Minion Regular, 22pt, flush left

3 · Body Text: Minion Regular, 13/13pt, flush left, .5pt line below

4 · Fact List: Minion Regular, 9/10pt, flush left

5 · Line: .5pt

The dotted lines on the top and bottom edges represent folds.

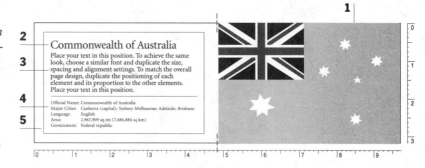

Commonwealth of Australia

Place your text in this position. To achieve the same look, choose a similar font and duplicate the size, spacing and alignment settings. To match the overall page design, duplicate the positioning of each element and its proportion to the other elements. Place your text in this position.

Official Name: Commonwealth of Australia
Major Cities: Canberra (capital); Sydney; Melbourne; Adelaide; Brisbane
Language: English
Area: 2,967,909 sq mi (7,686,884 sq km)
Government: Federal republic

Print the finished flags directly from your computer and have your group color them.

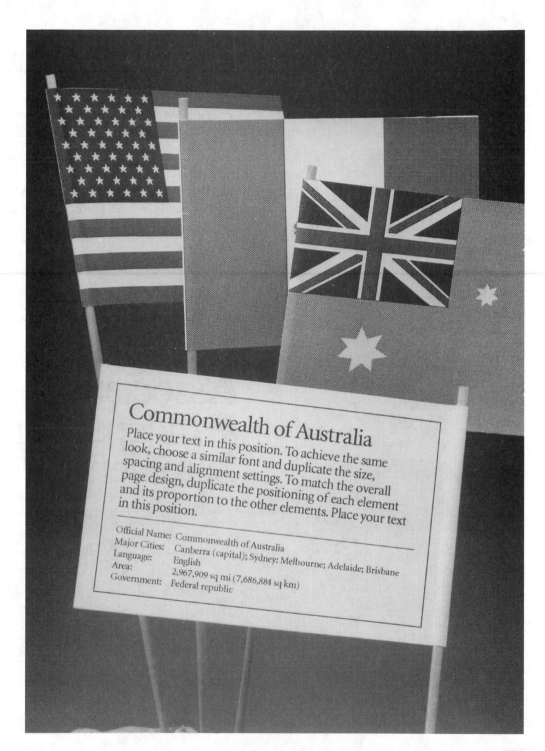

Commonwealth of Australia

Place your text in this position. To achieve the same look, choose a similar font and duplicate the size, spacing and alignment settings. To match the overall page design, duplicate the positioning of each element and its proportion to the other elements. Place your text in this position.

Official Name:	Commonwealth of Australia
Major Cities:	Canberra (capital); Sydney: Melbourne; Adelaide; Brisbane
Language:	English
Area:	2,967,909 sq mi (7,686,884 sq km)
Government:	Federal republic

Instant Signs

When you need quick changes

With a few clicks of the keys, you can transform a standard sheet of paper into a professional looking sign. All you need is a clear plastic frame and a little imagination. Need to change the message quickly? Just slide the old sheet out and the new one in.

The Idea Book example shows how a hotel might change signs day to day to welcome conference members.

For your version, personalize the sample design or create your own. When you're finished, step back 15' or 20' and see if it does the job. Print the sign directly from your computer on 24 lb bond stock. The display frames are available in both landscape and portrait orientations (*see* Source:)

Instant Signs Layout

1 · Top and Bottom Lines: 1pt

2 · "Welcome" : Times New Roman Italic, 52pt, flush left

3 · Headline: Times New Roman, 100/85pt, flush left

4 · "of" : Times New Roman, 48pt, centered, background box shaded with a 20% shade of black

5 · Dates: Times New Roman Italic, 24pt, flush left

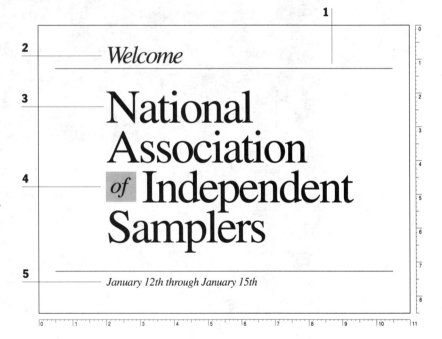

More sign headlines

Manager on duty:
Next week's sermon:
Quote of the month
Sales rep of the month
This week's interest rate

The Idea Book example shows how a hotel might change signs day to day to welcome conference members.

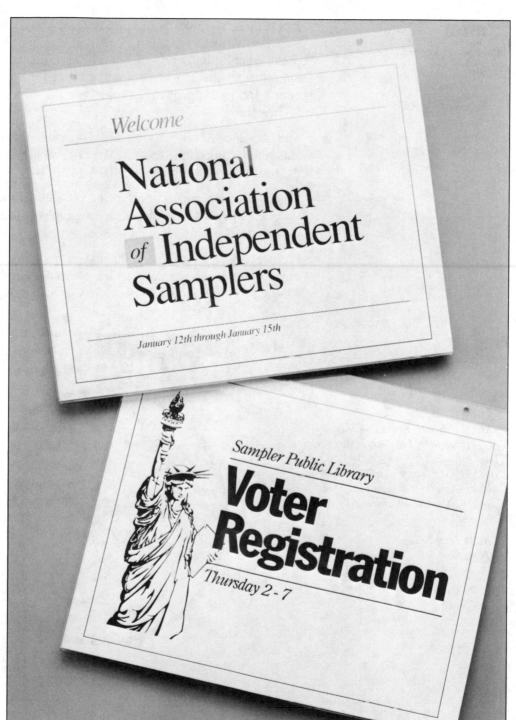

Welcome

National Association of Independent Samplers

January 12th through January 15th

Sampler Public Library

Voter Registration
Thursday 2 - 7

**Source:
Clear Plastic
Sign Displays**

The "Wall Mount Acrylic Display" (11" by 8.5") is from Beemak Plastics, Inc., 800-421-4393, 16639 South Gramercy Place, Gardena, CA 90247

Poster

*Make your pages larger
than life*

Just because you work with a printer that maxes out at an 11" by 14" page doesn't mean you can't create posters from your desktop. Most desktop publishing service bureaus print pages up to 18" wide by an unlimited length. The company that printed this example can print your 8 1/2" by 11" page in full color up to 42" by a whopping 12' (*see* Source:)!

The Idea Book example shows how a museum might use the poster to announce an upcoming exhibit. The original layout is 7 1/2" by 10"; the finished poster is blown up 400% to 30" by 40".

To create your version, select a first class clip art image and center your headline above it. Compose a paragraph to describe the details of the event and position it at the bottom.

Prepare and save the file using the instructions from the service bureau. On request, some service bureaus can also laminate the finished poster or mount it on a variety of materials.

Poster Layout

1 · Headline: Copperplate 33BC, 75pt, centered, all caps. "PLANET" is reverse (white) on a black background.

2 · Moon Clip Art: From DigitArt, Vol. 21, Fabulous Fifties, by Image Club Graphics Inc., 800-661-9410, Suite 5, 1902 Eleventh St. SE, Calgary, Alberta, Canada T2G 3G2 © Image Club Graphics Inc. All rights reserved

3 · Body Text: Times New Roman, 14/16pt, flush left

View the heavens through high-powered telescopes and learn fascinating facts about the night sky. At the Sampler Science Museum, 2nd Thursday of each month, 9:30 PM (clear nights only).

The Idea Book example shows how a museum might use the poster to announce an upcoming exhibit. The original layout is 7 1/2" by 10", but the finished poster is blown up 400% to 30" by 40"!

**Source:
Poster Prints**

Your poster can be printed in black and white or full color from a large variety of computer programs. The Poster (30" by 40") was printed by Reprographic Technologies, 800-236-8162, 2865 S. Moorland Road, New Berlin, WI 53151

CHAPTER 16
Specialty Projects

Bumper Sticker

Your bumper billboard

With a small investment, the right incentive and a minimum amount of desktop publishing effort, you can send your message around town or across the nation by bumper.

Keep your message short and your type big. Don't miss the opportunity to include your address or phone number so that those who see your sticker can get in touch.

Print one master copy of your artwork and send it to a printer that specializes in bumper stickers (*see* Source:).

Bumper Sticker Layout

1 · Organization Name and Address: Helvetica, 9pt, flush left

2 · Illustration: From "Old-Fashioned Silhouettes," edited by Carol Belanger Grafton, From Dover Publications, Inc., 31 East 2nd Street, Mineola, NY 11501 © Dover Publications, Inc. All rights reserved

3 · Headline: Shelley Allegro, 120pt, centered

4 · Subhead: Times New Roman, 45pt, centered

More Bumper Sticker Headlines

Win our contest . . .
I was there . . .
My hobby is . . .
I'm a member of . . .
I heart . . .
I support . . .

The Idea Book example shows a sticker that a wildlife park might sell as a souvenir or send as a thank you for contributions.

**Source:
Bumper Stickers**

The "Vinyl Bumper Strip" (3" by 10 7/8") is printed by Mo' Money Associates, 800-874-7681, PO Box 12591, Pensacola, FL 32574-2591. Mo' Money also prints hundreds of other promotional items. Call for their catalog.

279

Buttons

Wear your message

Because the cost of the equipment is so low, just about anyone can get into the button business. They are an affordable giveaway, a popular fundraiser, and a campaign requirement.

The "Air Show" example might be worn for identification. The "You are my top priority" version might be used by a retailer. And the "Visit!" button might be used to promote a charitable organization.

To create your own buttons, you need a button machine, a circle cutter and a supply of blank buttons (*see* Source:).

Print the finished artwork directly from your computer on 24 lb bond stock and trim it out with the circle cutter. Sandwich the button artwork between the metal shell and a plastic cover and seal it using the button machine.

Button Layout: Small

1 · "Sampler" : Times New Roman, 9pt, centered. Event: Copperplate 33BC, 16pt, centered, all caps

2 · Symbol: Adobe Carta Font, 36pt, centered, reverse (white) on a black background box

3 · "OFFICIAL" : Copperplate 33BC, 16pt, centered, all caps, reverse (white) on a black background

Button Layout: Medium

4 · "Y" : Shelley Allegro, 90pt. "ou" Shelley Allegro, 72pt, flush left

5 · Subhead: Formata Bold, 18/16pt, centered, overprints a box filled with a 20% screen of black

Button Layout: Large

6 · Headline: Franklin Gothic Condensed, 50pt, centered

7 · Subhead: Times New Roman, 12pt, centered

8 · Dog Cartoon Clip Art: From ClickArt Newsletter Cartoons by T/Maker Company, 415-962-0195, 1390 Villa Street, Mountain View, CA 94041 © T/Maker Company. All rights reserved

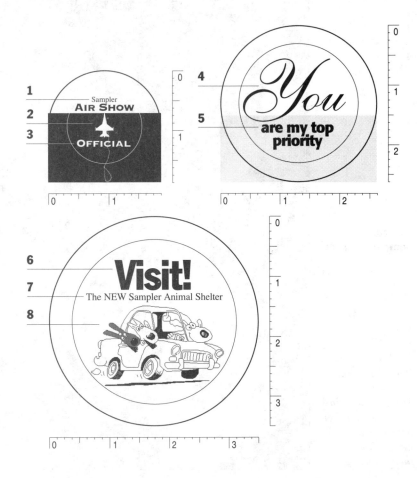

Use buttons for

Advertising
Campaigns
Concerts
Fundraising
Humor
Identification
Trade shows
Sporting events

**Source:
Do-It-Yourself
Button Machines
and Parts**

*These examples
were mounted on
a simple button
machine from
U.S.A. Buttons,
Inc., 800-777-
4992, 175
Progress Drive,
West Bend, WI
53095*

Coasters

Create an unusual keepsake

Old-fashioned wood pulp beer coasters have been around since the late 1800s. Although they serve an obvious purpose, they have become popular as souvenirs of the event or establishment they publicize.

The coarse wood pulp and the printing process are not ideal for highly detailed graphics, so keep your coaster artwork simple.

Print one master copy of your artwork and send it to a printer that specializes in beer coasters (*see* Source:).

Coaster Layout: Top

1 · "Class of" : Shelly Allegro, 40pt, centered. "1984" : Arcadia, 180pt, centered. "15th Reunion" : Formata Bold, 14pt, centered, reverse (white) on a black background box

2 · Line: 1pt

3 · Organization Name and City: Formata Regular, flush left or right

Coaster Layout: Bottom

4 · Line: 4pt

5 · Organization Name: Shelley Allegro, 32pt, centered

6 · Event: Minion Regular, 52pt, centered

7 · Nouveau Flower Clip Art: From Images With Impact!, Accents & Borders 1, by 3G Graphics, Inc., 800-456-0234, 114 Second Ave. S., Suite 104, Edmonds, WA 98020 © 3G Graphics, Inc. All rights reserved

Create coasters for your

Bar
Catering company
Company picnic
Festival
Party
Restaurant
Reunion
Wedding reception

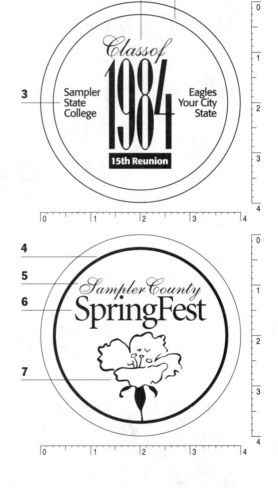

The Idea Book examples show how coasters for a reunion and a festival might look.

**Source:
Custom Coaster
Printing**

The "Beer Coaster" (4" round, 90 point) was printed by Craft Corporation, 718-417-1177, 54-01 Grand Ave., Maspeth, NY 11378

Decal

Send a clear message

Before the arrival of space-age adhesives and plastics, you soaked a decal in water and slid it off a sheet of paper onto glass. Today there are decals you just peel off and stick on, reusable decals that cling without adhesive, two-sided decals, and a super-quick laser version.

To create your version, keep your message simple and the type large enough to read from three or four feet away. Place graphics and text at least 1/8" from the edge.

Print the finished artwork directly from your computer on clear laser labels. Or print one master copy of your artwork and send it to a printer that specializes in decals (*see* Source:). The company that printed the example, Decals Unlimited, can print your artwork on every imaginable kind of decal and sticker. Call for their catalog.

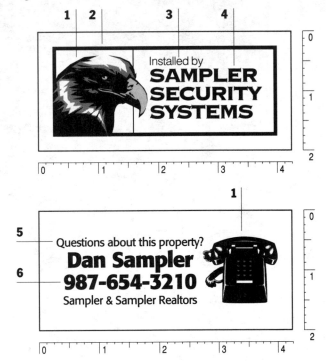

Laser Decal Layout: Top

1 · Eagle and Phone Clip Art: From Presentation Task Force by New Vision Technologies, Inc., 613-727-8184, 38 Auriga Drive, Unit 13, Nepean, Ontario, Canada K2E 8A5 © New Vision Technologies, Inc. All rights reserved

2 · Line: 4pt. Vertical Line: 1pt

3 · Subhead: Helvetica Light, 14pt, flush left

4 · Headline: Copperplate 33BC, 30/22pt, flush left, all caps

Static Cling Decal Layout: Bottom

5 · Subheads Top and Bottom: Formata Regular, 14pt, centered

6 · Name and Phone: Formata Bold, 26/26pt, centered

The first example shows a laser decal that a security company might use to ward off prowlers. The second decal is a reusable version that clings to glass with static. It shows how a realtor might identify a house he has listed.

**Source:
Clear Laser
Labels**

The "Clear Laser Labels" (4 1/4" by 2") are from Avery Dennison, 800-252-8379, 818 Oak Park Road, Covina, CA 91724

**Source:
Static Cling
Labels**

The "Static Cling" decal was printed by Decals Unlimited Inc., 800-826-8271, 1102 Spring Creek Rd., Mitchell, NE 69357. They can print every imaginable type of sticker and decal.

285

Message Magnet

Keep your message in sight

Message Magnet Layout: Top

1 · Headline: Format Bold, 18/18pt, centered

2 · Phone: Formata Bold, 18pt, flush right. Organization Name and Address: Formata Light, 9pt, flush right

3 · Talk Bubble Clip Art: From DigitArt, Vol. 21, Fabulous Fifties, by Image Club Graphics Inc., 800-661-9410, Suite 5, 1902 Eleventh St. SE, Calgary, Alberta, Canada T2G 3G2 © Image Club Graphics Inc. All rights reserved

4 · Phone Clip Art: From ClickArt EPS Symbols & Industry by T/Maker Company, 415-962-0195, 1390 Villa Street, Mountain View, CA 94041 © T/Maker Company. All rights reserved

Message Magnet Layout: Bottom

5 · Golfer Clip Art: From Presentation Task Force by New Vision Technologies, Inc., 613-727-8184, 38 Auriga Drive, Unit 13, Nepean, Ontario, Canada K2E 8A5 © New Vision Technologies, Inc. All rights reserved

6 · Subhead: Times New Roman, 12pt, centered, all caps, reverse (white) on a black background box. Phone: Times New Roman, 36pt, centered. Organization Name: Times New Roman, 12pt, centered

A message magnet is a simple transaction: in return for displaying your advertising message, the customer enjoys the convenience of having your phone number close at hand.

The first Idea Book example shows how a hardware store might encourage customers to call with home fix-it questions. The second shows how a golf course might remind players to reserve a tee time.

For your version, don't waste what little space you have on purely decorative graphics. Choose images that visually restate your message and text that prompts the reader to action.

Print one master copy of your artwork and send it to a printer that specializes in magnets (*see* Source:).

Use a message magnet for your

Club
Day care center
Delivery service
Fire department
Help line
Home services
News service
Police department
Rescue squad

Source: Magnets

The "Flexible Vinyl Magnet" (3 1/2" by 2") is from Mo' Money Associates, 800-874-7681, PO Box 12591, Pensacola, FL 32574-2591. Mo' Money also prints hundreds of other promotional items. Call for their catalog.

Placemat

Feast your eyes

Here's a practical project direct from your desktop to your tabletop.

Position your headline, text, and illustration inside a border. Center the border in a 6 1/2" by 6 1/2" box on a standard 8 1/2" by 11" page.

Print the artwork directly from your computer and trim out the box. Use spray adhesive to mount the box on a 18 3/4" by 12 1/2" sheet of colored stock. Have the finished sheet laminated with a 10 mil gloss film (*see* Source:).

You can also have a commercial printer reproduce your artwork on a thin sheet of paper for use as a disposable placemat. Add clip art for kids or trivia questions and answers for adults.

Placemat Layout

1 · Name: Copperplate 33BC, 85pt, centered, all caps

2 · Subhead: Formata Light, 20pt, centered, all caps, add one space between characters

3 · Sailboat Clip Art: From ClickArt EPS Business Art by T/Maker Company, 415-962-0195, 1390 Villa Street, Mountain View, CA 94041 © T/Maker Company. All rights reserved. The illustration overprints a box filled with a 10% shade of black.

4 · Decorative Line

5 · City, State: Formata Light, 18pt, centered

SAMPLER

SEAFOOD

Example Beach, State

Make permanent placemats for

Church dinners
Club luncheons
Home
Restaurant

Make throwaways for

Birthday parties
Company picnics
Holidays
Kids to color

Source: Laminating

The placemats are laminated by SLAM-LAM Inc., 800-331-7526, 652 West Randolph Street, Chicago, IL 60606-2114

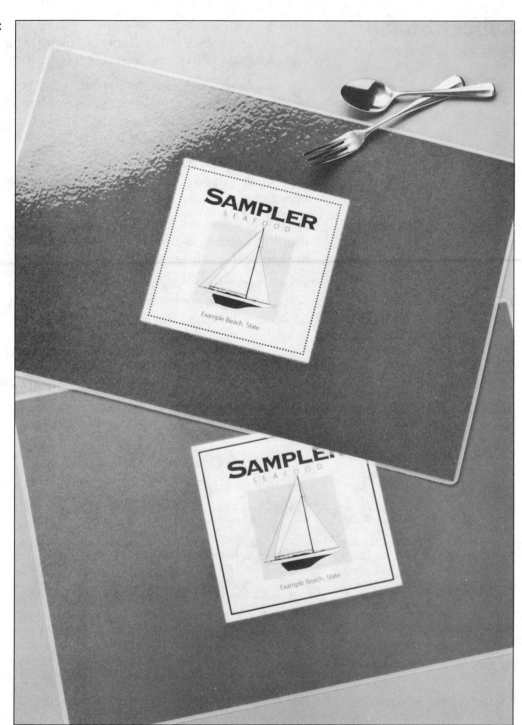

Rubber Stamp

Your hand-held printing press

Even with all our high-tech solutions, there is still nothing that matches the economy and versatility of a rubber stamp. The arrival of self-inking stamps has even eliminated the need for separate ink pads.

The Idea Book example at the top-left shows how a library might identify books; the example to the right shows how a supply company might label product samples; and the bottom example shows how a sales rep might add his name to invoices.

You can personalize these layouts or design your own. Print a master copy of the artwork and send it to a printer that specializes in manufacturing custom stamps (*see* Source:).

Keep your layout at a manageable size. Widths and heights greater than 3 1/2" are possible, but keep in mind that the larger the stamp the more difficult it is to get a clean impression.

If you're interested in manufacturing stamps in-house, call Jackson Marking Products for information about their stamp-making system for desktop publishers (*see* Source:).

Rubber Stamp Layout: Top-Left

1 · Subhead: Adobe Caslon Regular, 14pt, centered. Headline: Copperplate 33BC, 30/20pt, centered, all caps. Address and Phone: Adobe Caslon Regular, 14pt, centered. Circular Line: 1pt

2 · Symbol: Adobe Carta Font, 42pt, centered

Rubber Stamp Layout: Top-Right

3 · Subhead: Cochin, 14pt, centered. "Sampler Supply": Franklin Gothic Condensed, 24pt, centered, .5pt line around. Phone: Cochin, 18pt, centered

Rubber Stamp Layout: Bottom-Left

4 · Headline: Formata Bold, 12pt, flush left. Signature: Shelley Allegro, 36pt, flush right

The dotted lines represent the size of the final rubber stamp.

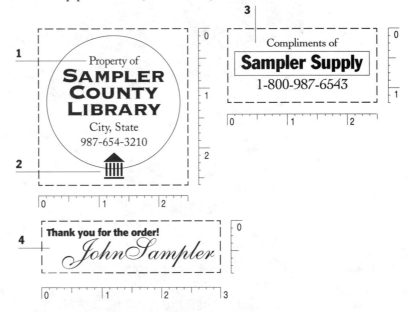

There is still nothing that matches the economy and versatility of a rubber stamp.

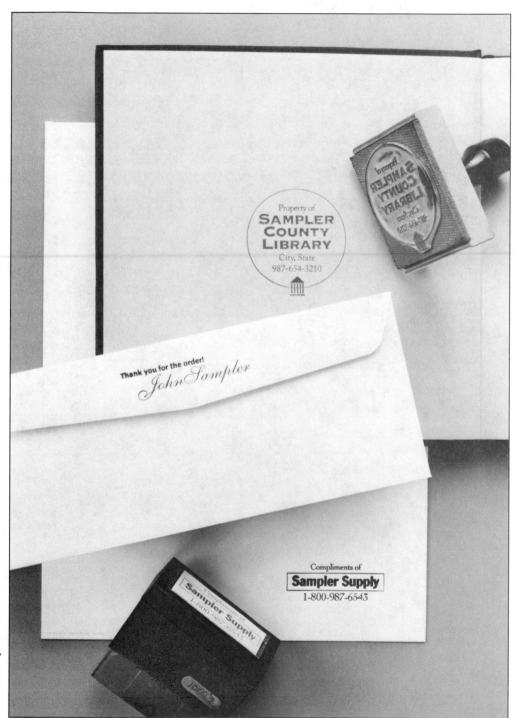

Source: Custom Rubber Stamps

Both self-inking and conventional rubber stamps are manufactured by Jackson Marking Products Co., Inc., 800-851-4945, Brownsville Road, Mt. Vernon, IL 62864-9736

CHAPTER 17
Tag & Label
Projects

3-in-1 Mailing Label

Your form, message, and label on a single sheet

If you ever send an invoice or packing slip along with a package, this *3-in-1 Mailing Label* is worth a look. It combines a mailing label and message area with a half-page form. The completed form is folded and inserted in an adhesive-back envelope and attached to the outside of the package (*see* Source:).

To create your version, place the form on the left-hand side and divide the right-hand side between the label and message. Declare "Invoice Enclosed" in the black bar at the top of the label panel. Print fill-in lines on the message panel so you can add last minute instructions.

Print the finished form directly from your computer on 24 lb bond stock. Use a yellow stock to contrast the white background of the envelope.

3-in-1 Mailing Layout

1 · Title: Formata Bold Italic, 18pt, flush left, reverse (white) on a black background box

2 · Organization Name: Formata Bold, 12pt, flush left. Phone and Address: Formata Light, 12/14pt, flush left

3 · Fill-In: Formata Light, 10/18pt, flush left, .5pt lines

4 · Line: 1pt

5 · "Thank You!" : Formata Bold Italic, 18pt, flush right

The dotted lines represent folds.

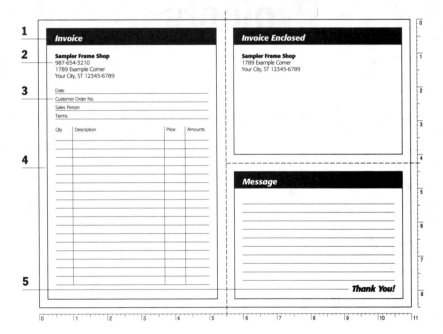

Or combine a label, message, and

Packing list
Warranty
Instruction sheet
Export document
Data sheet
Inspection document
Memo

The Idea Book example shows how a retailer might use the form to combine an invoice, a message form, and the shipping label.

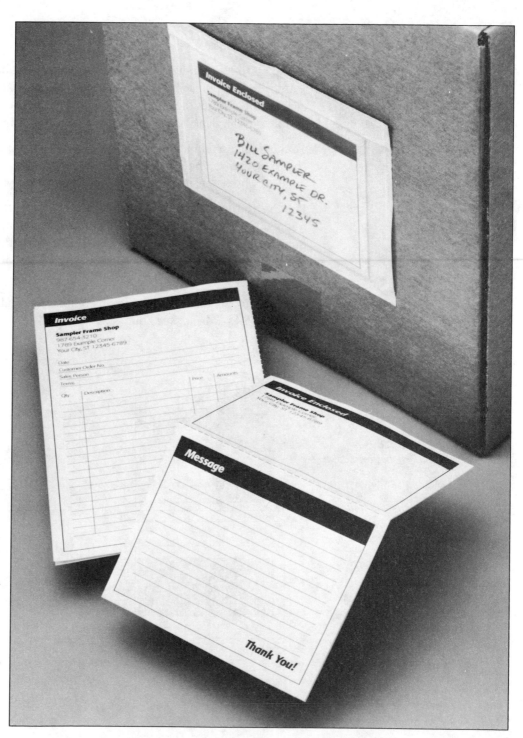

**Source:
Adhesive-Back
Envelopes**

The "Packing List Envelope" (adhesive back, clear face, 7" by 5.5") from Chiswick Trading, Inc., 800-225-8708, 33 Union Avenue, Sudbury, MA 01776

Computer Disk Labels

Put your disk labels to work

Disk labels can do more than catalog the contents of a disk. A little up-front work can save you plenty of time later.

Use the top-left example to label files by month and year. Include your name and phone number and use the fill-in to list file names. The check-off identifies the operating system used and whether the disk is double or high density.

To the right is a miniature memo for sending files to another user. The check-off names the operating system used and whether the disk is double or high density.

Use the example on the bottom to organize files by the program used to create them. Label the disks for spreadsheets, databases, desktop publishing, etc., or with the name of the actual program. Include your name, phone number, and the date. The check-off identifies the density of disk and whether it's formatted.

Print the labels directly from your computer on labels sized to fit 3 1/2" or 5 1/4" disks (*see* Source:).

Disk Label Layout: Top-Left

1 · Title: Helvetica Black, 10/10pt, flush left. Address and Phone: Helvetica Narrow Bold, 8/8pt, flush left. Both are reverse (white) on a black background box. Check Box Text: Helvetica Narrow, 8/10pt, flush left. Box and Fill-In Lines: .5pt.

Disk Label Layout: Top-Right

2 · "Memo" : Formata Bold Italic, 10pt, flush left, all caps. Headings: Formata Light Italic, 9/14pt, flush left, all caps. Fill-In Lines: .5pt. Check Box Text: Formata Light Italic, flush left. Box Lines: .5pt.

Disk Label Layout: Bottom

3 · Title: Helvetica Black, 10/10pt, flush left. Address, and Phone: Helvetica Narrow Bold, 8/10pt, flush left. Both are reverse (white) on a black background box. Name, Phone, and Date: Helvetica Narrow, 8/10pt, flush left. Fill-In Lines: .5pt.

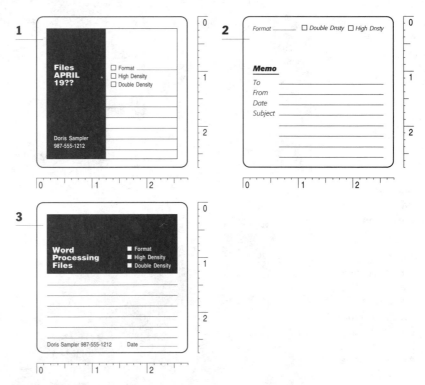

A little up-front work can save you plenty of time later.

**Source:
Diskette Laser
Labels**

The "Diskette Laser Labels" (3 1/2" and 5 1/4") are from Avery Dennison, 800-252-8379, 818 Oak Park Road, Covina, CA 91724

Name Tag

Create tags that tell the whole story

At a glance, a good name tag tells you the name, title, and affiliation of the person wearing it. This layout tells that and more.

For your version of the tag, you'll need the artwork, and a supply of name tag holders (*see* Source:).

Divide your tag into four sections. In the top section include the date, the name of the event, and the sponsoring organization. In the center section list the participant's name and title. In the bottom section identify the region, state, or organization the wearer represents. Use the box at the bottom right to code the badges for speakers, press, exhibitors, board members, etc.

Print the tags directly from your computer, trim them out and insert them into plastic holders.

Name Tag Layout

1 · Subhead: Formata Light, 14pt, flush left, reverse (white) on a black background box

2 · Headline: Formata Bold, 24pt, centered, reverse (white) on a black background box

3 · Name and Title: Formata Regular, 24pt, centered

4 · Code: Formata Bold, 24pt, centered

5 · Group: Formata Regular, 20pt, centered, overprints a box filled with a 20% shade of black

At a glance, this name tag tells you the event, the name, title, and affiliation of the wearer, plus a status code.

19?? Business Meeting & Conference
National Example Fund
Benjamin G. Sampler
Speaker
S
New Hampshire

**Source:
Name Tags**

The "Bulldog Clip Badges" (2 1/2" by 4") from Crestline Company, Inc., 800-221-7797, 22 West 21st Street, New York, NY 10010

Shipping Label

Finally, a simple, quick, custom label solution

If don't use labels often enough to justify ordering a custom version, that doesn't mean you have to do without. Print your own on ordinary paper, trim them out, and attach them with extra wide label tape.

Use the top example to list instructions and details, the number of boxes shipped (i.e., Box [2] of [3]), and contact information.

The bottom-left example creates a sense of urgency. Add an "Attention:" box for the name of the recipient and a subhead prompting, "Please Open Immediately."

Use example on the bottm-right to direct international packages and letters. Here, the "AIRMAIL" notice is composed in English, German, Spanish, and French.

Print the label on bright colored stock and seal it to the packages or envelope using 4" wide label tape (*see* Source:). The tape not only seals the label to the package, it protects it from the tears, moisture and grime suffered by ordinary labels.

Shipping Label Layout: Top

1 · Headline: Franklin Gothic Condensed, 42pt, centered. Subhead: Franklin Gothic Condensed, 30pt, centered, all caps. Both are reverse (white) on a black background box. Check Box Text: Franklin Gothic Condensed, 24pt, centered. Box Lines: .5pt. Phone, Name and Address: Helvetica Narrow, 11/12pt, centered, .5pt line

Shipping Label Layout: Bottom-Left

2 · "RUSH!" : Formata Bold, 72pt, centered, all caps. "SHIPMENT" : Formata Regular, 24pt, centered, all caps. "Attention:" : Formata Bold, 16pt, centered. Box Line: .5pt. Phone, Name and Address: formata Light, 11/12pt, centered

Shipping Label Layout: Bottom-Right

3 · Headline: Gill Sans Bold, 24pt, centered. Airplane Clip Art: From Presentation Task Force by New Vision Technologies, Inc., 613-727-8184, 38 Auriga Drive, Unit 13, Nepean, Ontario, Canada K2E 8A5 © New Vision Technologies, Inc. All rights reserved. The illustration overprints a box with a 6pt outline, filled with a 20% shade of black.

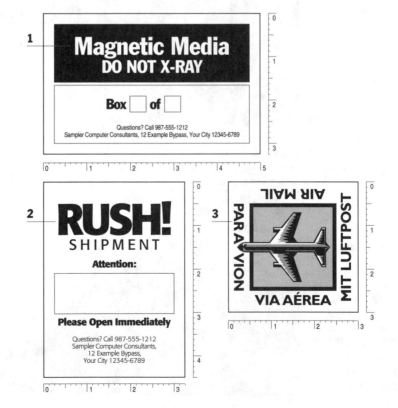

*Print your labels
on ordinary
paper, trim them
out, and attach
them with extra
wide label tape.*

**Source:
Extra Wide
Label Tape**

*The "Clear
Label Protection
Tape" (4") from
Chiswick
Trading, Inc.,
800-225-8708,
33 Union Avenue,
Sudbury, MA
01776*

Spot Label

Add your message to the products you resell

Spot Label Layout: Top-Left

1 · "FREE" : Format Bold Italic, 38pt, centered, all caps. "Sampler" : Formata Bold, 24pt, centered, reverse (white) on a black background box. "Quick..." : Formata Bold Italic, 32pt, centered, reverse (white) on a black background box. "Buy it..." : Formata Light, 11/11pt, centered

Spot Label Layout: Top-Right

2 · "SAMPLER..." : Copperplate 33BC, 16pt, centered, all caps. "CD" : Helvetica Black, 85pt, centered, all caps, reverse (white) on a black background box. "OF" : Copperplate 33BC, 18pt, centered, all caps, reverse (white) on a black background box. "the month" : Brush Script, 32pt, centered, reverse (white) on a black background box. "SAVE 20%" : Copperplate 33BC, 16pt, centered, all caps

Spot Label Layout: Bottom

3 · "Don't..." : Adobe Caslon Regular, 42/34pt, centered. "Aisle 4" : Helvetica Black Italic, 24pt, centered, overprints a box filled with a 20% shade of black

More spot label ideas

Your catalog is from this showroom . . .
We service this product . . .
We offer training for this product . . .
We finance this product . . .
We are the exclusive dealer . . .

If you resell another company's product, spot labels are a professional way to highlight your organization's name, and demonstrate the value you add to the sale.

The first Idea Book example (top-left) shows how a software dealer might alert the customer to a training incentive. The next example (top-right) shows how a music store might highlight and discount CDs. The final example (bottom) shows how a retailer might identify products that require batteries as a way to create a second sale.

You can personalize these designs with your information or dream up your own. Print the labels directly from your computer on 2 1/2" round laser labels (*see* Source:).

These Idea Book examples show how a software dealer, a music store, and a retailer might add their messages to the products they resell.

**Source:
Round Laser
Labels**

The "Round Laser Label" (2 1/2" diameter) is from Avery Dennison, 800-252-8379, 818 Oak Park Road, Covina, CA 91724

Tags

Create tags in all colors, shapes, and sizes

With off-the-shelf blanks you can create an amazing variety of tags. Just print your message on an adhesive-back label and apply it to a blank tag (*see* Source:).

Use the top example to communicate a simple message. Print the artwork on a clear laser label and apply it to a cardboard tag.

The bottom-left example protects operating instructions and keeps them with the equipment they describe. Print the artwork on a bright yellow stock, trim it to size, and insert it in the tag pocket.

Use the example on the right to identify the inspector. Print the artwork on a round laser label and apply it to a plastic disc.

Tag Layout: Top

1 · "Out" : Franklin Gothic Condensed, 62pt, reverse (white) on a black background box. "of order" : Franklin Gothic Condensed, 62pt, flush left

2 · Name and Phone: Times New Roman, 20/18pt, centered

Tag Layout: Bottom-Left

3 · Heading: Helvetica Black, 14/14pt, centered, reverse (white) on a black background box

4 · Instruction Text: Times New Roman, 16/18pt, flush left

Tag Layout: Bottom-Right

5 · "OK" : Helvetica Black, 52pt, centered

6 · Box For Initials: Times New Roman, 9pt, centered, .5pt line

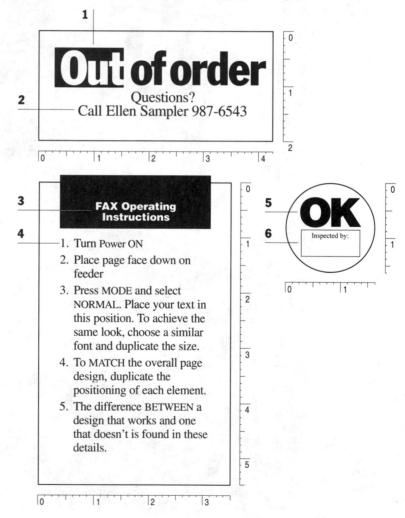

Out of order
Questions?
Call Ellen Sampler 987-6543

FAX Operating Instructions

1. Turn Power ON
2. Place page face down on feeder
3. Press MODE and select NORMAL. Place your text in this position. To achieve the same look, choose a similar font and duplicate the size.
4. To MATCH the overall page design, duplicate the positioning of each element.
5. The difference BETWEEN a design that works and one that doesn't is found in these details.

OK
Inspected by:

With off-the-shelf blanks you can create an amazing variety of tags.

Source:
Tags

The "Colored Cardboard Tag" (6 1/4" by 3 1/8"), "Vinyl Pocket" (3 1/2" by 5 1/2") and the plastic "Tuf-Tags" (3" diameter) are from Ready Made Safety Sign & Identification Products, 800-544-2440, 480 Fillmore Avenue, Tonawanda, NY 14150

Source:
Clear Laser Labels

The "Clear Laser Labels" (2" by 4 1/4") used for the "Out of order" tag and the "Round Laser Labels" (1 2/3" diameter) used for the "OK" tag are from Avery Dennison, 800-252-8379, 818 Oak Park Road, Covina, CA 91724

305

CHAPTER 18
Wearable
Projects

Baseball Cap

Stay on your customer's mind

Though wearables require a minimum amount of work, they produce some of the most spectacular results.

The Idea Book example shows a cap that an air charter service might hand out to clients. The second layout shows a cap that might be sold as a souvenir.

For your version, use words and pictures that are understood at a glance. Step eight or ten feet back from the finished artwork and see if it has the desired impact.

Print one master copy of the artwork and send it to a specialty printer (*see* Source:). The company that printed the example, Sales Guides, can imprint your artwork on everything from die-cast belt buckles to director's chairs. Call for their catalog.

Baseball Cap Layout: Top

1 · Headline: Helvetica Black, 160pt, centered

2 · Subhead: Formata Regular, 36pt, centered

Baseball Cap Layout: Bottom

3 · Symbol: Adobe Carta Font, 100pt

4 · Headline: Copperplate 33BC, 100/52pt, centered, all caps

5 · Subhead: Adobe Caslon Regular, 32pt, centered

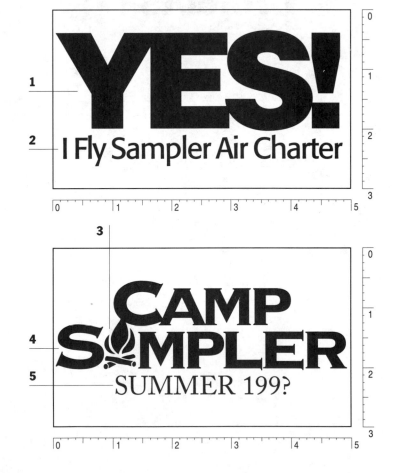

The first Idea Book example shows a cap that an air charter service might hand out to clients. The second example shows a cap that might be sold as a souvenir.

Source: Custom Printed Baseball Caps

The "Baseball Cap" is imprinted by Sales Guides, Inc., 800-352-9899, 4937 Otter Lake Rd., St. Paul, MN 55110

T-Shirt

Dress for success

Whether you sell them for profit or give them away as advertising, T-shirts attract a huge of audience.

To create your version, you'll need a bold headline, the highest quality clip art, and a little imagination. Keep your T-shirt design within an 8 1/2" by 11" area. Judge the success of the finished design from eight or ten feet back. Print in a color on white, black on a color, or use a color ink on a contrasting shirt.

Print one master copy of the artwork and send it to a specialty printer (*see* Source:). The company that printed the example, Sales Guides, can imprint your artwork on everything from die-cast belt buckles to director's chairs. Call for their catalog.

T-Shirt Layout

1 · Camping Clip Art: From Electronic Clipper by Dynamic Graphics, 800-255-8800, 6000 N. Forest Park Dr., Peoria, IL 61614-3592 © Dynamic Graphics, Inc. All rights reserved

2 · "S" : Formata Bold, 100pt, all caps, reverse (white) type on a black background box. "AMPLER" : Formata Bold, 100pt, centered, all caps

3 · "OUTFITTERS" : Formata Light, 50pt, centered, all caps

The Idea Book example shows how an outdoors outfitter might use the shirt as a promotion.

**Source:
Custom Printed
T-Shirts**

The "Cotton T" is imprinted by Sales Guides, Inc., 800-352-9899, 4937 Otter Lake Rd., St. Paul, MN 55110

CHAPTER 19
Web Projects

Float a Remote

Use a visual metaphor we can all relate to

Part of the excitement of web design is experimenting with how visitors navigate your site—and one way to make the process intuitive is to adopt a navigational metaphor that is already widely understood.

The example shows how a computer training firm might display their navigational menu in the form of the remote control you use to operate your TV or sound system. Though the similarity is obvious, the design of the remote is intentionally kept simple in order to keep from distracting the reader from the underlying page.

Does your remote control always sit on the same table, in the exact same position? No and neither should your virtual version. Place it in a different position on each page and use the same artwork rotated at various angles.

But the greatest advantage to the idea is this: when your menu is a separate, floating element, you are free to design your pages without restriction of a permanent menu in the same spot on every page. Plus your virtual remote won't get lost under a cushion on the couch.

More button ideas

Coming Soon
Exit
Guestbook
Home
Introduction
Recommended
Search
Store

Float a Remote Layout

1 · Body Text: Minion, 20/30pt, flush left.

2 · Computer Clip Art: From ClipTo Maniacs by ClipTo Art, 613-232-3567, 401 King Edward Ave., Suite 200, Ottawa, Ontario, K1N9C9 CANADA © ClipTo Art. All rights reserved. Organization Name: Trebuchet MS, 12pt, flush left.

3 · Remote Artwork: Composed from a piece of base button artwork from Screen Caffeine Pro by Jawai Interactive, Inc. 512-469-0502, 501 East Fourth St., Austin, TX 78701-3745 © Jawai Interactive. All rights reserved. Button Text: Trebuchet MS, 12pt, centered.

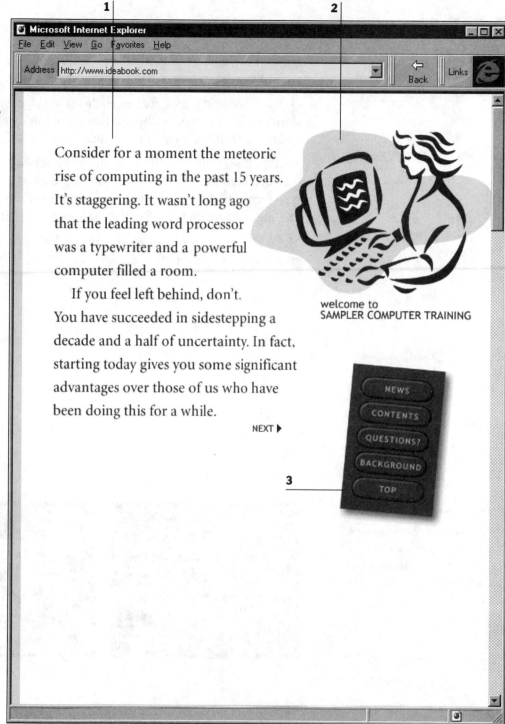

Consider for a moment the meteoric rise of computing in the past 15 years. It's staggering. It wasn't long ago that the leading word processor was a typewriter and a powerful computer filled a room.

If you feel left behind, don't. You have succeeded in sidestepping a decade and a half of uncertainty. In fact, starting today gives you some significant advantages over those of us who have been doing this for a while.

NEXT ▶

welcome to
SAMPLER COMPUTER TRAINING

NEWS
CONTENTS
QUESTIONS?
BACKGROUND
TOP

315

Quick Change Quotes

An easy way to keep your site fresh

On one thing most web experts agree—if you want people to visit your site often, you'll have to keep the content fresh. One way to make those changes obvious is to splash them all over the front page. The trick is to make the process manageable.

Quick Change Quotes makes it down right easy. The example shows how a veterinary clinic might use animal-related quotations and the date of the week, to keep their menu page ever-changing.

You do it all with a single plug-in image for each week or month (see the examples below.) The quotes are easy to find and the all type format makes the artwork easy to produce and the graphics fast loading. Too much text? Reduce the font size to fit.

Make five or ten modules at a sitting and plug them into the same spot each week or month.

More quick quote ideas

Use testimonials by customers
Quote industry experts
Present generic business ideas
Run a headline from an article
Say it in your own words

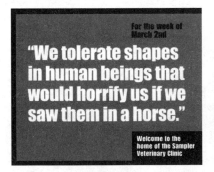

**Quick Change
Quotes Layout**

*1 · Date: Impact,
22/22pt, flush left.
Headline: Impact,
55/60pt, flush left,
reverse white.*

*2 · Organization
Name: Impact,
20/20pt, flush left,
reverse white.*

*3 · Button Text:
Trebuchet MS,
12/12, flush left.*

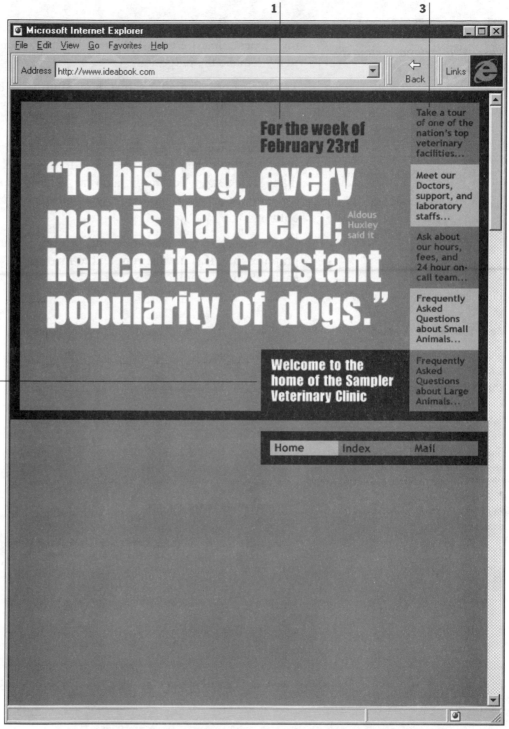

Theme Object

Design your page around a simple object

Does a web design have to be visually complicated to be interesting? Does it require lots of color and a fancy icon for every menu item? You be the judge.

The Idea Book example shows how simplicity has power of its own. One simple photograph forms a base from which to branch a series of menu items.

The ideal object is long and thin. That shape encourages the reader scrolling down the page to see the bottom and it keeps the file to a manageable size. You might also try using several copies of the same image or two of more different objects to divide the page into columns.

In this case, the section headings and body text shown are saved as graphics, but, if you want your text to load faster, you could just as easily use non-graphical text.

More theme object ideas

A gavel for a legal firm
A toy rocket for a science club
A wrench for a plumbing company
A whisk for a restaurant supplier

Photos: Gavel, wrench, whisk from CMCD Just Tools set, rocket from the CMCD Everyday Objects 1 by PhotoDisc Inc. 800-528-3472, 20132013 Fourth Ave., Seattle, WA 98121 © PhotoDisc Inc. All rights reserved

Theme Object Layout

1 · "Sampler": Franklin Gothic Heavy, 20pt, centered. "Writer's Club": Franklin Gothic Heavy, 60/45pt, centered. Typewriter Clip Art: From Commerce & Communications picture font by MvB from FontHaus, 800-942-9110, 1375 Kings Highway East, Fairfield, CT 06430 © MvB Design. All rights reserved

2· Pencil Photo: From CMCD Just Tools by PhotoDisc Inc. 800-528-3472, 2013 Fourth Ave., Seattle, WA 98121 © PhotoDisc Inc. All rights reserved

3 · Section Headings: Boulevard, 40pt, flush left. Body Text: Minion, 20/20pt, flush left

4 · Menu Text Top: Trebuchet MS, 12/12, flush left. Bottom: Trebuchet MS, 14/14, centered

SAMPLER Writer's Club

Home   Index   Mail   Search

News

January—Eric Sampler is teaching inmates to write... Historian Gregory Example headlines the new year... Our Publicity Committee makes a bold new proposal...

HelpDesk

Do you want to know the circumstances under which a verb becomes transitive? Do you know when a verb becomes transitive? Good we need you both...

Welcome

Stephen Leacock said "Writing is no trouble: you just jot down ideas as they occur to you. The jotting is simplicity itself—it is the occuring which is difficult"...

People

Our membership includes writers just starting out and a few who have topped the best-seller lists. Learn all about them and how to join the fastest growing club in the country...

Calendar

Have you been locked away for months pounding out the great American pesticide manufacturer's directory? (Hey we gotta make a living!) Time to surface for air...

Welcome | News | People | Help Desk | Calendar

Web Card

Remind your visitor of the people behind the screens

One tried and true way of grabbing attention is to do something your audience doesn't expect. On the Web, the last thing you'd expect to see is a conventional business card. But how many times have you printed out a web page to capture the name, street, or e-mail address of the publisher?

The Idea Book example shows how a realtor might use a graphic image that looks like, and is the same size as, his conventional business card, to provide the visitor with a tangible reminder of their visit. The headline "PRINT MY CARD AND CALL ME!" fills the void left by so many pages—with a distinct call to action.

To create your version, scan your business card or recreate it in a paint program. Add a dotted line around the outside as a cue for cutting it to size. At 72 pixels per inch, an image roughly 350 by 200 pixels prints at business card size.

Other documents for web printouts

A fax-back order form
A sheet of directions to your location
A certificate for completing a tour of your site or for sharing information

Web Card Layout

1 · "PIERCE SAMPLER": Frutiger 95 Ultra Black, 25/21pt, all caps, flush left. "AND": Frutiger 95 Ultra Black, 15pt, all caps, flush right. "REALTORS": Frutiger 95 Ultra Black, 17pt, all caps, flush left. House Clip Art: From Dick & Jane picture font by MvB from FontHaus, 800-942-9110, 1375 Kings Highway East, Fairfield, CT 06430 © MvB Design. All rights reserved

2 · Menu Text: Frutiger 45 Light, lower case, 12pt, flush left

3 · Section Heading: Trebuchet MS, 18pt, flush left. Body Text: Trebuchet MS, 14/18pt, flush left

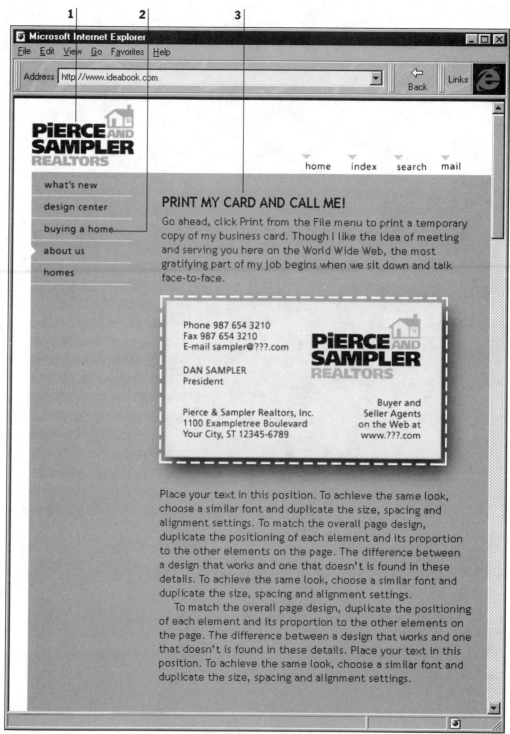

PRINT MY CARD AND CALL ME!

Go ahead, click Print from the File menu to print a temporary copy of my business card. Though I like the idea of meeting and serving you here on the World Wide Web, the most gratifying part of my job begins when we sit down and talk face-to-face.

Phone 987 654 3210
Fax 987 654 3210
E-mail sampler@???.com

DAN SAMPLER
President

Pierce & Sampler Realtors, Inc.
1100 Exampletree Boulevard
Your City, ST 12345-6789

Buyer and
Seller Agents
on the Web at
www.???.com

Place your text in this position. To achieve the same look, choose a similar font and duplicate the size, spacing and alignment settings. To match the overall page design, duplicate the positioning of each element and its proportion to the other elements on the page. The difference between a design that works and one that doesn't is found in these details. To achieve the same look, choose a similar font and duplicate the size, spacing and alignment settings.

To match the overall page design, duplicate the positioning of each element and its proportion to the other elements on the page. The difference between a design that works and one that doesn't is found in these details. Place your text in this position. To achieve the same look, choose a similar font and duplicate the size, spacing and alignment settings.

APPENDIX
Sources

Books

Clip Art Crazy,
The "greatest hits" of clip art on CD-ROM
I wrote *Clip Art Crazy* to show you how to find, choose, and use the best clip art on the planet. It includes 50 graphics-oriented projects, a big directory of companies, and a CD-ROM with 500 ready-to-use clip art images handpicked from the best artists in the industry.
By Chuck Green, 1996, Peachpit Press, ISBN 0-201-88361-9, www.ideabook.com

The E-Myth Revisited, *Why most small businesses don't work and what to do about it*
From a marketing angle, if you're planning to start a small business or you already own or work for one, and if the primary purpose of that business is sell a product or service, Michael Gerber has a surprise that could literally make or break it. Must reading.
By Michael Gerber, 1995, HarperBusiness, ISBN 0-88730-728-0

The Elements of Typographic Style
A surveyor plots the beauty of nature in practical terms—the beauty is unchanged, but the resulting map helps us find our way across the landscape. Robert Bringhurst offers a map of the typographic world—a style guide, a history, and a dictionary of terms—that will enhance your ability to navigate it.
By Robert Bringhurst, 1992, Hartley & Marks, Publishers, ISBN 0-88179-110-5

Guerrilla Marketing,
Secrets for making big profits from your small business
I like theory but I love specifics. Jay Conrad Levinson's updated classic is jam-packed with more proven marketing tips, strategies, and secrets than you could learn in a lifetime of hit and miss. The Guerrilla Philosophy will change the way you think about marketing.
By Jay Conrad Levinson, 1993, Houghton Mifflin Company, ISBN 0-395-64496-8, www.gmarketing.com

A History of Graphic Design, *Second Edition*
Why read history? It's a navigational tool—a guide to help us repeat the successes and sidestep the blunders. This heavily illustrated volume tells the story of design from its beginnings through the "Graphic Renaissance," the Industrial Revolution, the Modernist Era, and into the information age. Need a new perspective on your work? Look no further.
By Philip B. Meggs, 1992, Van Nostrand Reinhold, ISBN 0-442-31895-2

Looking Good In Print, *A Guide to Basic Design for Desktop Publishing, Third Edition*
Good design is difficult to create and even more difficult to explain. Roger Parker has a knack for making it understandable, testament to the fact that this is the best selling desktop publishing book ever written. He leads you through the basics of planning, the effective use of type and visuals, demonstrates design problems and their solutions, and gives you an in-depth look at projects and production.
By Roger C. Parker, 1996, Ventana Press, ISBN 0-940087-32-4, www.rcparker.com

Marketing With Newsletters, *How to boost sales, add members & raise funds with a printed, faxed or Web-site newsletter, Second Edition*
Newsletter expert Elaine Floyd details the six types of newsletter content. How to draw a research map. Why publishers like online delivery. How to write a news article using the inverted pyramid format. And hundreds of other newsletter-oriented insights. It includes a career's worth of trial and error.
By Elaine Floyd, 1997, Newsletter Resources, ISBN 0-9630222-4-5, www.newsletterinfo.com

Pocket Pal,
A Graphic Arts Production Handbook, Sixteenth Edition
Have a question about a specific printing process? A graphic arts term? Conventional or electronic prepress production? The weight of various types of paper? A technique of folding or binding? You'll find the answers to these and hundreds of other commercial printing questions in this industry standard history and how-to of printing.
International Paper, 1995, order direct: 800-854-3212

Web Concept & Design,
A comprehensive guide for creating effective web sites
If you're interested in designing a web site or hiring someone to design one for you, line up here. Crystal Waters shows and tells how to target your audience, choose the content, structure your site, design the graphics, and test the results. A terrific introduction to the web.
By Crystal Waters, 1996, New Riders Publishing, ISBN 1-56205-648-4, www.typo.com

Magazines & Newsletters

Before & After, *How to design cool stuff*
It's part newsletter and part magazine and it has no peer—every full color issue is brimming with projects, make-overs, ideas, and how-tos presented in simple, understandable terms. From the thinking behind a headline to the step-by-step process for creating a catalog, *Before & After* is a teaching machine for any desktop publisher—beginner or advanced. Bimonthly.
1830 Sierra Gardens Drive, Suite 30, Roseville, CA 95661, 916-784-3880, www.pagelab.com

Communication Arts
Any self-respecting industry professional has at least 150 pounds of CA magazines on the shelf—they're just too beautiful to throw away. If you're interested in seeing the latest work being done by the world's top art directors, designers, copywriters, illustrators, photographers and the organizations they represent—this is the place. Eight times a year.
410 Sherman Avenue, Palo Alto, CA 94306, 800-258-9111, www.commarts.com

Creative Business, *Business Standards for Graphic Design, Illustration, & Copywriting*
If graphics, illustration, or copywriting is your business, or you want it to be, you owe it to yourself to spend some time with this meat and potatoes newsletter—budgeting, management issues, case studies, and thoughtful advice. An unusual bonus to your subscription is an offer of free over-the-telephone business advice—anytime you want a second opinion they welcome a call. Bimonthly.
275 Newbury Street, Boston, MA 02116, 617-424-1368, www.creativebusiness.com

Dynamic Graphics Magazine,
The Idea Guide to Quick Desktop Success
It was conceived as a design publication for non-designers—a place for small business owners and corporate communicators to pick up tips for producing good-looking ads, brochures, packaging and to learn the basics about design and production. As it turns out, Dynamic Graphics Magazine has something to offer everyone. Bimonthly.
6000 N. Forest Park Drive, Peoria, IL 61614, Voice: 800-255-8800, www.dgusa.com

Publish,
The Magazine for Electronic Publishing Professionals
DTP industry news, software, hardware, and book reviews, advanced electronic production and how real organizations are making it work—its all in *Publish.* The project make-overs, done by a different designer each month, are second to none. Monthly.
501 Second Street, San Francisco, CA 94107, 800-656-7495, www.publish.com

Step-By-Step Electronic Design,
The How-To Newsletter for Electronic Graphic Designers
This publication and it's sister publication *Step-By-Step Graphics Magazine,* takes you behind the scenes to give you an over-the-shoulder look at how commercial designers and artists do what they do. You'll find preliminary sketches, work in progress, the finished products and hear the artists talk in detail about the techniques they use. The newsletter (monthly) focuses exclusively on the latest electronic design and production techniques using the most popular DTP and illustration software programs. The magazine (bimonthly) covers conventional *and* electronic design.
Dynamic Graphics, Inc., 6000 N. Forest Park Drive, Peoria, IL 61614-3592, 800-255-8800, www.dgusa.com

Products & Services

MAIL ORDER PRINTING

These companies specialize in reproducing your artwork on various papers and products.

Carl Sebastian Colour
Catalog pricing on standard-sized, color direct mail pieces, posters, postcards, brochures, etc.
436 E. Bannister Rd., Kansas City, MO 64131, 800-825-0381

Craft Corporation
Old-fashioned wood pulp beer coasters (page 283)
54-01 Grand Ave., Maspeth, NY 11378, 718-417-1177

Decals Unlimited Inc.
Static cling decals (page 285)
1102 Spring Creek Rd., Mitchell, NE 69357, 800-826-8271
www.prairieweb.com/decals

Folder Factory
Presentation pocket folders (page 37)
116-A High St., P.O. Box 429, Edinburg, VA 22824, 800-368-5270

HA-LO Marketing & Promotions
Custom printed 3M Post-it™ Notes (page 241)
1001 E. Main St. #917, Richmond, VA 23219, 800-474-4256
(ask for the Value Line Dept.)

Mo' Money Associates
Bumper stickers, message magnets (pages 279, 287)
P.O. Box 12591, Pensacola, FL 32574-2591, 800-874-7681

Reprographic Technologies
Page, to poster, to billboard sized file output (page 275)
2865 S. Moorland Road, New Berlin, WI 53151, 800-236-8162
www.getprints.com/rt

Sales Guides, Inc.
Hats and T-shirts (pages 309, 311)
4937 Otter Lake Rd., St. Paul, MN 55110, 800-352-9899

SLAM-LAM Inc.
Laminating (pages 269, 289)
940 West Monroe, Chicago, IL 60607, 800-331-7526

PROJECT MATERIALS

These companies offer products used to recreate specific projects.

20th Century Plastics
Photo album sheet protectors (page 59)
205 South Puente St., Brea, CA 90928, 800-767-0777

Avery Dennison
Laser printer labels, transparencies, lamination film, rotary cards (pages 33, 49, 115, 121, 225, 231, 237, 253, 261, 297, 303, 305)
818 Oak Park Road, Covina, CA 91724, 800-252-8379
www.avery.com

Associated Bag Company
Doorknob bags for flyers (page 267)
400 West Boden St., Milwaukee, WI 53207-7120, 800-926-6100

Bardes Products
Vinyl booklet envelopes (page 75)
5245 West Clinton Ave., Milwaukee, WI 53223, 800-223-1357

Beemak Plastics, Inc.
Acrylic plastic displays (page 91, 273)
16639 South Gramercy Place, Gardena, CA 90247, 800-421-4393

BrownCor International
Boxes and mailing tubes (page 221, 233)
770 South 70th St., P.O. Box 14770, Milwaukee, WI 53214-0770
800-327-2278

Chiswick Trading, Inc.
Adhesive back packing list envelopes and super-wide label tape (pages 295, 301)
33 Union Ave., Sudbury, MA 01776 800-225-8708

Crestline Company, Inc.
Bulldog clip name badges (page 299)
22 West 21st Street, New York, NY 10010, 800-221-7797
www.crestlinepromotions.com

Dick Blick Art Materials
Desktop picture frames (page 251)
P.O. Box 1267, Galesburg, IL 61401 800-933-2542
www.dickblick.com

DO-IT Corporation
Adhesive tab converts your business card to a rotary card (page 107)
P.O. Box 592, South Haven, MI 49090, 800-426-4822
www.do-it.com

Duo-Tang Inc.
Plastic strip binding (page 257)
828 Duo-Tang Road, Paw Paw, MI 49079, 800-852-0039

Freund Can Company
Blank coin cans and jars (page 229, 231)
155 West 84th St., Chicago, IL 60620, 773-224-4230

G. Neil Companies
Certificate presentation folders (page 249)
720 International Parkway, Sunrise, FL 33345-9111, 800-999-9111
www.gneil.com

Jackson Marking Products Co., Inc.
Conventional and self-inking rubber stamps (page 291)
Brownsville Rd., Mr. Vernon, IL 62864-9736, 800-851-4945
www.rubber-stamp.com

Modernistic
Easel backs for tabletop signs (page 245)
169 East Jenks Avenue, St. Paul, MN 55117, 800-641-4610

National Bag
Poly bags (page 235)
2233 Old Mill Road, Hudson, OH 44236, 800-247-6000

Paper Direct
Laser printer post cards (page 119)
P.O. Box 64429, St. Paul, MN 55164-0429, 800-272-7377

The Printer's Shopper
A desktop publisher's toy store. Hundreds of printing, graphic arts, and desktop publishing products and supplies.
111 Press Lane, Chula Vista, CA 91919-1011, 800-854-2911

Ready-Made Safety Sign & Identification Products
Blank cardboard tags and vinyl tag envelopes (page 305)
480 Fillmore Ave., Tonawanda, NY 14150, 800-544-2440
www.cornerstonedirect.com

R&M
Contest boxes (page 219)
P.O. Box 2152, Sante Fe Springs, CA 90670, 800-231-9600
http://r-and-m.com/home

Siegel Display Products
Acrylic plastic displays (page 91)
P.O. Box 95, Minneapolis, MN 55440, 800-626-0322

Southern Binding & Supply
Wire, plastic comb, and Velobind binding equipment and supplies (pages 63, 257)
P.O. Box 21489, Hot Springs, AR 71903, 800-331-5295
www.binding.com

U.S.A. Buttons, Inc.
Button machines and supplies (page 281)
175 Progress Drive, West Bend, WI 53095, 800-777-4992

Vulcan Binder & Cover
Audio and video cassette packaging (page 225)
One Looseleaf Lane, Vincent, AL 35178, 800-633-4526

Clip Art

3G Graphics, Inc.
Their *Images With Impact* collection features categories such as Business, Health, Cartoons, and Sports.
23632 Highway 99 #F407, Edmonds, WA 98026, 800-456-0234

Aridi Computer Graphics Inc.
Specializes in recreating historical graphics—borders, decorative initials, and ornaments—in digital form.
P.O. Box 797702, Dallas, TX 75379
800-755-6441
www.aridi.com

ARISEN Corporation,
Their *ARROglyphs* collection covers environment subjects such as energy, wildlife, recycling, and pollution.
P.O. Box 969, Milford, PA 18337
800-243-1515

Art Parts
Offers subjects as diverse as animals, health, business, holidays, travel, and finance all illustrated in Art Parts' trademark humorous style.
P.O. Box 6547, Santa Ana, CA 92706-0547, 714-834-9166

Artbeats Software Inc.
Focuses on backgrounds and images including a rich selection of textures such as leather, fabric, wood, stone, and marbled paper.
P.O. Box 709, Myrtle Creek, OR 97457, 541-863-4429
www.artbeats.com

Baudville Desktop Publishing Solutions
Their *Award Clips* collection features realistic and cartoon images in a delicate pencil illustration style.
5380 52nd St. S.E., Grand Rapids, MI 49512, 800-728-0888
www.baudville.com

Clip Art Crazy, *The "greatest hits" of clip art on CD-ROM*
It's as much a product as it is a book. In addition to 50 graphics-oriented projects and a big clip art directory, it includes a CD-ROM with 500 ready-to-use clip art images hand-picked from the best artists in the industry.
By Chuck Green, 1996, Peachpit Press, ISBN 0-201-88361-9
804-266-7996
www.ideabook.com

Clipto Art
Publishes the *Clipto Maniacs* collection with hundreds of subjects illustrated with a relaxed style in bright, bold colors.
401 King Edward Ave. Suite 200, Ottawa, Ontario, CANADA K1N9C9
800-741-6649
www.doubleexposure.com

Creative Media Services (CMS)
Offers *Megatoons*—a professional-quality library of business cartoons by Phil Frank the creator of Farley.
P.O. Box 5955, Berkeley, CA 94705
800-358-2278

Communication Resources Inc.
Their *Church Art Plus* is a large and ever-growing collection of Christian images.
4150 Belden Village St., Canton, OH 44718, 800-992-2144
www.comresources.com

CSA Archive Company
Specializes in both packaged and stock "retro" images from the 1920's through the 60's.
P.O. Box 581639, Minneapolis, MN 55458-1639, 612-339-1263
www.csa-archive.com

Digital Wisdom Inc.
Mountain High Maps is a library of meticulously detailed relief maps of the continents, countries, and ocean floors, and views of the globe.
P.O. Box 2070, Tappahannock, VA 22560, 800-800-8560
www.digiwis.com

DS Design
Maker of *KidBAG* clip art—electronic versions of drawings by kids in crayon, paint, marker, watercolor, pastel, and pencil.
1157 Executive Circle Suite D, Cary, NC 27511, 800-745-4037

Dover Publications, Inc.
Publishes an enormous collection of clip art and engraving in book form.
31 East 2nd Street, Mineola, NY 11501, 516-294-7000

© Art Parts

© Baudville

© CSA

Dynamic Graphics Inc.
Though they are one of the most experienced companies in the business, they remain a young-hearted organization with an ever-changing collection of stellar artwork.
6000 N. Forest Park Drive, Peoria, IL 61614-3592 , 800-255-8800
www.dgusa.com

FontHaus Inc.
In addition to their conventional fonts (page 332), they offer a large collection of picture fonts by top designers such as Mark van Bronkhorst.
1375 Kings Highway East, Fairfield, CT 06430, 800-942-9110
www.fonthaus.com

Iconomics
A coop of world-class illustrators who sell their illustrations as stock images (for as little as a few dollars per image) and who offer their services for creating custom art.
155 N. College Ave., Fort Collins, CO 80524, 800-297-7658
www.iconomics.com

Image Club Graphics Inc.
As the catalog arm of Adobe Systems, they develop their own clip art, fonts, and photo products *and* resell many others.
10545 West Donges Ct., Milwaukee, WI 53224-9985, 800-387-9193
www.imageclub.com

Imagine That! Publications
Offers fashion industry illustrations of individual clothing items, as well as the elements used to create them such as zippers, buttons, fabrics, and trimmings.
2229 Sherwood Ct., Minnetonka, MN 55305, 612-593-9085
www.techexchange.com/
imagin_that.html

Innovation Advertising & Design
Their *AdArt* is a vast collection of company logos and trademarks in computer form—useful to the companies themselves and to those who do business with them.
41 Mansfield Ave., Essex Junction, VT 05452, 800-255-0562
www.ad-art.com/innovation

Jawai Interactive, Inc.
Screen Caffeine Pro, a collection of buttons, graphics, textures, and scripts for multimedia and web page design.
501 East Fourth St., Austin, TX 78701-3745, 512-469-0502
www.jawai.com

Letraset USA
Their Fontek DesignFonts include a broad range of well designed, symbol-like graphics.
40 Eisenhower Dr., Paramus, NJ 07653, 800-343-8973
www.letraset.com

Metro Creative Graphics Inc.
Focuses on advertising artwork for retailers.
33 West 34th St., New York, NY 10001, 800-223-1600

Multi-Ad Services Inc.
A long time conventional and electronic clip art provider.
1720 W. Detweiller Drive, Peoria, IL 61615-1695, 309-692-1530

New Vision Technologies
Their *Task Force Collection* is everything a clip art collection should be—great content, deftly illustrated, so cheap you'll wonder how they make money. Their *Really BIG Edition* includes 10,000 images on CD-ROM, a 400 page color catalog, and a *Task Force Commander* utility for online searches and viewing.
38 Auriga Drive, #13 Nepean, Ontario, CANADA K2E-8A5
800-387-0732
http://fox.nstn.ca/~clipart

One Mile Up Inc.
Specializes in illustrations related to the U.S. Government—the executive, legislative, and judicial branches and the military.
7011 Evergreen Ct., Annandale, VA 22003, 800-258-5280
www.onemileup.com

© *Dynamic Graphics*

© *Imagine That!*

© *One Mile Up*

329

The Oswego Company
Creates photo realistic illustrations for prominent corporations and leading advertising agencies. Their *Illustrated Archives* set includes generic versions of a broad selection of products from electronics to transportation.
2701 NW Vaughn Suite 350, Portland, OR 97210, 800-275-1989

Daniel Pelavin
His illustrations have been recognized by all the top design magazines and professional organizations—they are both simple and beautiful.
80 Varick St., #3B, New York, NY 10013, 212-941-7418
www.inch.com/~dpelavin

Periwinkle Software
Specializes in republishing realistic style engravings from the 1700s and later including *Garden, Home, Transportation,* and *Sampler Editions.*
7475 Brydon Rd., La Verne, CA 91750, 800-730-3556
www.periwinkle.com

Planet Art
Their *Classic Graphics* series features everything from selected works of the renaissance artist Raphael to an eclectic collection of fabric, tapestries, wallpaper, and embroideries by eighteenth century poet and designer William Morris.
505 S Beverly Dr., #242, Beverly Hills, CA 90212, 800-200-3405
www.planetartcds.com

Judith Sutcliffe:
The Electric Typographer
Recreates ancient or historic paintings on, and carvings in rock (pictographs and petroglyphs) and applies the same unique styles to new designs.
501 First Avenue, Audubon, IA 50025-0224, 712-563-3799

T/Maker Company
Offers a mega-collection of artwork in just about every conceivable category.
1390 Villa St., Mountain View, CA 94041, 800-986-2537

TECH-M Company
Publishes *Pop-In Parts*—volumes of detailed line drawings of hardware, components, tools, objects, symbols, and hands at work.
9400 Fourth St. North, Suite 160, St. Petersburg, FL 33702, 800-576-1881
www.cent.com/techm

TechPool Studios
Their *LifeArt* collection focuses on subjects such as anatomy, medicine, emergency care, nutrition, and safety featuring illustrations of everything from CPR procedures to detailed diagrams of the body's structures.
1463 Warrensville Center Rd., Cleveland, OH 44121-2676
800-543-3278
www.lifeart.com

Ultimate Symbol Inc.
Has created a category unto itself. Their *Design Elements–A Digital Reference* features graphic elements such as geometrics, pointers, pictorial symbols, dingbats, printers' ornaments, and all manner of shapes—a terrific collection for, among other things, creating logos.
31 Wilderness Dr., Stony Point, NY 10980, 800-870-7940

Youth Specialties Inc.
Their *ArtSource* offers a useful collection of Christian images with a youth-oriented sense of humor and design.
P.O. Box 4406, Spartanburg, SC 29305, 800-776-8008
www.youthspecialties.com

© Daniel Pelavin

© Tech-M

© Ultimate Symbol

Royalty Free & Stock Photography

ROYALTY FREE PHOTOGRAPHY

Classic PIO Partners
It was a stroke of genius when these partners decided to search Hollywood prop rooms for vintage objects, such as jukeboxes, radios, microphones, and business equipment and to sell them to a world that can't get enough of retro.
87 East Green St. Suite 309, Pasadena, CA 91105, 800-370-2746
www.classicpartners.com

Digital Stock Corporation
Features a big collection of images on CD-ROM including categories such as holidays, landmarks, graffiti, outdoor activities, business, manufacturing, medicine, lifestyles and concepts.
400 South Sierra Avenue, Suite 100, Solana Beach, CA 92075
800-545-4514
www.digitalstock.com.

Image Farm Inc.
Don't overlook the smaller independents that represent the work of a single or a small group of photographers—they often offer the niche subject matter you won't find elsewhere. Image Farm offers a stunning collection of textures and backgrounds.
110 Spadina Avenue, Suite 309, Toronto, Ontario, CANADA M5V 2K4, 800-438-3276
www.imagefarm.com

PhotoDisc Inc.
Publishes CD-ROM collections such as PhotoDisc Volumes; organized by subject matter, such as *US Landmarks & Travel* and *Modern Technologies*. The Background and Object Series; organized by type, such as *Fruits & Vegetables* and *Toolshed*. And The Signature Series; organized by the artist, such as *Everyday People* by Barbara Penoyar.
2013 Fourth Ave., Seattle, WA 98121
800-528-3472
www.photodisc.com

STOCK PHOTOGRAPHY

Archive Films/Archive Photos
Claims the "largest and most comprehensive historical photo still libraries in the world, with more than 20,000,000 photographs, engravings and drawings." Includes categories such as news photos, publicity photos of cars, appliances, etc., color stock shots, Hollywood behind-the-scenes and movie stills, and personalities (royalty, politicians, sports figures, authors).
530 West 25th Street, New York, NY, 10001, 800-447-0733
www.archivefilms.com

Comstock Stock Photography
Has a library of over 5 million photos composed by leading photographers primarily for stock usage.
30 Irving Place, New York, NY 10003, 800-225-2727

Corbis
In accordance with their mission to "become the world's premier provider of high-quality digital content" Corbis, has acquired the rights to collections from respected organizations such as the Philadelphia Museum of Art, the Sakamoto Archive, and the National Gallery of London, and the Bettmann Archive—a collection of 16 million-plus photographs and illustrations covering every conceivable subject matter.
15395 SE 130th Place, Bellevue, WA 98007, 800-260-0444
www.corbis.com

Index Stock
Represents the work of more than 400 professional photographers.
23 West 18th Street, 3rd Floor, New York, NY 10011, 800-729-7466
www.indexstock.com

Tony Stone Images
Represents the work of more than 1000 international photographers.
500 North Michigan Ave., Suite 1700, Chicago, IL 60611
800-644-1658
www.tonystone.com

© Image Farm

© PhotoDisc

Fonts

Active Images
Since I was a kid, I have wished I had the kind of handwriting I found on the pages of my comic books—now the wait is over. Richard Starkings, the man whose exquisite hand lettering graces the pages of comic books such as Batman, Captain America, and Spider-Man, is making them available to us in font form. The collection includes balloon, caption, display, and sound effects lettering.
430 Colorado Avenue #301, Santa Monica, CA 90401, 310-458-9094
www.comicbookfonts.com

Adobe Systems
You likely know Adobe as the publisher of PageMaker and Photoshop, but Adobe also has a serious commitment to typography. They employ their own staff of type designers among them Robert Slimbach the designer of Minion, and Carol Twombly who designed Charlemagne, two fonts used throughout the Idea Book. Adobe also pioneered the PostScript language—the standard for creating high-quality output on desktop computers—and look to be a major player in the development of font solutions for the Internet. They market their fonts through many resellers and their catalog division: Image Club Graphics.
1525 Greenview Drive, Grand Prairie, TX 75050, 800-661-9410
www.imageclub.com

Font Bureau
This is where powerhouse publishers such as The New York Times and Condé Nast commission the design of the fonts that give their publications such a unique typographic style. A few remain the exclusive property of the publications, but most are also available to you and me. Ain't life great?
175 Newbury Street, Boston MA 02116, 617-423-8770
www.fontbureau.com

Fonthaus
They started out as a reseller but have blossomed into a full-fledged type foundry. They offer hundreds of exclusive typefaces and picture fonts in addition to the collections of most of the other major designers.
1375 Kings Highway East, Fairfield, CT 06430, 800-942-9110
www.fonthaus.com

Fonthead Design
Ethan Dunham is one of those designers who creates type because he loves it—and the fact that he loves it shines through. Finding his site on the Internet reminded me how important it is to continually prospect for sources outside the mainstream.
1872-B Darryl Drive, Tallahassee, FL 32301-6017
www.fonthead.com

House Industries
Among all their other shenanigans, these guys went out and found Ed "Big Daddy" Roth, the father of "Rat Fink," moon eyes, and custom cars, and put his 60's era art and type in font form. Enough said.
P.O. Box 30000, Wilmington DE 19805, 800-888-4390
www.houseind.com

Monotype Typography Inc.
Looking for a single answer to your font questions? Monotype has joined forces with another type mega-distributor, Agfa, to offer a comprehensive pick-and-pay CD-ROM. It includes the Monotype and Agfa libraries plus those of Adobe, Fontek, FontHaus, ITC, many small foundries, and some highly respected independent type designers—over 4000 fonts. Wow.
985 Busse Road, Elk Grove Village, IL 60007-2400, 800-803-6964

Castle Systems
Look on the pages of *House & Garden, Outside,* and *Sports Illustrated for Kids,* and you'll find some of the many, exquisite fonts created by Castle Systems.
1306 Lincoln Avenue, San Rafael, CA 94901-2105, 415-459-6495
http://home.earthlink.net/~castlesys

Walden Font
Their focus is to resurrect typefaces of historical importance. Their Civil War Press collection, for example, includes 14 original typefaces and over 70 images used in the advertising of the period.
P.O. Box 871, Winchester, MA 01890, 800-519-4575
www.waldenfont.com

types of type

Good Dog Cool Font
Fonthead Design

Style

Agenda Bold Ultra Condensed
Font Bureau

President's Signatures
Walden Font

Index

300
Includes all the
Idea Book projects
plus 200 more

projects on CD-ROM!

by Chuck Green

All the Idea Book projects, plus 200 others are now available on CD-ROM as part of Chuck Green's *PrePage Templates for PageMaker* (call or visit www.ideabook.com for upcoming versions for other programs).

The idea is simple—modifying a document is far easier than starting from scratch. Chuck has researched, designed, and meticulously formatted 300 extraordinary templates, you just select a design, add your message, and print. (Fonts and clip art are not included.) And they're not just pretty pages—*PrePage* templates help you present information in a way that captures attention and moves your reader to action.

To order the *PrePage* CD-ROM for just $99.00 plus $5 S&H call 804-266-7996 or mail your order to Logic Arts Corporation, P.O. Box 3192, Glen Allen, VA 23058-3192 or visit www.ideabook.com.

For credit card orders or more info

Call 804 266 7996

Mon-Fri, 9-6 EST

Continue the conversation at
www.ideabook.com